An Asian American Theology of Liberation

Wong Tian An

LEVER
PRESS

Lever Press (leverpress.org) is a publisher of pathbreaking scholarship.
Supported by a consortium of higher education institutions focused on, and
renowned for, excellence in both research and teaching, our press is grounded
on three essential commitments: to be a digitally native press, to be a peer-
reviewed, open access press that charges no fees to either authors or their
institutions, and to be a press aligned with the liberal arts ethos.

DOI: https://doi.org/10.3998/mpub.12789659
Print ISBN: 978-1-64315-055-0
Open access ISBN: 978-1-64315-056-7

Published in the United States of America by Lever Press, in partnership with
Michigan Publishing.

To all who love more fiercely than they dare believe.

Contents

Having

Power

Member Institution Acknowledgments

Lever Press is a joint venture. This work was made possible by the generous support of Lever Press member libraries from the following institutions:

Amherst College
Berea College
Bowdoin College
Carleton College
Central Washington University
Claremont Graduate
  University
Claremont McKenna College
Clark Atlanta University
College of Saint Benedict &
  Saint John's University
The College of Wooster
Davidson College
Denison University
DePauw University
Grinnell College
Hamilton College
Hampshire College

Harvey Mudd College
Hollins University
Iowa State University
Keck Graduate Institute
Knox College
Lafayette College
Macalester College
Middlebury College
Morehouse College
Norwich University
Occidental College
Penn State University
Pitzer College
Pomona College
Randolph-Macon College
Rollins College
Santa Clara University
Scripps College

Skidmore College
Smith College
Spelman College
Susquehanna University
Swarthmore College
Trinity University
UCLA Library
Union College
University of Idaho
University of Northern
   Colorado
University of Puget Sound

University of Rhode Island
University of San Francisco
University of Vermont
Ursinus College
Vassar College
Washington and Lee
   University
Whitman College
Whittier College
Whitworth University
Willamette University
Williams College

Acknowledgments

In a critical reading of acknowledgments in academic historical works, Emily Callaci writes that acknowledgments, at their best, "dismantle the myth of the lone, self-contained genius-at-work, and instead expose the messy interplay of institutional support, finances, intellectual genealogies, and interpersonal chaos that shape how an idea is brought into the world."[1] They reveal truths we intend to share as well as many that we do not. In such acknowledgments, one can often read between the lines to find privileges of citizenship, financial sponsors, mobility, and heteropatriarchy such as men thanking their wives for typing, for childcare, for their long-suffering, for footing the bill of social reproduction costs. In contrast to these are those that instead recognize their abundant care networks as having performed work or labor, signaling "I had help. If you are going to do this, you will need help." (In Callaci's field of history, those who admit this are reportedly disproportionately women of color.)

So, I had help. Lots of it. While most of this book is written in a historical and theoretical style, its underpinnings and motivations arise from experiences that I have come to think of as informal ethnographic fieldwork, or what anthropologist Clifford Geertz called "deep hanging out."[2] My intellectual development has not been so much through books as through the people who read them, who live in the world. From regularly attending Ming Hui-Tseng's family's Taiwanese church in Flushing to Grace Lee's family's Korean churches in Valley Stream and Long Island City to the Ascension community in Forest Hills, I came to be a part of the Asian American Christian experience primarily from immigrant communities in New York City in the time of Occupy Wall Street and Black Lives Matter. I also got glimpses into Filipino communities through Kay Hautea's family, Kirklyn Escondo, and Chauncey Velasco; South Asian communities through Jesssica Chandras, Shemon Salam, and Amna Ali; and Hong Kong communities through the Lausan Collective.

Many a night was spent in a cramped apartment with Tiamba Wilkerson, Shemon Salam, and Grace Lee arguing the possibility and futility of Black–Asian relations, Whiteness, abolition, queerness, and revolution on the horizon. The POC oasis we had carved out in rural Massachusetts on the White side of the "Tofu Curtain" showed what intractable problems remained in the absence of Whiteness. I'm also grateful to the mostly online Progressive Asian American Christian community that flourished, starting from Liz Lin's lamentation on the loneliness of being a progressive Asian American Christian, through which I found valuable support in Grace Ji-Sun Kim, Joe Cheah, Grace Kao, Suejeanne Koh-Parsons, and, later, Jonathan Tran who helped me navigate the academy and publishing as an outsider; in Esther Yuen who rounded up the Vancouver contingent for an early testing of ideas; and the Detroit Metro folks who gave us a place to land in the final leg, especially Da Ding, Drew, and Erin Pineda. Through all of these, I have to a degree "gone native" in the best possible sense—a problematic phrase, to be certain, but from the perspective of standpoint epistemology or situated knowledge quite a useful thing—yet my secure attachment to family and friends in Malaysia grounds my commitment to not completely assimilate into the settler-colonial fabric of the United States.

One can read in these acknowledgments a degree of mobility, but there is also the interruption of the coronavirus lockdown:

much of this book was written in a time of social distancing, which afforded the isolation one often needs to write. But its formation runs over a decade and across continents. So, the deepest, most obvious thanks go to Grace, for the charity to go along with all of it, for the social reproduction, for the years of shared intellectual, spiritual, and political growth.

To paraphrase Walter Rodney's own acknowledgments in *How Europe Underdeveloped Africa*, not all the mistakes in here are my own. They are committed in imperfect community, struggle, and love. I will always wish I had written a better book. It will always be incomplete, imperfect; there will always be more to say, to improve, to revise. I had no institutional support. For that reason, I am grateful to David Stiver at the Graduate Theological Union, who scanned portions of the PACTS archive for me when I could not afford to travel in person to California, and to *Inheritance Magazine* that published my first thoughts based on these in 2019. But what I did have was some institutional access as a mathematician embedded in the academy and personal networks through the generosity of friends and strangers. Much thanks also to Sean Guynes at Lever Press, who believed in the project and helped to finally bring it into the world via open access.

I am ever grateful to my angels unaware: the brief, divine encounters where we never knew each other's name for longer than a minute, on the streets of Poughkeepsie, New York City, and all across the destitute landscape of North America; the organic intellectuals who know firsthand the violence of the state, the callousness of humans, the harshness of getting by, yet are the warmest of all. You teach me ways of being in the world: what it means to wander, to trust, to need, to thirst, to wait, to remember, to live, to die. Angels who sleep on sidewalks, who beg for change, who share the abundance of their lives. And the ghosts of this land that haunt me in waves of retrojective grief: the afterlives of slavery, lynching, and genocide.

This book is written with my younger selves in mind, also my second-generation Asian American Sunday School students, many of whom by now are facing the world as fully grown adults, for those wishing for a way to love both God and neighbor without compromise. As we grow older, we sometimes grow wiser—by our missteps, if nothing else—and there comes a time to accept that we have somehow become someone's elders, that our words carry meaning, have weight. At the same time, our dreams fade and our fires wane and our bones ache: we can only hope that the inheritance we have to offer is worth the pain.

My attempts to theologize liberation has sometimes been met with a forgivable skepticism or surprise, given my lack of credentials. But if you think about it for just a moment, this is precisely what liberation and its theology demands: it cannot be primarily the domain of specialists, kept behind the gates of the academy or even the church. No, it belongs in the burning streets and collective farms, dancing and laughing and making music, food, love, and peace. A theology of liberation for us and by us, free. If you are reading these words, it is yours also to claim. And reshape. If you see yourself in any and all of this, then this book is a love letter and call to arms to you and the communities you belong to. The world awaits.

INTRODUCTION: LIBERATION THEOLOGY UNBOUND: FOR SUCH A TIME AS THIS

When he had thus spoken, he cried with a loud voice, "Lazarus, come forth!" The dead man came forth, bound hand and foot with grave-clothes, and his face wrapped in a cloth. Jesus said to them, "Unbind him, and let him go."

—John 11:43–44

Religious suffering is, at one and the same time, the expression of real suffering and a protest against real suffering. Religion is the sigh of the oppressed creature, the heart of a heartless world, and the soul of soulless conditions. It is the opium of the people. The abolition of religion as the illusory happiness of the people is the demand for their real happiness. To call on them to give up their illusions about their condition is to call on them to give up a condition that requires illusions. The criticism of religion is, therefore, in embryo, the criticism of that vale of tears of which religion is the halo.

—Karl Marx, "Introduction" to
A Contribution to the Critique of Hegel's Philosophy of Right

The dreams of the colonial subject are muscular dreams, dreams of action, dreams of aggressive vitality. I dream I am jumping, swimming, running, and climbing. I dream I burst out laughing, I am leaping across a river and chased by a pack of cars that never catches up with me.

—Frantz Fanon, *The Wretched of the Earth*

What time is it on the clock of the world?

—Grace Lee Boggs, *The Next American Revolution*

Here is a book that should have been written long ago. It should have been written by any of the theologians or activists or laypersons who articulated an "Amerasian" or "Asian American" theology of liberation in the early 1970s, whose writings have instead been relegated to archival documents in libraries and seminaries.[1] Methodist bishop Roy Isao Sano, director of what was then the Asian Center for Theology and Strategies (ACTS, and later PACTS) in Berkeley, California, compiled two readers on the nascent subject, with contributions from dozens of Japanese, Filipine, Chinese, and Korean American Christians reflecting on the growing consciousness around their personal identity and cultural heritage. They connected it with the new Black theology that was being developed alongside the Black Power movement and Third World Liberation Front, against the backdrop of White racist domination at home and military imperialism abroad.[2] Copies of the readers were distributed but never published, unlike *Roots: An Asian American Reader* (1971), the first publication of UCLA's Asian American Studies Center Press. The press was created to address the "lack of appropriate materials in readily accessible form,"[3] as the field of Asian American studies was newly established after the 1968 strikes for ethnic studies in San Francisco State College (now San Francisco State University) and UC Berkeley. In his introduction to *The Theologies of Asian Americans and Pacific Peoples: A Reader* (1976), Roy I. Sano expressed the hope that a third edition would be sufficiently inclusive of representative voices, so that a publisher would consider printing and distributing the volume to a wider audience. As history would have it, this was not to be.

One would be hard-pressed to learn about this brief history of Asian American theology of liberation. Only a few books surveying Asian American theology or liberation theology mention it, if at all, in a few short paragraphs or as a footnote. When I learned about this, I was fortunate enough to be visiting the University of British Columbia mathematics department, where the Vancouver School of Theology up the road held a copy of the 1976 reader. This was in

2019, in the middle of the Trump era and at the end of a turbulent decade of global unrest. I had been in the United States on and off for about a decade—what was the place of Asians or faith in the ongoing struggles? Even in 2015 I remember raging and grieving and searching inside as a I sat listening to a dispassionate sermon the Sunday after a White supremacist murdered nine people at Emanuel AME Church in Charleston. Why did I have to dig so deep to find any trace of liberation theology from an Asian American point of view? How much more now, in the wake of the COVID-19 pandemic?

To my knowledge, only two other libraries carried copies of Sano's reader, one in Berkeley and one in New York City. The one I found looked, as New Testament scholar Seung Ai Yang described, "very much like one of today's 'readers' used for a course in colleges and graduate schools. Its handwritten page numbers, ring-binding, and different typefaces for each article reveals the urgency and necessity Sano felt for this work at that time as a pioneer in this field."[4] Most of these works remain hidden in dusty archives, their existence known only to scholars and historians and perhaps other seekers of liberative Asian American theological traditions.[5] The tattered, yellow pages with handwritten page numbers document the powerful activist theological energy of a bygone era. Here was a once loud, communal force that cried out for the liberation of Asians in the United States, in the civil rights era, for a theology of one's own, and for solidarity with oppressed people everywhere. This is our inheritance.

While Black, Latin American, and White feminist theologies of liberation are able to point to texts that mark the inauguration of new ways of doing theology beyond the White Western male norm, such as James Cone's *Black Theology and Black Power* (1969) and *A Black Theology of Liberation* (1971), Gustavo Gutiérrez's *Teología de la Liberación* (1971), and Mary Daly's *Beyond God the Father* (1973), the concurrent but informal reader *AmerAsian Theology of Liberation* (1973) was not followed by a similar landmark publication to inspire later generations of Asian American theologians.[6] This present book is in part a retrieval of this lesser-known history of Asian American contributions to liberation theology and at the same time a rearticulation of an Asian American theology of liberation that is urgently needed today. As such, this book is about fifty years too late and, hopefully, just in time.

Of course, any theology of liberation today must first address its own relevance in the twenty-first century. To do so, it is necessary to honestly assess the failures and the successes of earlier theologians and activists without reservation if we are to build forward. For one, theologies of liberation are now by and large the domain of academic study rather than the bottom-up, grassroots theologies of the masses they were intended to be. They have, in the sense of Marcella Althaus-Reid, become decent. According to her, the Latin American Christian discourse of liberation assumed that nothing had been outside of Christianity, declared the poor asexual, and did not challenge women's subordination or the sexual insubordination of the favelas or shanty towns.[7] Liberation theology as such became a recognized theology, a commercial enterprise that made it fashionable to those on the margins, and "what is fashionable, sells."[8] European theologians, suddenly interested in the Latin American poor, projected a colonial image of liberation theology through church tourism and theological voyeurism.

The material suffering of the people was expropriated from the oppressed classes and became the intellectual property of the owners of the intellectual system of production: the theologians.[9] Theology became a surplus value of human suffering: "It alienates by taking possession, extorting from others what belongs to them, dismantling any relation that the workers may have with the sacred. The process gives value to human suffering as merchandise, objectified as an abstract commodity and sold for a price: the continuation of oppressive political systems in alliance with ecclesiastical ones."

All of this to say that theological reflection, even in liberation theology, can become a commodity and betray the people. More recently, in assessing the place of liberation theology in a capitalistic theological market in 2000, Althaus-Reid writes:

> A cultural shift took place. In recent years, in order to produce some difference in its analysis, especially since postcolonialism was underlying the liberationists' contradictions on issues of identity and agency, liberationists discovered the native people from the Original Nations who sometimes were not Christians ... Instead of Christ and the poor, the new discourse was on Christ and the Mayan. Christianity suddenly became more plural. It was Christianity and *Mestizaje*; Christianity and *Santería* worship, or Umbanda; Christianity and Andean theology.[10]

The same can be seen in Asian American theological production where Christianity and Asian culture dominates. Theologies of liberation, whether willingly or unwillingly, have become irrelevant as a driving force of liberation, or even as a comrade of liberation movements, and instead have become what Althaus-Reid calls "theological science fiction," morally constructing its subjects as an undifferentiated and innocent mass. At least in the United States, they have been effectively decoupled from the masses in all but a handful of churches. Therefore, any attempt to deploy them today must first answer the question: Why now?

THEOLOGIES OF LIBERATION: WHY NOW?

We have been in crisis. I started writing this book before the coronavirus pandemic and the global rebellion that was ignited by the resurgence of the Black Lives Matter movement. The list that started with Trayvon Martin grows longer every day. Global White nationalism had been on the rise with mass shootings and White supremacist rallies throughout Europe and its settler colonies. Geopolitical instability and climate change are causing mass migrations—refugees from Syria and Yemen fleeing war risk death to arrive on European shores; over a million Rohingya Muslims fleeing ethnic cleansing in Myanmar live in the world's largest refugee camp in Bangladesh; asylum seekers from Guatemala and Honduras are fleeing violence and economic hardship only to be faced with violence, family separation, and detention at the US–Mexico border.[11] Millions of Muslim Uyghurs are being detained and "reeducated" in China's Xinjiang region, as Han Chinese take over Tibetan homes and erase their culture. Increasing tension in US–China relations threaten war, hot or cold.

Multiple climate reports indicate that the planet will soon become largely uninhabitable in just a few decades. The climate crisis can no longer be prevented, only mitigated, and we must instead ask after climate adaptation in the wake of the oncoming societal collapse, which itself will be unevenly distributed, disproportionately affecting poor people, communities of color, and the Third World.[12] The climate catastrophe will press deeper into the preexisting fissures in the social fabric just as the coronavirus pandemic has already provided a preview: from protective-equipment hoarding to vaccine nationalism to unvarnished xenophobia. Frighteningly, the end of the world as we know it is no longer hyperbole but hard science. The question is, What is the world to come?

While in some sense there is nothing new under the sun, it is also true that this is far from normal, and things are not okay. There is no ecological precedent for the future that our planet is hurtling toward. As it were, it had become fashionable for a time for social scientists to theorize about what geologists call the Anthropocene, the geological age in which destructive human activity is the defining event, where plastic is becoming a part of the rock record as plastiglomerate, a novel part-plastic, part-mineral rock formation.[13] Microplastics have been found in the remotest regions from the Alps to the Artic and in fetuses.[14] It literally permeates our being and the air we breathe: the ongoing ecological collapse and societal collapse are inseparable. And yet, as much as global crises are beginning to unfold at an alarming rate, everyday life remains business as usual for many. Until it isn't.

Numerous social movements have swept across the globe in the past decade, such as the 2011 Occupy movement, which finds roots in the earlier Arab Spring and which inspired Hong Kong's Umbrella Movement in 2014 and antiextradition protests in 2019;[15] the Black Lives Matter movement against police brutality in the United States that began in 2013 and reignited in 2020; the #MeToo and subsequent #ChurchToo movements against sexual harassment and rape culture; Indigenous movements in North America such as the Idle No More, the Standing Rock #NoDAPL protests, and the Missing and Murdered Indigenous Women, Girls, and Two-Spirit People (MMIWG2S) movement; school climate strikes calling for climate action; worker strikes against tech giants; blockades on highways and ports resisting the flow of weapons, oil, and capital at large. Mass movements are now taking place with increasing frequency such as in Puerto Rico, Haiti, Sudan, Hong Kong, Hawai'i, Thailand, Myanmar, and Sri Lanka at such a pace that it is difficult keep up. In short, the irruption of the poor, the refugee, the queer, and the abused is here.

The social upheavals that continue to reverberate on a global scale demand an adequate and unequivocal theological response. This book focuses on struggles that link Asia and the United States, tracking how these struggles flow and interweave through the diaspora and form networks of solidarity. The mass protests and other direct actions against authoritarian regimes, against inaction toward climate change, and against the systematic dehumanization of others are a clarion call to action. Quite literally, the people are crying out. There is no ethical middle ground, no time to be lukewarm as global suffering reaches a crescendo. The coming years will see unprecedented turmoil, which the last decade has already foreshadowed. We cannot stand idly by.

White theology and Asian American theology, inasmuch as it

tries to approximate the latter, are not up to the task. By theology here I do not mean primarily the academic work of professional theologians, though theory will play a significant role in what follows, but rather the "God-talk" that is done in day-to-day churches and over kitchen tables by poor lay people of color. Asian American theology, as it stands, is ill-equipped to critique and interpret the structural and epistemic violence that are being dealt nor the institutional and cultural frameworks that have cultivated the present crisis. Nor is it capable of grounding and empowering the activism, solidarity, and engagement with such social movements that are waging attempts against the forces which collectively threaten human existence itself. Its interlocutors often have middle-class origins and concerns and skew East Asian.[16] What has been lost for the sake of respectability? What was given up in exchange for the wages of Whiteness, for the comfort of tenure and the riches of nonprofit grants?[17] How are we serving the people?

We desperately need a theological framework that has the firepower to engage the events of today, to enter into the fray. The landscape of Asian America has changed dramatically from the arrival of the first Filipinos with the Spanish ships in the 1500s to the various immigration laws and refugee acts in the mid-1900s. The younger generation on the streets today fighting for racial and economic justice, burning police cars and redistributing looted goods, and providing mutual aid must guide our theological reflection, not the other way around. At the same time, in order to close the loop on the hermeneutical circle, these reflections must be communicated back to the people in plain language. In this book, I draw on *Asian American* as a social location and coalitional identity that coheres a critical discourse and deconstructive analysis, and on *liberation theology* as the interpretive structure that grounds our struggle and constructive praxis.[18] The vast heterogeneity of Asian Americanness, with the complexities of migration, belonging, and refuge that attend it provides an analytic, a vision of coalitional politics for a US future that is "majority-minority" and a global future upended by climate change. It is no accident that the imperial and colonial violence and accumulation that have precipitated the current global disorders are also constitutive of Asian American identity. As the saying goes, we are here because you were there.[19]

Liberation theology is the interpretive key by which we apprehend God's actions as revealed in history and act faithfully according to this revelation. Theologies of liberation burst onto the scene in the 1960s, remaining forceful and influential until the 1980s, expanding and deepening their analyses of oppression and reflection on praxis. I use *oppression* here to mean the adverse effects of unequal power relations produced by those with power over others in disadvantaged positions. In the following decades, theologies of liberation began to lose their critical edge even as they gained respect and acceptance into the theological academy and the middle class. Today, theologians debate the usefulness of liberation theology. But theologies of liberation have always been aware of the chasm between vision and reality, the already and not-yet. The same is true of any kind of radical prefigurative politics. As Gayraud Wilmore's "A Revolution Unfulfilled but not Invalidated" and Eleazar Fernandez and Fernando Segovia's volume *A Dream Unfinished* both insist, the fundamental claims of theologies of liberation have not been falsified, only unrealized.[20] To put a spin on Marx and Engels, the specter of liberation is haunting us. If anything, the events of the last decade only underscore their continuing relevance. Rather than doing away with liberation theology, as some have suggested, what is needed is a deeper commitment to the principles of liberation and, as with all activist work, to view the work as a lifelong struggle that must be passed on from generation to generation.

The task at hand, I shall argue, is to realize an Asian radical tradition, learning from the past and building for the future. The poor you have with you always, Jesus pointed out. For theology to center the oppression of the poor is not simply a passing fad but rather a cornerstone of Christian theology, the grammar of God-talk.[21] Asian American theology, in particular, must become radical, returning to its prophetic role in Asian American liberation. To do so, we must first ask what the proper sources of an Asian American theology of liberation are.

ASIAN AMERICAN THEOLOGY OF LIBERATION: SOURCES

Asian American theology finds its roots in Asian American liberation theology.[22] This historical consciousness is the first source of a radical Asian American theology. Asian theologians such as Shoki Coe, Aloysius Pieris, and Peter Phan emphasized the need to inculturate theology in Asia. Early Asian American theologians, too, called for producing a theology indigenous to Asian Americans. An Asian American theology of liberation cannot survive playing by the rules of respectability and identity politics, dictated by Whites who know nothing of the experience of Asian Americans. Neither is it primarily articulated by Asian Americans in ivory towers, who know little of the suffering of working-class migrant Asians at risk of deportation, economic precarity, and sexual exploitation. The role of Asian American theologians is to interpret the signs of the times, to recognize the work of God in the liberation of poor Asians in diaspora. As the readers compiled by Roy Sano reveal, the early Asian American theology was not articulated by erudite scholars or professors chasing tenure or the next book deal but instead by dozens of lay people and clergy personally invested in the struggles of their communities. They knew how to apply insights from social theory and other forms of knowledge. They saw the social movements of their time fighting for the liberation of the colonized Third World and of what they saw as the internal colonies of the United States and sought to build a theology that did not turn away from the call of these movements, from the suffering of the oppressed.

The lived experiences, migration histories, and cultural memories of the Asian American community are the primary sources for an Asian American theology built from the bottom up. It is precisely because of the distinctiveness of the Asian American experience that White theology has nothing of practical use to say to Asian Americans, and even Black, Latine, and other theologies can only be in dialogue with the Asian American community.[23] They cannot determine the content of Asian American theology, even if they may have a great deal to teach us. At the same time, not all Asian American experiences are equally valued. While a select group of Asians rise in prominence, whether as political candidates, billionaire tech executives, or Hollywood stars, their narratives often fit into a model-minority myth of the so-called Asian American dream and do little to interrogate or challenge the US settler-colonial and racial capitalist empire.

Instead, it is the subaltern experience of Hmong, Vietnamese, Cambodians, Bangladeshis, Nepalese, Filipine, and similarly overlooked Asians in the United States—undocumented, undereducated, and disadvantaged—that serves as the touchstone for a radical and grounded Asian American theology. The Asian American church cannot stay silent as people cry out against sexual abuse, police brutality, economic oppression, and environmental racism. It cannot stand idly by when people are fighting and dying in the streets for freedom. Asian American theology must point to the God who is for the poor and against the rich, who speaks from the mouths of Asian children participating in strikes and protests. There is no neutral ground for Asian American theology to stand upon: it can only be against oppression and repression of any kind in any place, aligning itself with the masses, the 99 percent, the minjung.[24] As activist Grace Lee Boggs writes, rather than viewing "the masses" as a faceless abstraction to be mobilized in increasingly aggressive struggles, we should see ourselves as organizing a community base of caring individuals transforming ourselves and becoming the change we want to see.[25]

Another source of Asian American theology is of course Asian theologies, which have given corrective insights that look beyond the borders and concerns of the US mainland. It is highly significant that many theologies generated from the Asian continent share liberation as a central theme, though they may not use such language. While "liberation" as a concept is itself European in origin, the struggle for freedom is universal. Theologies of liberation attend to their respective social contexts, making no claim to universality as White theology does. At the same time, they recognize that each struggle is linked to one another through global capitalism, imperialism, neocolonialism, and heteropatriarchy. As theological traditions in Asia continue to develop in their own distinct manner, it will be important to dialogue with these creative sources that provide a counter-narrative to White theological traditions and a grounding for Asian American reflections, with neither nostalgia nor idealization. To be radically Asian American calls for an outright decolonial refusal of Asian American activism as merely a politics of inclusion and representation bounded by the nation-state. Instead, it needs to be fiercely internationalist in outlook and identity.

Besides working against frameworks of nationalism and citizenship, Asian American theology also complicates binaries of race, class, nationality, religion, and gender that structure US cultural politics. Liberation theologies draw upon social analyses in order to sharpen their theological critique of power, without allowing themselves to be subsumed into totalizing theories. It was a fear of such totalization that led the Vatican to condemn the early Latin American liberation theology's use of Marxism. The same fear also animates conservative Christian anxiety surrounding postmodernism, more recently critical race theory. Asian American theology cannot afford to ignore these insights; it is also strengthened by dialogues with Black, Latine, feminist, queer, and Indigenous theologies. While the particularity of liberation theologies is easily mistaken for a kind of narrow-minded theological identity politics or tribalism, in reality the shared struggle for collective liberation must be waged through the richness of particular contexts and solidarities between struggles without ignoring the real differences and tensions between groups. We bring our whole selves to the fight.

Unbeknownst to many, Asian American theologies of liberation have already existed in the past, inspired by Black theology and Third World revolutionary movements. They sought to establish a theology relevant to the Asian American experience of White racist domination and US empire, to interpret God's work of liberation in their own communities. Today, the social upheavals witnessed worldwide in the last decade and the deepening crisis call for a renewed Asian American theology of liberation for such a time as this, a theology that learns from past theologies of liberation, especially those arising from struggles in Asian contexts and leverages the complicated nature of Asian American identity to reveal the different forms of violence that are produced by ideologies of race, class, gender, sexuality, religion, and nation. A radical approach to Asian American theology renews the commitment to the liberation of working-class, migrant, and colonized Asians while expanding the view to include queer and refugee Asians.

This book is concerned about the lived experiences of Asians in relation to structures of power and domination. As theology is a reflection on praxis, or what Latin American liberation theologians call *la caminata*, the see-judge-act hermeneutic circle of suspicion exemplified by the Indigenous Zapatistas in Chiapas, Mexico, through questioning while walking, *preguntando caminamos*, we will also do theology by discussing social theory in subway trains, washing dishes in kitchens, and struggling in protests everywhere. Moreover, I shall argue that liberation theology is better said to be reflection *through* praxis, to emphasize that it is only in love and struggle that we realize what is liberation theology. More than just God-talk, it is a God-walk, or theopraxis.[26] There is no such thing as "liberation theology for armchair theologians," as Miguel de la

Torre, in a booklet of the same ironic title, insists that the very ethos of being a liberation theologian is the *doing* of liberation theology.[27] And, I would add, all those who *do* liberation theology are the true liberation theologians.

CHAPTER OUTLINE

To set the stage, chapter 1 begins with a disambiguation of inculturation and liberation, followed by a retrieval of Asian American theologies of liberation. The latter can be found in the archival material of the early 1970s, squarely within the zeitgeist of Asian America's becoming, traditionally understood. While this might seem ironic given that I shall argue against a nostalgia complex in dominant Asian American historiography relating to that era, by locating Asian American liberation theology in direct colineage with Asian, Black, and Latin American theologies of liberation, I show this project resonates with a rich theological tradition of liberation, even as it takes into account historical, theological, and intellectual developments in the intervening time.

This is not an inherently innovative project that presents a novel theological method ex nihilo, but neither is it one frozen in the twentieth century or that dreams of failed 1960s-era coalitions. Instead, our mandate is to renew and reinterpret tradition in ways that preserve the memory and honor the lives, losses, and loves of those gone before us. Indeed, in doing so we will make completely new mistakes of our own, which future generations will have to correct for. In fact, any theology of liberation *requires* such dynamism: the hermeneutic circle connecting immanent reality and theological reflection is what animates it. Or, as Frantz Fanon writes, "Each generation must discover its mission, fulfill it or betray it, in relative opacity" and "for us who are determined to break the back of colonialism, our historic mission is to authorize every revolt, every desperate act, and every attack aborted or drowned in blood."[28]

With these clarifications in place, chapter 2 turns to the perpetual question of who is Asian American and who are the subjects of Asian American theology, considering views both from the state and from below. The first is intimately related to representational politics, how Asians are discussed and portrayed in the public sphere. The second invokes a subaltern politics: Asian Americans farmers, garment workers, and others who have organized around labor, against racial discrimination and exploitation in the workplace, followed by refugees and victims of sex and labor trafficking.[29] The construction of Asian American identity has several touchstones. They are all worn out. Its genesis is invariably located in the fight for ethnic studies in San Francisco and Berkeley in the late sixties. On the other side of the 1965 Immigration Act, it is the murder of Vincent Chin and the Los Angeles riots that underpin most attempts to outline a hagiography of Asian American existence through a narrative of legal and extralegal exclusion.[30] Look at how we have never been wanted. These events are unified by a thread of victimization or resilience; in some versions a moralistic parable of overcoming adversity, of attaining success in spite of discrimination—the immigrant American dream par excellence. No matter how much they reject us, we still love them back, like a fucked-up Gospel story. While these violent ruptures indeed define Asian America in important ways, not least in its own self-conception, they also elide alternative genealogies of Asian resistance and radicalism in the forms of labor organizing, anti-racist coalitions, and anti-colonial struggles.

With these in mind, chapter 3 turns to the fraughtness of Asian American theological identity, drawing from Asian American scholar Kandice Chuh's notion of the *subjectlessness* of Asian American studies. At a certain point this will seem to be an overly academic endeavor and have nothing to do with the liberation of human beings, but from a theological standpoint the question of who, what, and how we are is a central one, one that will be taken up again in chapter 5. I draw also on the combination of psychoanalytic and critical race theoretic analyses of David Eng and Shinhee Han that propose racial melancholia and racial dissociation as the psycho-affective character of certain Gen X and Gen Y Asian Americans, suggesting that the Chuh's subjectlessness as a theoretical intervention is also an accurate diagnostic.[31] Relating our lived—racialized, gendered, and bordered—experiences to the power structures that determine them is the work that the subjectlessness does for us: the psychic instability that Asian Americans feel about their social location has a grounding in material reality. Simply put, the difficulties we have in agreeing on what we mean by *Asian American* has everything to do with the larger forces of imperialism, racial capitalism, colonialism, orientalism, and sexuality.

The external reality of oppression and historical trauma is in constant dialectical relation with our internal worlds. The negotiation of these two realities is called intersubjectivity, which opens up into what Eng and Han call a racial third space, a space of play that forms but one aspect of the liberation that I am attempting to describe. Play, here, is a psychoanalytic expression of the notion of free response, and which I later revisit on different registers through Walter Benjamin's divine violence (Chapters 8) and queer theology (Chapter 9). The thrust of these considerations is that we must constantly be aware of the tentativeness of Asian American theological identity and in doing so we are freed to weaponize it for both critique and coalition-building. Its inherent constructedness—subjectlessness—should free us from trying to fit into preconceived notions of who we are and move toward adaptive racial dissociation: being able to be many and one without collapsing in on ourselves. As David Graeber, one of the key figures of the Occupy Wall Street movement, asserted: the ultimate, hidden truth of the world is that it is something that we make and could just as easily make differently.[32] The same is true of the malleable and fluid thing that is Asian American identity. It is ours for the making.

Having laid the foundation of subjectivity, I turn to the first steps of a theological construction. Building an Asian American theology of liberation for the future requires, first and foremost, a decolonization of contemporary Asian American theology, thus a reckoning with Asian settler colonialism, with our positionality that Hawaiian activist Haunani-Kay Trask refers to as "settlers of color."[33] With this in mind, chapter 4 dialogues with Indigenous scholars and theologians, in particular Vine Deloria Jr. and George Tinker whose works lay out the realities that any form of settler or non-Indigenous theology in North America must confront. In contrast to these claims, I argue that Asian American theology is characterized by *landlessness*—a foreignness in perpetuity that must be in solidarity with Indigenous struggles for sovereignty and resurgence.[34] In other words, Asian American theology must not seek to indigenize or be grounded in any territorial sense but rather embrace its inherent transnationality and dislocation. I draw also from Naim Ateek's Palestinian liberation theology, which, along with Native American theologians, rejects the problematic Exodus narrative, a paradigmatic text of liberation theologies, and constructs a theology of freedom that centers concern for the land and its stewards. This theology of landlessness is in dialectical opposition with earlier Asian American theologies that seek particular forms of belonging within US settler society, whereas a theology of landlessness proposes a capitulation of any such desire. There is no ultimately defensible position for inclusion in the anti-Black US settler-colonial empire.

Having cleared the way for an Asian American theology of migration that is in harmony with the land and its Indigenous people, chapter 5 turns to Asian American theology as a means of critiquing Asian anti-Blackness and learning from the Black radical tradition, Black liberation theology, and Dalit theology. Historical Black–Asian coalitions lay a foundation for an Asian radical tradition that might begin to parallel Cedric Robinson's articulation of the Black radical tradition.[35] The real question, still, is: How do we struggle alongside each other today? Dalit theology can serve as a point of contact for an Asian American theology of liberation that is able to build power and solidarity despite incommensurable differences and Afro-pessimist arguments. Indeed, a closer reading reveals resonances between the open invitations of Black and Dalit liberation to non-Black and non-Dalit communities to, as in Hebrews, "go to him outside the camp and bear the reproach he endured," he who "suffered outside the gate."[36] So are we called to a kenosis of social death and nonbeing, to become outcaste or, as James Cone writes unambiguously, to become Black.[37] At the overlap of Dalit theology, Afro-pessimism, and Fanonian theory is the problem of the human being, the possibility of a new humanism at the horizon of decolonization, abolition, and the ontological rupture required by Afropessimism. In approaching the confluence of these multiple horizons, Asian American theology must divest from not only Whiteness but the ontology of non-Blackness and the hierarchical structure of casteism in favor of nonbeing, or *beinglessness*.

Chapter 6 turns to the means of struggle and visions worthy of revolutionary action in the current political moment of mass movements around the world and in the wake of the coronavirus pandemic. The struggles of Hong Kong serve as a crucial point of reflection, connecting with an earlier Korean minjung theology and a theology of the multitude, in the sense of Kwok Pui-Lan and Joerg Rieger. Understanding Asian American theology of liberation as a grassroots theology, it is necessary to consider the multitude, the 99 percent, the masses whom Jesus had compassion on, as the movement out of which theological reflections must be grounded in and whose sufferings must be shared. Parallel to the earlier calls for divestment, I draw upon Jonathan Tran's notion of the aftermarket of racial capitalism, to locate Asian Americans within racial capitalism. Tran locates Asian Americans within the material reality structured by anti-Black racism: the political-economic afterlife of slavery, we might say. This framing is critical as the demographic shift in Asian Americans post-1965 resulted in the average Asian

American being upper-middle class, despite protestations about the internal economic inequalities and experiences of racism. For a theology that intends to be for the poor and oppressed, this places most Asian Americans in an awkward spot. The material consequences of the previous chapter's call to beinglessness are now brought to bear in what I call *havelessness*, which simply harkens to Jesus's unambiguous invitation to "sell all that you have," or what Tran calls dispossession. I propose that the only way out is through, a path that lies in the revolutionary calls of Amilcar Cabral to "return to the source," Walter Rodney's "groundings with my brothers," and Filipino theologian Eleazar Fernandez's theology of struggle. This is the prerogative of so-called middle minorities, the petite bourgeoisie, or what Afro-pessimist Frank Wilderson calls civil society's junior partners, in service of revolution. Building upon these, a theology of class struggle emerges that must undergird future struggles of mass movements and activists. We are workers together with God, yes, as the apostle Paul writes, but we are also workers together with those who work in Amazon warehouses, nail salons, nursing facilities, restaurant kitchens, factory lines, and industrial farms.

With this in view, I broach in chapter 7 the question of violence in the context of revolutionary struggle and liberation. At the opposite end is the quasireligious adherence to nonviolence, which Ward Churchill demonstrates to be pathological and counter-revolutionary. The false moral high ground of absolute pacifism mirrors what Eve Tuck and K. Wayne Yang refer to as a "settler move to innocence" whereby settler identity is deflected through equating different kinds of oppressions and privileging decolonization in the abstract while continuing to enjoy settler privilege and occupy stolen land.[38] Setting aside the pathology of pacifism allows for clearer thinking around the question of violence. For that, the riddle of John Brown presents itself as a useful prism through which it might be apprehended. Brown's use of deadly violence as a White abolitionist poses ethical and political problems not otherwise present in considerations of Black abolitionists or, say, anti-colonial fighters. (This parallels the problem that the preferential option for the poor poses to wealthy Asian Americans.)

Drawing on theologian Ted Smith's use of political theology to circumscribe the limits of ethics, in particular what Smith calls the "frame of universalizable immanent ethical obligation," I place Smith's interpretation of Walter Benjamin's notion of divine violence and relief of law in conversation with Fanon's treatise on violence in the context of decolonization. Whereas Smith's analysis locates revolutionary violence outside the limit of ethics, Fanon's diagnosis finds violence to be all but necessary for the liberation of the colonized, closer perhaps to the assessments of Black revolutionaries in the United States. I argue that *both* perspectives inform the Asian American position, caricatured as timid and non-confrontational, as opposed to the rich history of militancy and protest in Asia and Asian America. We can and must also hold in view the totality. We are not yet free as long as any of us is not free.

Chapter 8 is a supplement to the previous one, considering the problem of anti-Asian violence, with an emphasis on the spectacle of a Black male assailant and Asian female victim. Even though such incidents make up only a small fraction of what might be called anti-Asian racism, it is a hard conversation to have, one that liberal establishments carefully avoid but also permeates private chats on Kakao, WeChat, and WhatsApp. In this brief meditation, I offer an interpretation of such events as a subconscious, metabolic waste product of racial capitalism, wherein the actual solution to all forms of anti-Asian violence must include Black liberation. I also draw on Iyko Day's analysis of Asians as the "new Jew" and Anne Annlin Cheng's notion of ornamentalism, drawing together again Marxist and ontological readings as a means of understanding the social location of Asian American women. Combined with the themes of the previous chapters, this points us to a broader will to *powerlessness*, a call to relinquish the desire for retribution and an exploration of what it might mean to love one's enemies.

With each notion of subjectlessness, landlessness, beinglessness, havelessness, and powerlessness, I outline a nonlinear path
for building an Asian American theology of liberation that remem-
bers its history, works in solidarity with others, and is not afraid of
the fight. Broadening the field of vision, in the concluding chapter
9, I draw all these threads together to suggest that Asian Americanness, understood through each of these refusals of rigid binaries, opens up into a queer future of liberation, where freedom is
marked by indeterminacy, free response, and free identification.
Such is the in-between space that is neither/nor, rather than both/
and, echoing the Christian notion of the already but not yet. For
the unbounded joy at the horizon, I call this the erotics of liberation, drawing from Althaus-Reid's indecent theology and archbishop Rowan Williams's meditations on the body's grace. Whereas
the disorders of racial melancholia and racial dissociation, the
psychic and geographic nowhere, the anxieties of being a racial
middleman are all inscribed on the Asian body, the resolution of
these tensions—muscular tension according to Fanon and sexual
tension according to Freud—is also manifested in release and liberation through the body, both sexual and spiritual. The freedom
to be found in Asian American liberation is a deeply queer space.
"The borderlands," according to Gloria Anzaldúa, "are physically
present wherever two or more cultures edge each other, where
people of different races occupy the same territory, where under,
lower, middle, and upper classes touch, where the space between
two individuals shrinks with intimacy."[39] Liberation, likewise, is a
space of limitless potential and creativity, just as Fanon declared,
"In the world I am heading for, I am endlessly creating myself."[40]

LIBERATION THEOLOGY UNBOUND

Anthropologist Patrick Wolfe wrote in the context of settler colonialism that invasion is a structure, not an event.[41] So is liberation
also a structure and not an event. That is to say that freedom, as

with the Jewish concept of shalom, is a pervasive, jubilant presence that must be built and sustained through structural means, forbidding hegemonic systems of domination to take root and requiring expansive and prophetic visions of new Jerusalems. It is a journey without destination, a means without end.

To declare liberation theology unbound is a nod to historian Gary Okihiro's *American History Unbound*, a historical and anti-historical project that writes with and against existing representations of Asians and Pacific Islanders in the United States. In it, Okihiro narrates from the perspective of ocean worlds, assigning historical significance to oceans and islands over continents, which are also islands in themselves, seas of islands connected by water. Oceans and Oceania, according to Okihiro, are decolonizing discourses and material conditions, fluid worlds untethered from the seemingly fixed, immobile continents.[42] In the unbinding of liberation theology I also mean to gesture to a complete abolition of borders and boundaries that yet maintains selfhood and integrity, as in Fanon: "When there are no more slaves, there are no masters."[43] Beyond the horizon of liberation is a new humanity—a new ontology, a fundamental transformation of every social relation, love without end.

This book is written with Asian Americans in mind, those who have found themselves theologically unmoored and adrift in the wake of the last decade's social upheavals, Asian Americans who have found themselves like me, as Nikki Toyama-Szeto put it, spiritually homeless.[44] I write for the community of those who have found White theology to be an irredeemably bankrupt modern-day Pharisaism and have found other liberation theologies, while inspiring and challenging, to be outdated or one step removed from the Asian American struggle. I write against armchair theologians for whom class struggle, deportations, and poverty are abstract issues to theorize about and profit from. I write for a street-fighting Asian American theology of liberation, unapologetic and unreserved in its commitment to the liberation of oppressed and exploited Asians and Asian Americans, for a theology most concerned with the plight and freedom of the global diaspora of Asian working-class poor, migrant laborers, asylum seekers, and trafficked persons.

There is a place for subtle arguments and systematic theories about theology, race, power, and so on; this is not the place. At the same time, even as I draw from academic theologies and theories to scaffold an Asian American theology of liberation, this by itself is *not* the content of liberation theology: it is in the "groanings which cannot be uttered," in which the Spirit of God dwells, in the riots and strikes and barrios and ghettoes and street corners. The work of theology is to interpret these groanings, to perform the negating work of divine violence. Such reverberations can be felt in the aftermath of Hurricane Katrina in 2005 where the Catholic Vietnamese American community in New Orleans participated in the rebuilding process, of which the regional director of the National Association of Vietnamese Service Agencies James Bui remarked, "This is the first time I've seen the Vietnamese church practicing liberation theology."[45] It is this liberation theology that Bui intuitively reached for that this book is about.

While liberation theology is meant to be theology from the ground up, theological reflection on the suffering of the poor and the downtrodden, theology that participates in a hermeneutic circle of reflection and praxis, it may not always be immediately legible to the people whom it is written for. Fanon opposed this opaqueness plainly:

> But if we speak in plain language, if we are not obsessed with a perverse determination to confuse the issues and exclude the people, then it will be clear that the masses comprehend all the finer points and every artifice. Resorting to technical language means you are determined to treat the masses as uninitiated. Such language is a poor front for the lecturer's intent to deceive the people and leave them on the sidelines. Language's endeavor to confuse is a mask behind which looms an even greater undertaking to dispossess. The intention is to strip the people of their possessions as

well as their sovereignty. You can explain anything to the people provided you really want them to understand.[46]

In attempting to translate and synthesize ideas from the academy in service of the people who live outside of it, this book has quite possibly failed in this regard. Time will tell.

Liberation theology is reflection through praxis, and it is only in love and struggle that our theology is realized. There is nothing new under the sun. We already know enough to do justice, love mercy, and walk humbly before our God. In the context of the struggle for Algerian independence, Fanon asserted:

> We would not be so naive as to believe that the appeals for reason or respect for human dignity can change reality. For the Antillean working in the sugarcane plantations in Le Robert, to fight is the only solution. And he will undertake and carry out this struggle not as the result of a Marxist or idealistic analysis but because quite simply he cannot conceive his life otherwise than as a kind of combat against exploitation, poverty, and hunger.[47]

And again: "We would be overjoyed to learn of the existence of a correspondence between some black philosopher and Plato. But we can absolutely not see how this fact would change the lives of eight-year-old kids working in the cane fields of Martinique or Guadaloupe."[48] James Cone similarly asserted: "It is so easy to make [Jesus's] name mean intellectual analysis, and we already have too much of that garbage in seminary libraries. What is needed is an application of the name to concrete affairs. What does the name mean when black people are burning buildings and white people are responding with riot-police control? Whose side is Jesus on?"[49] Though this book is primarily for and about Asian Americans, it is the unyielding, revolutionary spirit of Fanon and Cone that burns within, who set their faces like flint toward the complete annihilation of colonialism and Whiteness. So fiercely must our love burn.

I am not myself a theologian, nor the child of a theologian. I write in the urgency of the now, from the social location of a Malaysian resident alien in the United States, as glaciers melt and social unrest boils over. I wrestle with my own complicity in the settler-colonial state and complicated relationship with the term *Asian American* itself. Despite any misgivings of my own, Thomas Szasz writes that in the human kingdom the rule is define or be defined, and so do the activist roots of Asian American identity remind us that what we are called can also be weaponized.[50] Of course, the master's tool will not dismantle the master's house, as Audre Lorde famously wrote, but in claiming Asian America in all its contradictions we may still assert a coalitional politics that builds power across incommensurable differences, to bring about radical change and loving resistance.[51]

Paradoxically, the emptiness of Asian American identity is also its strength: it provides a deconstructive lens through which it may be apprehended that in liberation Asian Americanness will also pass away. I thus write from outside the fold of professional theology, as it were, offering an invitation to the Asian American church to struggle for the total liberation that God has redeemed us for. It is for liberation that the Messiah has liberated us. The Indigenous peoples of the Americas, Africa, and Asia have all lived through the end of the world after the Europeans arrived. Soon the climate catastrophe will bring again an end of the world to the masses, this time including the Europeans. As the ecological collapse begins, as we look back half a century to the political awakening of Asians in the United States and the liberation theology they had begun to build in the 1970s, we must ask if fifty years on others will look back on the 2020s and be inspired or disappointed. That is up to us. This book is not the first word on Asian American liberation theology, nor will it be the last. This is an opening salvo, as we follow God into the streets and rebuild a movement, working out our salvation with fear and trembling.

1.

A HISTORY WE NEVER KNEW WAS OURS

Retrieving Asian American Liberation Theology

> *What they have actually delivered when they promised assimilation is only to make asses out of the suckers who bought the line.*
> —Roy Sano, "Toward a Liberating Ethnicity."

Liberation theology burst onto the scene in the 1960s, beginning with Latin American Roman Catholic priests inspired by the outcome of Vatican II. They developed a theology of liberation whose point of departure was the Christian poor, who in turn formed the ecclesiastical base communities in Latin America and suffered under the effects of globalized capitalism. Concurrently, in the United States, revolutionary movements arose such as the Black Power movement and the involvement of the Black church in the civil rights movement. Malcolm X and Martin Luther King Jr. inspired a young James Cone to develop a Black theology of liberation, which radically interpreted Blackness—Black suffering especially—as the primary source of theological reflection in the United States and liberation from oppression as the principal task of theology. Also, riding the current of second-wave feminism was a White feminist liberation theology, which interrogated the heteropatriarchal power structures deeply embedded within churches and sexist hermeneutics, challenging the maleness of God and the Messiah, opening the way for broader theological conceptions of both.

These movements helped inspire indigenous theological movements elsewhere, in conjunction with the Third World revolutions and decolonization, leading to various Third World liberation theologies, including African and Asian liberation theologies attending to the transition from colonial imperialism to primarily capitalist nation-state apparatuses. The driving force of liberation theology is the condition of freedom, or liberation, establishing an anti-racist, anti-capitalist, and anti-imperialist stance through its critiques of systematic oppression and hegemonic domination. According to Gustavo Gutiérrez, liberation theology theologizes from the viewpoint of the oppressed, hence a theology "from below" that inverts the direction of theological knowledge-production and asserts the preferential option for the poor, a cornerstone in Catholic social teaching and Methodism. It is a theological reflection through praxis, *preguntando caminamos*, and must be engaged in class struggle. Viewed as a hermeneutic circle of suspicion, theological reflection through critical interrogation and persistent action calls for conceiving of Asian American theologies as critical theologies of difference. The early emergence of an Asian American consciousness brought with it the development of Asian American theologies, initially conceived as theologies of liberation and inculturation.

To set the stage, I begin with a survey of the lay of the land. Contemporary Asian American theology, I argue, has pursued a project of construction without deconstruction when in fact both are necessary. It has, as a whole, not mounted the necessary theological critiques of the multiple intersecting axes of gender, race, class, and nation that constitute United States nationalism and imperialism, let alone the self-critiques of Asian American complicity in perpetuating these relations of power through institu-

tional church structures, individual notions of piety, and conformity to the model-minority myth.[1] As Jonathan Tran's recent work
powerfully argues, and which I shall return to in chapter 5, critical
attention to the political-economic dimensions of race is necessary for Asian American theological reflection. For now, a review of
contemporary accounts of Asian American liberation theology and
Asian American theology will orient us and, in so doing, reveal that
the two have often been conflated, and that articulating a contemporary Asian American theology of liberation requires retrieving
a historical form of Asian American liberation theology. In order
to excavate this history, a detour is necessary to outline the broad
contours that distinguish inculturation and liberation theologies.

ASIAN AMERICAN THEOLOGY: INCULTURATION
VERSUS LIBERATION

Liberation theology stands in contrast, but not in opposition to,
the inculturation or identity-building projects attempted by Asian
American interpretations of hybridity, marginality, and story theology. Both inculturation and liberation theologies are contextual theologies, a notion first proposed by Taiwanese theologian
Shoki Coe in 1968, theological methods that attend to the cultural
contexts in which a theology is articulated.[2] Inculturation is the
process of localizing an apparently universal or foreign theological
formation, translating abstract theological concepts into culturally
relevant terms. Asian American and other "ethnic" theologies are
commonly categorized as contextualized theologies in the sense of
sociocultural contexts, leaving intact presumptions of the universality of European or White articulations of theological concepts.
In other words, it's rarely acknowledged that White theology is
also contextual.

Autobiographical theologies that narrate the social location of
Asians are valuable as counter-narratives to hegemonic theological discourse, but inculturation projects do not interrogate the

relations of power and difference that constitute Asian Americanness. That is, while it is good and well to make "our" voices heard, it is far from the same as asking what, or why, "we" are. It is therefore important to differentiate between the two. Theological discourse generated from experiences of marginalization may implicate racism and discrimination but often only abstractly. Inculturation as an identity-building project does not interrogate bourgeois Asian American politics that precludes solidarity with oppressed people. Any project of contextualization, according to Filipino American theologian Lester Edwin J. Ruiz, cannot avoid addressing the dangers of being absorbed into the "US-led western project" of empire and, furthermore, the dynamics of power and privilege that accompany other empire-building projects such as those of Europe or China.[3]

In developing an Asian theology of liberation, Sri Lankan Jesuit Aloysius Pieris proposed a theology of inculturation in terms of Asian religiousness and a theology of liberation responding to the poverty and oppression of the Asian masses, which present apparently competing modes of liberation and are reconciled in an Asian context through the (non-Semitic) "religiousness of the poor," articulating a "theology of liberation for our continent and simultaneously announc[ing] the birth of genuine local churches of Asia."[4] In doing so, Pieris points to interactions between inculturation and liberation theology, the latter being understood through the Latin American framework of poverty, and interprets liberation as being from Western models of Christianity and spirituality. But the territorialization of Asia and the Americas as discrete, bounded geographies ignores the complex interactions of colonialism, empire, migration, and capitalism. As such, Pieris's Asian theology of liberation is closer to an inculturation project, despite the overlapping aims of liberation and inculturation.[5]

Elsewhere, in articulating an Asian American liberative ethics, Sharon Tan presents liberation as moving from marginality to liminality, from racism to solidarity, and from imperialism to story.[6] Tan offers a succinct description of various Asian American theological paradigms. In the first case, Tan draws upon theological interpretations of Asian American identity: as hybridity following Wonhee Ann Joh, as interstitial integrity following Rita Nakashima Brock, and as liminality following Sang Hyun Lee. In the second case, Tan discusses the Korean concept of Han, which is "the pain of and resentment that comes through experiencing injustice on a personal, social, and structural level," which can be contrasted against Anselm Min's "solidarity of others," proposed as the new paradigm needed to replace liberation theologies that have "almost exhausted themselves."[7] In the third register, Tan draws upon Choan-Seng Song's notion of story theology, which focuses on "telling the stories of people's religious experience and deriving meaning from the stories." This is closely related to auto-biographical theology, which Peter C. Phan describes as theological reflections on personal experiences, invoking being "betwixt and between," and suggests that Asian American theologians are attempting to "construct an 'intercultural theology' for a new context characterized by the phenomenon of globalization."[8] This all is good and well, but these methodologies synthesized by Tan are constructions of an Asian American theological subjectivity rather than critical or liberative theological discourses. That these outline a liberative ethics is not as clear. In other words, these theological methods are better understood as inculturation theologies rather than liberation theologies, which, again, does not preclude creative interactions and cross-fertilizations between the two while being analytically differentiated.

To summarize, the various Asian American theologies that have been articulated can be distinguished by their core themes of inculturation, hybridity, and liberation. While interrelated concepts, they are different in their ends. From the point of view of liberation, inculturation can be seen as the first step in decoupling Asian American theologies from White theologies, often assumed to be universal and thus context free.[9] Notions of hybridity and marginality are by and large also inculturation projects, making efforts toward identity formation in the context of Asian American communities, in harmony with autobiographical theological methods that stake one's claim outside of White Christianity. But the diversity that is celebrated through these methods can often elide uncomfortable differences in order to present a unified subject. Liberation is about how we all get free.

What about Asian American feminist theologies? Where do they fit in? These, I argue, find their genealogies in the matrix of Third World liberation theologies, Asian feminist theologies, and Asian American theologies. Thus they are constituted by a forceful synthesis of inculturation through narrative modes, themselves forms of resistance within heteropatriarchal systems, and of liberation through critiques of power and gender oppression. Their power was in not only speaking up but also speaking against. Asian feminist theological voices were consolidated as early as 1989 in the collection *We Dare to Dream: Doing Theology as Asian Women* edited by Virginia Fabella and Sun Ai Lee Park, examining the intersections of poverty and religion as both Asians and women. [10]

At around the same time was the Asian women's theology of Chung Hyun Kyung, identifying with the second generation of liberation theologians in Asia who "do not spend our energy reacting mainly against the colonial legacy. We now spend our energies naming our experience with our own terms and creating alternatives that are liberative for us."[11] Kyung suggests that Asian women theologians should realize that they themselves are the text while the Bible and traditions of the Christian church are the contexts of their theology. The inherently intersectional theologies articulated by the first generation of Asian American feminist theologies and interpretations provide a rich corpus of feminist scholarship upon which later generations have built upon. At the same time, those in North America cannot yet abandon critical theology for constructive theology alone: we very much live in a colonial present that must be destroyed.

In addressing postmodern critiques of liberation theology, Kwok Pui-lan suggests that the challenge will be how the option for the margin will engage postmodernity in new ways and generate new insights for theological, social, political, and economic thinking and that the preferential option for the poor requires much unpacking if we are to avoid monolithic constructions of "the poor."[12] In a similar vein, the transformation of the "poor Asian woman" into a nationalist symbol in the context of post–World War II nation-building enterprises and into the heroine of Asian feminist theology has been critically examined by Wai-Ching Wong, tracing the generation of the "oppressed woman" through the politics of First and Third World feminist discourse and urging attention to the particularities and diversities of experience of Asian women, which resists universalization.[13] Thus we are reminded that the Asian American feminist theological subject must also resist the imposition of uniform subjectivity and, viewed thus, Asian American feminist theologies are not separate from but complement and challenge Asian American liberation theologies in important ways.

RETRIEVING AN ASIAN AMERICAN LIBERATION THEOLOGY

Having established Asian American liberation theology as a project distinct from current Asian American theological endeavors, I turn to the question of what *was* this thing called Asian American liberation theology? It had in fact existed in the sixties and seventies, alongside Black, Latin American, and feminist liberation theologies, though there is little record of it. I begin with Japanese American Methodist theologian Roy Isao Sano, now professor emeritus of United Methodist Studies at the Pacific School of Religion in Berkeley, California. One of the early prominent Asian American theologians that emerged in the 1960s, Sano's childhood experience of the Japanese concentration camp in Postone during the

Second World War shaped his theological worldview and conscientized him to the issues of marginalization and liberation. Sano became an early advocate of Asian American liberation theology, patterned after the Black liberation theology articulated by James Cone and Gayraud Wilmore of the first generation of Black liberation theologians.

An Asian American liberation theology was articulated primarily by Japanese, Chinese, Filipine, and Korean Americans, which together constituted the majority of Asian Americans at the time. This theology differed from other liberation theologies in that it traces its genealogy in part to the experience of Japanese incarceration, or internment, which forced Japanese American Christians to develop a theology of suffering, one that could speak to their trauma. In a 1986 sermon, Jitsuo Morikawa, who was held at Poston Internment Camp in Arizona, explained how Japanese Americans' experience of rejection and collective incarceration showed them "the extravagance of God's grace, that even pain, suffering and injustice He often transforms into blessing."

Another former Postonite, Paul Nagano developed a theology of marginality, concluding that his marginality within America was a permanent predicament and that the church must "mean the humanness of the minorities as well as the majority—the majority freed from their peculiar arrogance and the minorities freed to be what God has meant them to be as persons."[14] Similarly, Korean American theologian Jung Young Lee, a contemporary of Sano, believed the loneliness, alienation, and suffering that he experienced was due to being an immigrant, and that the "liberation of Asian Americans as a marginal people could only come about if the people at the center are liberated from their exclusivist and discriminatory worldviews."[15] Thus Nagano and Lee both argued that liberation involves both the oppressor and the oppressed.

Yet, what little historical remnant that is left of this movement is mostly archived in a collection of twenty boxes containing documents from the Pacific and Asian American Center for Theology and Strategies (PACTS), which grew out of the need to "re-think faith and reorient ministries in light of the emergence of ethnic consciousness" in the late 1960s. It was designed to be "an ecumenical center for research, resourcing, recruiting, training, and consciousness-raising which sought to promote the fulfillment of God's mission through the ministries of the churches and the service of community groups."[16] These archival boxes contain the writings of an earlier generation of Asian Americans, revealing the intense theological activity and conscientization during that period. As the first director of PACTS, Sano compiled two unpublished readers: *AmerAsian Theology of Liberation* (1973) and *The Theologies of Asian Americans and Pacific Peoples* (1976). In a preface to the 1976 reader, Sano wrote that "the 'internal colony' which we have experienced has rendered far too many of us speechless, convinced we have nothing to offer. If liberation means anything, it should release the wealth of stories, insights, vision, and courage which God has given us. 'Where the Spirit of the Lord is, there is freedom.' (II Corinthians 3:17)." From the PACTS collections, there are many insights already to be excavated, which provide historical grounding for new articulations of Asian American theologies of liberation. In what follows, I quote from these texts at length as an exercise in retrieving these theological voices from a forgotten historical moment.

In the same reader, Dennis Loo asks and answers the question: "Why an Asian American theology of liberation?" Arguing that "the type of dominance which has continued historically until the present cannot continue any longer if we claim to be the church, the body of Christ which includes all the different peoples of the world," Loo detailed the myths of excessive Asian American ethnocentrism, of success as model minorities, and of being a problem-free racial group, altogether reinforcing oppression among Asians in America. There is a need for Asians in America to rethink, to articulate, and to appropriate an interpretation of the Christian faith, Loo continued, which combats rather than perpetuates oppressive thought patterns and encourages the development of an Asian American frame of reference, making its own unique contribution to the developing Third World theological dialogue, to the global theological task, and to liberation movements in the United States and in the world.[17] In doing so, Loo made clear the connections between the possibility of Asian American liberation theology and the struggles of Third World liberation theologies and movements internationally.

Elsewhere, Sano cites Harold Cruse's *The Crisis of the Negro Intellectual* and Wilmore's *Black Religion and Black Radicalism* as sources of reflection on oppression and internal colonialism. Considering cultural oppression as more basic and inhumane in some ways than political and economic oppression, and in questioning the institutions that deal with them, Sano held that "we will in every case come to the same conclusion as historians of Black communities," that "although the church has played into the hands of those who would subject ethnic minorities to cultural genocide, the cultural function of the church also facilitated the humanizing qualities as well." Drawing from Cone and Gutiérrez, Sano held that liberation had become the critical norm to determine the primary theology category, and that liberation is "not only the basis for reconciliation, it may unite diverse movements for liberation. The diverse colorful peoples within the United States and abroad in the Third World can find in the theme a uniting task," including "feminist, gay, poor or defrauded whites" as those who may also find cause to combat oppression as well.[18] Signaling the characteristic grounding of liberation theology in praxis, Sano concluded the consultation with a quotation, saying, "There is nothing quite so practical as good theory and nothing so good for theory-making as direct involvement with practice."

Elsewhere, in a preface to the proceedings of the Second Conference on East Asian and AmerAsian Theology held in Berkeley in 1975, Sano expressed regret in complaining at an earlier time that "ethnic minorities in the United States of America have so many pressing needs loading them down that they had no time for additional involvements in international issues in East Asia." At the same conference, Harold Hak-won Sunoo pointed out that the church "identifies with the economic and political power in the present system," having become "friends of the rich, not of the poor; friends of power, not of the oppressed; friends of the rulers, not of the ruled." So the class problem of Asian American embourgeoisement is hardly new. Sunoo asked, "Are we able to challenge the present-day condition of America which is dominated by giant corporations and centralized bureaucratic system, and corporate capitalism and militarization?" and suggested that the new theology, theology of liberation, theology of hope, or "whatever you might call it," is found among "social actions; no other source. Social actions simply mean serving the people—the masses of the poor, the dispossessed, and the oppressed. We, the Asian Americans, are the oppressed ones."[19] It is important to register here that these Asian Americans were less interested in liberation theology as a theoretical exercise and more as a vehicle of social change and revolution. Their unvarnished indictments are striking. All of these invocations remain as relevant today as they were then.

Describing the American dream as one that has "shattered into a nightmare schizophrenia" and "the logic of industrialization," Sunoo held that we need to resist all the dehumanizing effects of the old inequality, and that "the church must arm [sic] with a new hope, a new theology of social justice. American church, [sic] in other words must have a Third World perspective, because God has revealed Himself through the masses of the poor." And finally, the concern of all the Third World people revolves around the relationship of oppression and liberation: "We, the Asian-Americans, are very much involved with this liberation movement. This historical task we must accept with joy and hope." Sunoo, in describing an ethics of liberation, pointed to the Christ who knew that "poverty, hunger, injustice, exploitation, alienation, racism and war are all products of men's greed for wealth and power. To be a good Christian, then, meant to stop such men so that all persons might benefit from the earth as God intended." And under capitalism, "being is displaced by having." According to Sunoo, the Marxist concept of "class-revolutionary consciousness" derives from "no other place than from the historical Christian vision of man," and that the "fullness of liberation" is a free gift from Christ; the meaning of total liberation is communion with God and with other men: "I cannot be a free man when my neighbor is a slave."[20]

These brief snapshots display the breadth and depth of historical Asian American voices seeking to establish a theology of liberation relevant to Asian American contexts. The theologies articulated drew from the biblical hermeneutics of other contemporary liberation theologies and connected them to liberation struggles on a global scale. For example, Wesley Woo invoked Gutiérrez's understanding of theology as critical reflection through praxis, indissolubly linked to historical praxis. He proposed that theologizing from an Asian American perspective must "keep integrity with faith in a God who calls us to full and authentic humanity," generate "insight-action" in the sense of providing insight that leads to, and manifests itself in, action, and be done in a corporate context, allowing "the corporate body to criticize, validate, and enrich our theologizing." Woo noted that the new "Asian-American" identity created a tangible expression of corporate identity but cautioned against reducing "pluralistic understandings of the Gospel to one format." He suggested that one of the characteristics for an Asian-American perspective is a prophetic message that involves the "debunking" or "de-reifying" of dehumanizing realities, realities that deny authentic humanity to peoples and instead perpetuates oppression, pointing to the need to conceive Asian American theology through difference rather than identity.[21]

Many of these theological and autobiographical writings display what might seem to some today a brazenness in critiquing White racism. Sano, for example, referred to race relations in most Protestant settings as "nothing more than race-erasion."

Relations between "the colorless and the colorful," Sano argued, is an encounter and confrontation, and that "some Protestants say they have no racially separated or segregated structures," which goes to show that "they have only appealed to what students would now call bastardized ethnic minorities, or anaesthetized ethnics": "What they have actually delivered when they promised assimilation is only to make asses out of the suckers who bought the line." But their criticism is also constructive. As Sano wrote, "The price whites will have to pay to make the yellow peril into a pearl is to bury the Melting Pot theory which in practice turned out to be a crock of baloney," and addresses "the recovery of ethnicity of a lighter of the colorful ethnic minorities which has always been tempted to pass as colorless, namely the Yellows or Asians."[22]

Early Asian American feminist perspectives were also clearly articulated in these collections. For example, June I. Kimoto, on the other hand, named the "collusion of the Institutional Church as an active participant to the Asian Dilemma," zeroing in on the combination of "the Asian sense of Shame and Christianity's Guilt." "There needs to be special focus on us—Asian women," Kimoto asserted, "as we are seeking commonality with other minority races, the 'three-steps behind' syndrome has also been Third World Women's entrapment." The solidarity of Asian American liberation theologies with Third World movements must continue to be grounded in Third World feminisms and decolonization and undergird the radical and revolutionary Asian American spirits that combat systemic oppression and produce meaningful solidarity with other communities of color. Kimoto pointed to Vine Deloria Jr.'s works on Native American theology; Dee Brown's *Bury My Heart at Wounded Knee*, which "gives exhaustive documentation of the persistent and relentless pursuit of American Indians and offers Asians an insight into the workings of White thoughts"; and *Black Rage* by psychiatrists Grier and Cobbs, who "expose the problems of Black Folk—there are parallels that can awaken the Asian minds."[23] Solidarity, thus conceived, is built upon shared struggles against oppression, revealing the differentiated forms of power as it relates to other groups, in a collective effort to raise consciousness.

Another contributor, Leslie Loo, asked a series of questions: "Can I add that [Asian women] are also trying to come to terms with the desire of many American men of all colors to think of us as exotic dolls and sources of mystery? Can I say without hurting feelings that American women (especially in the church) think of us only as 'superb' tea pourers or subconsciously as sources of cultural education for their families?" And further, in wondering whether Asian women as second-class citizens among minority Americans have maintained an acceptable passivity in order to survive, Loo asked, "Would it be more nearly correct to say that as minority persons we have been powerless and therefore had situations such as the Japanese concentration camp era forced upon us?," linking the material consequences of oppression to the mental subjugation of internalized racism. "Do you realize that labor conditions and legislation improved for American women at a point in history when the United States began to use the labor of women and men in Third World countries? Are you aware that Third World women make the lowest wages in American industry?"[24] Loo thus problematized White women's feminism through global capitalist extraction of Asian women's labor and connected with the struggles of Third World women by identifying as an Asian woman. The vigor of Asian American women's theological critiques at the intersections of race, gender, and class provided a robust foundation and heritage for later generations of Asian American feminist theologies.

In sum, the contributions of Asian Americans in the 1970s to an "AmerAsian" theology of liberation laid the groundwork upon which contemporary rearticulations of Asian American theologies of liberation can build. Already from this handful of excerpts we can see the rich theological imagination, drawing inspiration with the Black, Indigenous, feminist, and Third World struggles against oppression.

The coming and passing of these Asian American theologies

of liberation took place against the backdrop of the transition between what historian Timothy Tseng described as the first and second waves of Asian immigration to the United States. The first wave began in the 1850s, with Asian labor arriving in Hawaii and California, characterized by nationalism, social support, and Roman Catholicism or mainline Protestantism, and ended by the exclusion acts; the second wave marks the post-1965 era, and amid the growing Muslim, Buddhist, and Hindu migrations, the Protestant Christian subpopulation shifted from mainline to evangelical or Pentecostal orientations, exhibiting stronger "separatist tendencies."[25] The constantly changing face of Asian America necessitates a constant reevaluation of Asian American theological subjectivity, particularly given the half century that has passed since an Asian American theology of liberation was first articulated. This reevaluation will carry us into the next two chapters.

NO LONGER OPPRESSED? CONTRADICTIONS OF ASIAN AMERICAN LIBERATION TODAY

Fifty years later, Asian American liberation theology has faded from the Asian American theological consciousness. One might point to the fact that in the 1980s, Ronald Reagan oversaw the decimation of social services funding, which many organizations in the early Asian American movement depended upon. It could also be argued that the disappearance of Asian American theologies of liberation from collective memory was a result of the lack of material production with regards to these knowledges, in contrast to the intellectual outputs of Black, feminist, and Latin American liberation theologies that have the landmark texts of Cone, Daly, and Gutiérrez, respectively, and persist in theological imaginations. Indeed, no mention at all of Asian American theologies of liberation is made in historian Lillian Barger's recent account of the intellectual history of liberation theology.[26] This erasure is glaring, in light of the PACTS archives.

Nonetheless, the theological writings of later generations of Asian Americans reflect two major streams that flowed from the remnants of this historical Asian American liberation theology: theologies of inculturation that sought to build an Asian American theological identity through reflections on marginalization, hybridity, and liminality, and Asian American feminist theologies that drew upon social science critiques such as postcolonialism and feminism to produce a distinctive theological voice and important critiques. The latter carries some of the fire of theological critique that speaks truth to power, perhaps due in part to the nature of the "double bind" of being a person of color and a woman or gender-nonconforming person. Moreover, given the patriarchal structures of almost all settler North American and Asian cultures, this places Asian American women in yet another double bind, on top of the racist oppression inscribed upon Asian female bodies through labor exploitation and sexual objectification. In this sense, the liberation theologies articulated by Sano, Nagano, and others did not die off but influenced the next generation of Asian American theologians.

Asian American feminist theologies, in conversation with Asian feminist theologies, drew heavily on postcolonial critiques, such as the works of Edward Said, Homi Bhabha, and Gayatri Spivak.[27] While undoubtedly valuable advances, such critiques tend to focus on the discursive rather than structural relations of power and the lasting effects of colonization on the psychological level. They ultimately lack firepower when deployed within the ongoing settler-colonial US empire rather than in the decolonized Third World. Here, *anti*-colonial praxis is more relevant than *post*-colonial theory. Asian American theology must rise to unapologetically confront ongoing systems of oppression such as capitalism, racism, sexism, and settler colonialism. Liberation theology can deliver a more incisive critique when it engages the structural and systemic nature of power and oppression. And unlike these theories, what liberation theology has to offer is an emphasis on theopraxis, a radical political commitment to action, colaboring with God and the proletariat.

Today, "Asian American" is an established demographic category, even as the racial group it intends to signify continues to grow in increasing complexity through immigration, transnational flows, and class difference. It is the fastest growing racial group with the largest economic disparity in the United States. Yet, its problems are not new: Sano had already pointed out that many ethnic minorities arrive in the promised land and forget that there can be new forms of oppression in the land of promise, drawing on Cone's reading of the book of Judges, and that they have become part of "the system of oppression not knowing that their penetration into existing white dominated structures and their success in moving up have only placed them in a position of an oppressor."[28] Later Asian American theologies largely address racism in the abstract, a fantasy of racism without racists, sexism without sexists, marginality without marginalization. Reducing Asian American theology to a single dimension of hybridity and marginality leaves intact Asian American success through participation in systems of oppression, as previous Asian American liberation theologians have already pointed out.

In relation to this, Christian ethicist Ki Joo Choi complicates theologian Sang Hyun Lee's notion of Asian American hybridity, pointing to intra-Asian hostilities and prejudices. Citing a study of Asian American interracial politics which concluded that "Asian Americans and Blacks, in particular, appear to lack extensive contact and shared experiences that facilitate coalition building," Choi brings attention to the fact of Asian Americans inhabiting new instantiations of White racism and privilege, or an "Asian American whiteness." This stands in stark contrast to the immense influence of the Black Power movement and Black liberation theology on Asian American liberation theology and the latter's attempt to find common cause with the Black liberation movement.

Lee argues that the moral promise of hybridity offers a way to call out and resist Asian American reinscriptions of Whiteness. But this requires intentionality and self-critique. Echoing Sano, Choi argues that inattention to conscious and unconscious attitudes and behaviors that mimic White racialized hierarchies as a consequence of their growing socioeconomic achievements may have Asian Americans "sleepwalking into the very forms of life that perpetuate exclusion and marginalization, including their own."[29] For this reason, it is not immediately obvious whether Asian American identity can be "conceived in a manner that advances solidarity and cooperation between Asian Americans and non-Asian Americans of color."[30] Put differently, many Asian Americans simply do not *feel* oppressed.

Fumitaka Matsuoka also recognized this problem: Asian American professionals, having grown up in a system in which class identification is perceived as more important than race, are often astonished at the individual acts of racism directed against them. They expect their professional status to protect them, Matsuoka writes, and not only on the individual level—Asian American churches, too, have adopted the myth of power based on class identification, or the view that power is gained through institutional and economic access and upward mobility, the exact opposite of the beatitudes. "Perhaps the severest critique we can direct upon Asian American churches is that to a certain extent they have co-opted into the very racist structure of society and thus have come to neglect the most alienated people in society, the poor and underclass, even among our own Asian Americans," and the price to be paid for middle-class advancements is found in "our alienation from the poor within the Asian American community. In our effort to overcome racial subordination, Asian American churches have come to perpetuate the very ills of the society we critique."[31]

Choi instead proposes a "tragic conception" of hybrid identity, which calls attention to the "discriminatory traps" of reproducing racism and inattentiveness to the persistent inequalities between Asian Americans and Whites. Tragic hybridity does not assume that Asian American Christian ethics is inherently liberatory. Instead, its potential for liberation and racial solidarity arises only from a commitment to interpreting Asian American experience through sustained self-criticism or, in other words, to critical theology.[32] Asian American culture and Asian American identity, Choi argues, arise from a social logic—cultural choices that are more akin to strategies of negotiating social realities more so than a mediation of those circumstances. That is, it is more than just a reflection of social conditions; it is an adaptive response. According to sociologists Min Zhou and J. V. Gatewood, US-born Asian Americans "usually do not seize on traditional cultural symbols" and instead "tend to build their identities on the basis of mediating *interpretive memories* of homeland cultures in which they have never personally lived, and their own diverse life experiences in the United States"[33]—a projected nostalgia.

This negotiation echoes David Eng and Shinhee Han's conception of racial formation as both an intersubjective and intrasubjective experience, the racial melancholia of homeland cultures never directly experienced, which I shall draw on more fully in Chapter 3. It brings to bear the external reality of racial discrimination whose persistence in Asian American life hybridity fails to attend to.[34] Thus, to be Asian in North America is not simply a matter of fact but a process of racialization that involves unequal power relations and, all too often, violence. In this sense, hybridity or liminality takes a shortcut to liberation or borderlessness by sanctioning the appropriation of various cultures in an attempt to construct a coherent yet hybrid racial self.

The work of constructing Asian American theologies proper is an impossible yet unavoidable task. As Matsuoka points out, it's unavoidable that issues of "ethnically based identity" will continue to be a primary concern among Asian Americans and will remain a major theme in Asian American theological thought as long as the forces of cultural alienation and oppressive racism in American society persist.[35] Said otherwise, whether the category "Asian

American," let alone any Asian American theology of liberation, is useful remains an open question, but the reality of its persistence is evermore clear in the wake of COVID-19. The question is not whether "Asian America" will continue to define us but what we can make it do for us and others.

Liberation theology is distinct from inculturation theology. The two converge when, as theologian Eleazar Fernadez argues, "the final thrust of contextualization is liberation, not for the sake of mere inculturating or indigenizing a theological given."[36] Asian American liberation theology as a struggle for collective freedom should be differentiated from other Asian American theologies as inculturation or identity-building projects while drawing from and pointing to the sustained work of Asian American feminist theologians. The 1970s Asian American theology of liberation lies in the past, but it is a sufficient foundation to build upon half a century later. At the same time, the terrain has shifted greatly, and a new accounting is necessary, as indeed Fanon wrote that each generation much discover its mission and fulfill it or betray it.

The first question that must be reassessed, then, is who "we" are and how "we" come to be. Deconstructing the Asian American theological subject, grounding it in difference rather than identity, will clear the path toward a critical theological discourse upon which Asian American theologies of liberation can begin to be reconstructed with sustained reflection through praxis. The goal of the remainder of this book, then, is to carry out the self-critical analyses along these multiple intersecting axes of nation, race, class, gender, and sexuality as required by any Asian American theology of liberation, or tragic hybridity, and to directly confront the issues that attend Asian American subjectivity and prevent solidarity.

SUBJECT

2.

"WE ARE HERE BECAUSE YOU WERE THERE"

Asian American Theology as a Theology of Migration

> It's important that we all understand that the main terrorist and the main enemy of the world's people is the U.S. government. Racism has been a weakness of this country from the beginning. Throughout history, all people of color, and all people who don't see eye-to-eye with the U.S. government has been subjected to American terror.
>
> —Yuri Kochiyama, *Heartbeat of Struggle*

> But I feel that the greatest message that could be given from the Chol Soo Lee movement is that, as Mr. K. W. Lee said, is the purity, the unselfishness, the integrity of people, giving to a stranger. And I think that message needs to be brought back to the Asian community. I think we live in a world of selfishness. All the past movements, the civil rights to gain the right to attend schools and so forth and now that education is being used for "everything is for me." We have no room to share with others. I think that if [my] story could be told, yes there is small room there. There are still deprived people, even more deprived people than in the past. The need to give today is far greater than in my own time.
>
> —Chol Soo Lee, "A Conversation with Chol Soo Lee and K. W. Lee."

Because all our lives, I mean I lived it, Koreans have no identity in America because in the previous 100 years, Korea had no identity because Korea was a land that was wiped off the map; so there was no identity. So it's very important that Koreans must come to realize that they are Koreans here. Nobody is going to give a fuck for them. In other words, the Chol Soo Lee case is the first time that Koreans had to wake up. Otherwise, what do you have at all? That is why I was emphasizing it. This was also an education for Koreans, including myself. Listen, I am not doing just for him. I am doing it for myself too—trying to find my place in America. If the Koreans don't give a shit about their own people, especially an absolutely powerless voice like him, then what is the future of Koreans in America? The voiceless people and the power-less people must have a chance in America.

—K. W. Lee, "A Conversation with Chol Soo Lee and K. W. Lee."

It's not fair.

—Vincent Chin's last words

In April 2018, the Trump administration implemented a "zero tolerance" policy along the Mexico–United States border to deter immigration, informally referred to as the family-separation policy under which children were separated from their parents or guardians. Adults were held in federal jails to be prosecuted while children were held by the United States Department of Health and Human Services. The policy was implemented in response to the increasing number of Central American asylum seekers arriving at the border, many fleeing economic instability and gang violence. While the policy was formally ended after two months following major public outcry and protest, thousands of children were separated as a result and less than half were eventually reunited.

In part, the tragedy was manufactured by Donald Trump's insistence on the existence of a crisis at the Mexico–United States border that warranted the construction of a border wall, on which

Trump based much of his 2015 presidential campaign. In June 2019, the Trump administration announced that 1,400 migrant children would be detained in Fort Sill, Oklahoma, in what used to be the long-time prison of Apache leader Geronimo until his death in 1909 and a Japanese incarceration camp during World War II. The plans were eventually halted, once again due to public opposition. Less publicized was the fact that during the Obama administration, several hundred migrant children were also held in the same facility in 2014.

At another concentration camp in Manzanar, California, which held over 120,000 Japanese and Japanese Americans from 1942 to 1945 under Franklin Roosevelt's Executive Order 9066, there was an uptick in Muslim visitors following the September 11, 2001, attacks. The Muslim visitors saw clearly the parallels with the thousands of people of Arab and South Asian descent who were swiftly detained following the attacks. Visitors again increased in 2017 when Executive Order 13769 was signed by Trump, informally referred to as the Muslim ban, suspending the entry of Syrian refugees indefinitely and severely restricting the entry of people from Iran, Iraq, Libya, Somalia, Sudan, and Yemen. At that point, the Council on American–Islamic Relations had already been organizing pilgrimages to Manzanar for over a decade, connecting Muslim Americans to Japanese American survivors and activists. The Muslim ban was answered with major protests, beginning at JFK International Airport in New York City and spreading to the rest of the country. The crisscrossing of these systematic forms of xenophobia and Islamophobia signals the interconnectedness of various struggles against state violence and racism.[1]

The Japanese concentration camps also hold a key to a historical Asian American theology of liberation. While the revolutionary movements led by the Black Power movement in the United States during the 1960s were indeed joined by Asians, at the time racialized as Orientals rather than Asian Americans, it was from the painful experience of mass incarceration that Japanese American Christians found the raw material to develop a theology of struggle and suffering. These experiences, according to historian Anne Blankenship, encouraged lay Japanese Christians to develop new lived theologies and accelerated the evolution of new structures and theologies, building a foundation for Asian American liberation theologies articulated in the 1960s and 1970s.[2] This is not to say that Asians had not suffered since the Spanish ships first landed with Filipino deckhands, some of whom deserted as early as 1763 to form the first Asian settlement of Saint Malo in Louisiana and becoming the Manilamen or Tagalas with the help of the Indigenous inhabitants there.[3] Later generations of Asians seized upon Asian American identity as a political weapon, which forms the historical bedrock for building a contemporary Asian American theology of liberation. To do so, we must first ask who its subjects are. What *is* Asian America?

ASIAN AMERICA: THE VIEW FROM ABOVE

Asian American theology is unquestionably a theology of migration, because the story of Asians in the Americas cannot be told without migration and movement across the oceans. While some may find the historical recollections of this chapter banal, these rehearsals are necessary preparations for the later chapters. The fact that the mere existence of Asian American studies was and continues to be a site of struggle highlights the lack of avenues for structured learning of these histories. This lack of a historical consciousness manifests in a collective amnesia. The historical vignettes presented in this chapter are only a small selection of the deep and vast history of Asians in the Americas. While it may seem futile to attempt to hold it all in view, an ahistorical approach is an indefensible one. History is not enough to guide us, but it must surely ground us.

To speak of Asian America is never a simple discussion. Inasmuch as Asian American identity was first established as an oppo-

sitional identity for the purpose of politically organizing disparate groups of Asians people in the United States, it is largely a
demographic label today.[4] Not only does it elide the suffering of
poorer Asians, the 2020 US Census definition of Asian excludes
those from the Middle East and Central Asia.[5] Among the latter,
many prefer to identify as White rather than Asian or "Other," further problematizing the internal cohesion of Asian identity in the
US. (A "Check it right, you ain't white" campaign leading up to
the 2010 US census encouraged those of Arab and Iranian descent
to not identify as White.) The relationship of Asian Americans to
Whiteness depends in part on where one falls on the color line—a
brown paper bag test for Asians.[6] The absorption of those of Middle Eastern and North African descent into the White category
is just the latest instance of the malleability of Whiteness, where
before it was the Italians, Irish, and Jews, however conditional their
acceptance.[7]

Nonetheless, by these standards, the Pew Research Center,
using 2013–2015 survey data showed that the Asian population in
the US grew from 11.9 million to 20.4 million between 2000 and
2015, the fastest growth rate of any major racial or ethnic group,
the second being the Hispanic population. Undocumented Asians
make up about 13% of the 11.1 million undocumented or "unautho-
rized immigrants" in the US, mainly coming from India, China,
the Philippines, and Korea. Put together, we see that about one
in every seven Asian immigrants in the United States is undocumented.[8] Economically, the Asian population in the United States
as a whole appears to fare better than average, with median annual
household incomes of $85,800, compared with $61,800 among all
US households. By this measure, most Asian households earn more
than most US households. But disaggregating the data by national
origin reveals that while Indians ($119,000), Filipine ($90,400), Japanese ($83,000), and Chinese ($82,000) have the highest median
income while most other groups fall below the median. At the
lower end of the spectrum are Nepalese ($55,000) and Burmese

($44,400) households. Similarly, Mongolian and Burmese had the highest poverty rates among Asian groups (25 percent each), even as Asians overall had lower poverty rates compared to the general US population.[9] Importantly, the Southeast and South Asian populations indexed here are largely refugees, asylum seekers, undocumented, or working-class migrants.

Given the limitation of large surveys for reasons such as narrow definitions of nationality, citizenship, race, and household, not to mention the inherent difficulties in producing reliable demographic statistics, I lean but lightly on data such as this.[10] At the same time, such broad outlines provide a necessary, even if inadequate, grounding for interpreting Asian American theology, as we want to be talking about the real and tangible experience of Asians, which can be measured in various ways, however inaccurately.

The census, as a tool of the state, provides a view of Asian America from the eyes of the nation-state. The 1820 census first introduced the racial category "free colored," later expanded in 1890 to include Negroes, Chinese, Japanese, and civilized Indians, and by 1920 also Indian, Filipino, Hindu, Korean, Hawaiian, Malay, Siamese, and Māori. This represents the first wave of migration and exclusion of Asians to the United States and, as Lisa Lowe argued, the first layer of the legal structure of the racial formation of Asians in the United States through a series of immigration acts.

Whereas Filipino and other Southeast Asians first arrived on the American continent over four hundred years ago, popular accounts often describe Asian American history as being only about 150 years old. Persons of Asian origin first appeared in the US census in 1870 with "Chinese or Mongolian," then in 1890 "Japanese." In 1860, "civilized Indians" were also first counted, meaning the Indigenous people. The 1930 census grew to include Mexican, Filipino, Hindu (South Asian), and Korean populations, indicating the need to track the changing migrant labor populations of the time. At around the same time, the first laws systematically excluding immigration according to race were passed, beginning with the

1875 Page Act banning immigration of "cheap Chinese labor and immoral Chinese women," the 1882 Chinese Exclusion Act banning Chinese immigration entirely, the Gentlemen's Agreement of 1907 in which Japan agreed to ban emigration to the United States, the Immigration Act of 1917 designating the so-called Asiatic barred zone spanning much of Asia and the Pacific Islands, and finally the 1924 Johnson-Reed Act, which included the Asian Exclusion Act, effectively banning all immigration from Asia.[11] The Philippine Independence Act of 1934 established the process for the Philippines to transition to independence but at the same time limited immigration from the Philippines. It was quickly followed by the Filipino Repatriation Act of 1935 that provided one-way passage back for Filipine in the United States, similar to the repatriation of Mexicans during that time.

This exclusionary trend reversed course beginning with the 1945 War Brides Act, allowing alien spouses and children of members of the US Armed Forces to immigrate to the United States. Given the earlier Exclusion Act, this benefited Chinese women greatly, and in the following year "war brides" from the Philippines and India were also allowed to immigrate under the Alien Fiancées and Fiancés Act of 1946, amended the next year to also allow for Korean and Japanese women. These together with the Page Act indicate the sexual dimension of Asian immigration, continuing today with trafficking and other sexually differentiated forms of migrant labor. Indeed, Roy Sano's use of the term "AmerAsian theology" underscores the limitations of the vocabulary of his time: the Amerasian was a specific form of racial mixing, most often the product of a US military man and an East Asian woman whereby the Asian woman's body becomes the archetypal symbol for the imperialist and colonial penetration of the United States empire into the Orient.[12]

The second wave of Asian immigration to the United States began with the watershed Hart-Cellar Act in 1965, which followed the Civil Rights Act of the previous year, abolishing the immigration quotas based upon the existing populations within the United States. It is important to note that the Black struggle for civil rights paved the way for Asian inclusion and also that these struggles played out in the theater of the Cold War, making geopolitically expedient certain legal concessions made to people of color. That is, the United States had to present its liberal democracy as more favorable than communism to people of color. The 1965 Act, together with the 1975 Indochina Migration and Refugee Assistance Act bringing in refugees of the United States' proxy wars from South Vietnam, Laos, and Cambodia, transformed Asian demographics in the United States from consisting of largely migrant labor to include highly educated professionals and asylum-seeking refugees from greater portions of the Asian continent. Later, the Immigration Act of 1990 reformed the 1965 act to allow more skilled and educated immigrants in comparison to family-based immigration. These ebbs and flows of Asia migration reflect the racialized nature of labor in the United States. In contrast to the transatlantic slave trade through which African America was created, the cycles of Asian immigration reveal Asian labor to be a fungible commodity—an expendable, infinitely replaceable resource, a particular form of racialized surplus labor that Iyko Day calls alien capital.[13] On the other hand, the growing class difference within Asian subpopulations points to Asian American heterogeneity, foreclosing naive forms of solidarity.

The racial formation of Asian Americans is circumscribed by legal acts and court cases, as suggested by critical race theory, a concept which emerged from the field of critical legal studies, not least Kimberlé Crenshaw's important notion of intersectionality.[14] Intersectionality draws attention to the multiple layers of oppression such as race and gender, which produce multiplicities and inequivalent experiences that cannot be accounted for through any single approach. As a coalitional politics, Asian American theology must recognize the intersections of Asian identity with other dimensions of class, gender, sexuality, and nation. And as US legal history shows, the figure of the Asian, along with Hawaiians, Mexicans, Africans, and others, plays a crucial role in the construction and maintenance of Whiteness in the United States.

But what is Whiteness, from a legal standpoint, and how did Asians relate to it? The federal district ruling *In re Ah Yup* (1878) first denied naturalization to Chinese immigrants on the basis of being non-White and was later followed by dozens of challenges to the legal definition of Whiteness. The Supreme Court decision in *Takao Ozawa v. United States* (1922) ruled that "White" referred to Caucasians and that Ozawa, a Japanese man who argued he was White as defined by cultural practices and loyalty to the nation-state, was not Caucasian. Yet in *United States v. Bhagat Singh Thind* (1923), Thind, a South Asian man, argued that he was Caucasian based on the controversial theory that Northern Indians were the result of Indo-Aryan migration, sometimes known as the Aryan invasion theory. But here the US Supreme Court ruled instead that "White" and "Caucasian" are terms of common speech and not of scientific origin, revealing the social construction of Whiteness and its flexibility in including or excluding others according to convenience.[15]

So what are we to make of Asian Americans? Yến Lê Espiritu describes Asian Americanness as a pan-ethnicity, one that encompasses the world's largest continent's heterogeneous population, and finds itself in the United States.[16] It is hopeless to narrowly define what Asian American means. Instead, it more properly functions as a fluid and open-ended signifier, unbounded by geography, citizenship, or sociological definitions. This points to the "subjectless" approach to Asian Americanness proposed by scholar Kandice Chuh, for whom the construction and deconstruction of Asian American identity reveals the ways in which race, class, gender, sexuality, religion, and nation are discursively constructed, an idea I shall return to in chapter 3.[17] In other words, apprehending the problems inherent in trying to establish a neat Asian American identity leads to a better understanding of the ways in which various ideologies benefit some and disadvantage others. Asian American theology must pay constant attention to just whom exactly its presumed subjects are and are not. In the tradition of theologies of liberation, this is particularly important as it compels us to seek out the nonhuman, the other, the nonbeing with whom God's spirit dwells.

In practice, I shall rely on what postcolonial theorist Gayatri Spivak refers to as a strategic essentialism, which understands that a signifier can be at once problematic because it reifies what is fluid but also useful because race structures everyday life in the United States and can be useful for politics. Strategic essentialism describes the unavoidable usefulness of something that is very dangerous. This tension was already understood by the early Asian American movements, but it must be held even more clearly in view now as Asian Americans form the most heterogeneous demographic in terms of household wealth, national origin, and educational attainment than any other racial group.[18] The rise of select groups of Asians into places of prominence and power, while itself presenting an obstacle to solidarity with the powerless and invisible, signals the potential value of organizing under the banner of Asian America. As Toni Morrison writes, the function of freedom is to free someone else. What power and liberation accrued by Asian Americans are not to be hoarded, a light hidden under a basket but set on a hill, giving light to all that are in the house. Rather than think of power-sharing as a zero-sum game, any Asian American liberation must seek the liberation of all.

With this in mind, Asian American churches must also be in dialogue with Asian churches, recognizing that each one's struggle against oppression is deeply interconnected with that of others. White racism and anti-Blackness are global imperial projects, as are capitalism and heteropatriarchy. For us to have any hope of truly opposing them we must free our thinking from the confines of the national borders drawn by White Europeans or any other neocolonial power. It is worth noting that in their later works, both James Cone and Gustavo Gutiérrez acknowledged that their respective theologies of liberation, in their first iterations, suffered from a lack of gender analysis and Third World perspectives. Hence, as important as it is for us to be well-informed about the coloniality of power and how Asian American identity is constituted through legal and institutional discourse, in order to discover the means of resistance, we have to privilege the view from below.

ASIAN AMERICA: THE VIEW FROM BELOW

Any Asian American theology of liberation must be rooted in the lived experiences of Asians in the Americas and the lives of their spiritual communities. It is a grassroots theology. Indeed, any theology of liberation is measured by its praxis ("I will show you my faith by my works"), its preferential option for the poor (therefore incompatible with model-minority aspirations), and its capacity to free the oppressed and marginalized among our own communities. That this is not clearly happening in Asian American theologies and churches is a sobering indictment of Asian American theology. Despite its intellectual roots in liberation theology and historical roots in Asian liberation movements, it is clear that Asian American theology is under what Soong-Chan Rah calls Western cultural captivity, but are the trends in immigrant, ethnic and multiethnic churches that Rah points to enough to deliver it from this captivity?[19] Should evangelicalism or Christianity at large be saved? Whom does it serve anyway?

To place ourselves in the viewpoint of the oppressed, as Gutiérrez's Latin American theology of liberation does, I return to the Filipino crewmembers sailing from Manila to New Spain on the Mexican Atlantic Coast as early as 1565. They were called Indians or *indios*, the term for all native people of Spain's colonies. The crew on these Spanish ships were made up of mostly Filipinos and Chinese sailors, but there were also Japanese and South Asians. The ones who survived the treacherous voyage were paid less than Spanish crewmembers and often deserted ship after arrival.[20] This was the largest source of Asians in the Americas at the time. While the Indigenous populations were being decimated by war and disease, slaves made up the next largest group of Asians arriving in the so-called New World. Portuguese slave ships carried enslaved people from Africa, stopping in Malacca and Manila, colonies of the Portuguese empire, bringing along hundreds of enslaved people from Macao, Myanmar, Malacca, Java, India, and the Philippines, referred to collectively as *chinos*.[21] The enslaved ranged from skilled to unskilled workers, both men and women, with some of the women being sold as sex slaves. According to historian Erika Lee, Manila became a center of transpacific slave trade in the sixteenth and seventeenth centuries, until in 1672 when enslaved Asians were emancipated in New Spain, and in 1700, a royal Spanish order prohibited the Asian slave trade.[22] As these people did not have the means to document their own history, any history from below must often resort to official reports and documentation, which only tell an incomplete story. The prerogative is to perform a retrieval of the subaltern or, in this case, an Asian American history told through sex, labor, and war.[23]

Beginning in the eighteenth century, hundreds of thousands of migrant or indentured laborers travelled from South Asia as coolies to British West Indian plantations in Guyana, Trinidad, and Jamaica, and from China to Cuba and Peru, for example. These movements of Asian labor were spurred by the end of African slavery in those places, recruited through kidnapping, coercion, or deception, often arriving on the same crowded and unsanitary ships previously used in the slave trade.[24] By 1891, South Asian indentured laborers made up over 80 percent of the workforce on British Guyana sugar plantations, often working alongside free Africans. Female South Asian indentured laborers were also sexually exploited by plantation managers or, as in one estate, they were brought in by a South Asian overseer to serve as prostitutes for male South Asian workers.[25] At the same time, planters and colonial officials wanted only "virtuous women," either widowed or having husbands, who would be able to tame the mostly male population. These interlocking forms of oppression remind us to remain attentive to the dynamics of sexual and power relations. Despite the intentions of their bosses, South Asian workers proved to be militant, conducting work strikes, mass marches, violent demonstrations, and mass desertions throughout the labor system in the West Indies. By one estimate, one hundred strikes occurred between 1886 and 1889 alone, and another 141 erupted between 1900 and 1913.[26]

Also of note is the Ghadar Movement, formed in 1913 by a coalition of Punjabi migrant workers and Punjabi intellectuals and students in San Francisco. Many of its Punjabi Sikh male members were veterans of the British Indian army, seeking to overthrow the British Empire through armed revolution. Claiming members and branches around the world, the Ghadar party circulated its newspaper *Ghadar*, meaning revolt or rebellion, in India where it was immediately banned. It was also banned in China, Japan, South Africa, and throughout Southeast Asia.[27] Though the party mobilized nearly eight thousand Indians in diaspora to return to India to overthrow British rule, with hundreds arrested by British officials even before arriving, the Ghadarites were not so well received by Indians in India. Leaders of the Indian National Congress, priests of important Sikh gurdwaras, and other nationalist leaders in India denounced the group.

Many Chinese, on other hand, migrated in the wake of the Opium Wars, civil unrest, and natural disasters in the mid-nineteenth century, Chinese laborers began arriving in Cuba and Peru in *la trata amarilla*, the yellow trade, bringing Chinese coolies together with enslaved Africans to work in plantations, mines, cities, or on railroads. In response to similarly exploitative work conditions, they often slowed the pace of work, sabotaged equipment, stole from plantations, committed suicide, and even joined Cuban anti-colonial insurgents.[28] Large numbers of Chinese coolies sought passage to California during the Gold Rush, beginning in 1849. During this era, Asians organized around labor rights in notable events such as the 1867 Chinese railroad worker strike in the Sierra Nevada region of California involving thousands of Chinese working on the transcontinental railroad, ending after supplies and food were cut off from the workers, and the 1920 Oahu sugar strike from January to July involving thousands of Filipino and Japanese laborers. This latter multiethnic coalition is significant for the fact that laborers were brought to Hawaii from various regions, particularly the Philippines, Japan, and Korea, to prevent solidarity among the workers; if one ethnic group went on strike, the others worked as strikebreakers, defeating the strike. Also, in 1965 was the Delano Grape Strike in California, lasting almost five years, led by Filipino farmworkers such as Larry Itliong and Philip Vera Cruz, who were soon after joined by Cesar Chavez, Dolores Huerte, and other Mexican farmworkers.[29] This period also saw the formation of the Japanese–Mexican Labor Association (JMLA), one of the first multiracial labor unions in the United States.[30]

Asian women, though fewer in number, similarly organized in areas such as in the garment industry. In 1938, over a hundred Chinese women garment workers organized against unfair labor practices at Joe Shoong's National Dollar Stores sewing factory, forming the Chinese Ladies' Garment Workers' Union and going on strike for fifteen weeks. It was the longest strike in the history of San Francisco Chinatown at the time. Later in 1974 was the Jung Sai garment workers strike in San Francisco consisting of over a hundred Chinese women conducting strike activities leading to sixty-four arrests and court injunctions.[31] The strikes formed a part of the Third World workers struggles that were taking place at the time in the United States. In the summer of 1982, twenty thousand workers from union garment factories in and around Canal Street in New York City Chinatown flooded the streets to demand a fair contract after union contract negotiations were blocked by a small group of Chinatown employers. This massive fourteen-week strike was organized by the International Ladies'

Garment Workers' Union, made up of largely immigrant women. In the realm of sex work, in San Francisco in 1910, Presbyterian missionary Donaldina Cameron joined local police on brothel raids to "rescue" Chinese immigrant sex workers and take them into her mission home, called Nine-twenty. At Nine-twenty, the women were made to cook and clean and sew in preparation for being Christian wives, but many of the rescued women eventually escaped their "rescuers."

According to the historiography of Asian American identity, Asian American subjectivity was first claimed in the revolutionary movements of the 1960s—what some historians refer to as "the Long Sixties." In echoing Simone de Beauvoir, that one is not born but rather becomes a woman, writer Karen Ishizuka contended that one is not born but willfully becomes Asian American. The creation of "Asian American" as a political identity was an attempt to unite the struggles of various Asian American communities toward common goals of racial justice and equity. In the words of Jeff Chang's foreword to Karen Ishizuka's account of the making of Asian America, there was a time when the word *Asian American* was not merely a demographic category but "a fight you were picking with the world."[32] While the initial movement beginning in 1969 was mainly realized through agitating for the establishment of Asian American studies programs in the San Francisco Bay Area, largely confined to universities and the West Coast, the broader acceptance of the label was catalyzed in 1982 through protests following the death of Vincent Chin, a Chinese American working in Detroit who was beaten to death at his bachelor party by White autoworkers angered by the negative impact that the Japanese automobile industry had on the US domestic market at the time. In the wake of heightened anti-Asian violence during the COVID-19 pandemic, the figure of Vincent Chin was revived as a symbol of the perpetuity of anti-Asian sentiment, while the twenty-thousand strong Chinatown garment workers strike was little remembered.

The political ferment of the sixties saw pan-ethnic Asian collaborations such as the Yellow Power movement, the revolutionary student magazine *Gidra*, and the Third World Liberation Front. The latter, inspired in part by the National Liberation Front in South Vietnam during the war, was a coalition of Black, Latine, Filipine American, Asian American, and Mexican American student organizations. These movements understood the struggles for Black, Asian, Indigenous, Chicane, and Third World liberation as being deeply connected. As contributor Patsy Chan wrote in an issue of *Gidra*, "The vicious imperialism which seeks to commit total genocide against the proud people of Indochina is the same imperialism which oppresses those of us here in the US by creating dehumanising conditions in our Asian communities, barrios, Black ghettos and reservations."[33] In invoking the people of Indochina, Chan was referring to the Vietnam war—or the American war, as it is referred to in Vietnam—and the covert wars in Laos and Myanmar, in which Black Americans served and later contributed to the formation of the Black Panther Party. The movement was not without its flaws, as the term *Yellow Power* foregrounded Japanese, Chinese, and Filipinos who then made up the majority of Asians in the United States, marginalizing others such as South Asians, West Asians, Black Asians, and queer Asians.

An important event in this historical moment was the International Hotel, or I-Hotel, a low-income residential hotel in San Francisco. Originally established as a luxury hotel in 1854, it was relocated and rebuilt after the 1906 earthquake and fire in San Francisco. By the 1930s, thousands of Asian workers came to reside in the hotel, and the area surrounding it grew into a ten-block Filipino American enclave along Kearney Street known as Manilatown. Amid the urban redevelopment of San Francisco, the real estate company Milton Myer & Co. issued eviction notices to the tenants in 1969, with plans to demolish the I-Hotel and replace it with a parking garage. Thus began a long campaign by tenants and Asian American activists, including students from San Francisco

State University and the University of California, Berkeley. In 1973, Four Seas Investment Corporation, a Thai company, bought over the hotel but continued with plans to demolish it and rebuild on the site. It was finally in 1977, when a court ordered the eviction of the tenants and four hundred riot police physically removed them despite over three thousand protesters attempting to surround and barricade the I-Hotel, marking the end of an eight-year struggle and solidarity between Asian American activists, workers, and elders of various backgrounds.

At around the same time, another rallying point for the burgeoning Asian American movement was the Free Chol Soo Lee movement. Lee immigrated from Jeolla Province in South Korea to San Francisco Chinatown at twelve years of age in 1964. He was wrongly convicted at the age of twenty-one for the murder of a Chinatown gang leader in 1973 and sentenced to life in prison. In 1977, Lee fatally stabbed a neo-Nazi inmate in an altercation, claiming self-defense, but because of his prior murder conviction he was sentenced to death and transferred to San Quentin's death row. At the time of Lee's initial arrest, he received little outside support; those believing his innocence feared retaliation from the Chinatown gang and corrupt police officers. One of Lee's earliest and strongest supporters was personal acquaintance Ranko Yamada, a Sansei (third-generation Japanese American) college student, and Tom Kim, a local third-generation Korean American community organizer. Kim brought the case to the attention of K. W. Lee, a *Sacramento Union* reporter who felt sympathy because he had a nephew of the same name who was studying for a PhD in engineering.[34] In a retrospective interview in 2005, K. W. Lee said: "There are many, many Chol Soo Lees right now in prison. And that is what makes me mad. There are so many of them. Do you hear anything about them in Asian America? You don't. That is what makes me feel sick."[35] K. W. Lee published a two-part investigative report in 1978, bringing into question the police investigation and subsequent trial of Chol Soo Lee, which worked to garner strong public support and led to the formation of the Chol Soo Lee defense committee.

Lee was finally released from prison in 1983, his first murder conviction overturned and his second downgraded to second-degree murder without admission of guilt. The long fight represented one of the early Asian American movement's first major political campaigns—and indeed successes—involving young US-born Asian activists, elderly immigrants, religious organizations, white-collar professionals, left-wing communist groups, and legal assistance organizations. But as Chol Soo Lee's memoir *Freedom without Justice* reveals, Lee's personal struggle for survival in prison happened in parallel to the legal and political struggles outside on what Richard Kim called a "different order of moral complexity, defined by a hypermasculine prison code that dictates an ever-ready willingness and capacity to use unrestrained violence against fellow prisoners."[36] Equally important is the fact that Lee's reentry was difficult, plagued by what Lee himself believed to be post-traumatic stress disorder, falling into depression and cocaine addiction. He served eighteen months in prison in 1990 on a drug possession charge and in 1991 suffered third-degree burns on 85 percent of his body after a failed arson attempt while working for a Hong Kong triad. Lee eventually died in 2014 due to medical complications arising from his burns.

All told, Chol Soo Lee was as human as any of us, no perfect victim or picture of innocence that an easy mythology could be built upon. When reflecting on why Vincent Chin's murder, which took place toward the end of Lee's imprisonment, was taught in classrooms more than Chol Soo Lee, Lee surmised that it was a "safer issue for Asian Americans to take up." Even if Lee's case laid a foundation for the activism around the Chin case—not to mention being more successful in court—it was a "controversial case" that K. W. Lee "had to walk a straight line with." In a moment of self-reflection, and perhaps even despair, Chol Soo Lee wondered aloud, "Maybe Chol Soo Lee forgot himself. He could not adjust to . . . after coming out of prison, could not adjust to life on the outside."[37] Still, Lee felt that the greatest message to come out of the Free Chol Soo Lee movement is "purity, the unselfishness, the integrity of people, giving to a stranger," and "the need to give today is far greater than in my own time."[38]

However, as Ishizuka writes, these days the term *Asian American* has been neutralized into a mere adjective, barely more than a census label. Its activist history has been lost except mostly to other activists and scholars. The shifting demographics post-1965 continue to change the face of Asians in the United States, with flows of high-skilled workers and refugees and undocumented people. The generational shifts in migration histories lead to differences in the psychic structure of Asians and their own attitudes toward race. Asian migrant labor continues to operate in forms rendered invisible in representations of the Asian: Filipine domestic and trafficked workers, for example, some working as nannies and housekeepers to wealthy families, who were professionals in the Philippines. Photographer Xyza Cruz Bacani, who worked in Hong Kong as a maid for nine years, and her mother, in the same household for twenty years, connected the invisible labor of Filipine domestic workers in Hong Kong, New York, and New Jersey through photography and with help from nonprofits such as the Damayan Migrant Workers Association in New York City.[39] By turning the gaze onto domestic workers and their transnationality, Bacani makes visible the embeddedness of migrant Asian women within the larger structure of racial capitalism in contrast to prominent, high-achieving upper and upper-middle-class Asians with elite educations who fulfill the role of the model minority.

Migrant Asian women working in service industries are a particularly vulnerable group. Not bound to a specific trade, they often move between working in restaurants, nail salons, grocery stores, dry cleaners, and massage parlors. Over Thanksgiving weekend in 2017, thirty-eight-year-old Yang Song jumped off the third floor of a massage parlor in Flushing, New York, during a Vice

Enforcement Unit police raid and died in the hospital shortly after. Song, who was from Shenyang, China, had been working in illegal massage parlors for several years and had been arrested four times before. She also claimed to have been sexually assaulted by a man who flashed a badge and gun and claimed to be an undercover cop. Song's death led to the creation of the organization Red Canary Song, supporting the grassroots organizing of migrant sex workers, focusing on the Chinese community of massage parlor workers in New York City. It organized internationally with Butterfly, a group of over two hundred Asian sex workers in Toronto, and Les Roses D'Acier, a group of over five hundred Chinese migrant sex workers in Paris. As Red Canary Song's work shows, police raids against and deportation of migrant sex workers point to the nexus of power, borders, sexuality, and race working in concert and the ways in which sexualized and racialized forms of migrant labor are expropriated by capitalism. Activism surrounding sex work, particularly among Asians, surged momentarily in the wake of the 2021 Atlanta spa shootings and quickly died down once media attention faded.

Besides migrant workers, refugees from Vietnam, Cambodia, and Laos—many of whom were infants in refugee camps—are often deported on the basis of having a criminal conviction, hence "bad immigrants." In the prison-to-deportation pipeline, incarcerated persons are transferred to immigration authorities immediately upon release from prison. The narrative of criminality aside, other complex cases also arise from the capriciousness of immigration enforcement and bureaucratic loopholes, such as the deportation of international adoptees. While Asian deportations typically number only in the hundreds, it is crucial to view this within the framework of the expansion of the United States Immigrations and Customs Enforcement (ICE), "border protection," and White nationalism at large. While ICE has focused its deportations and raids on Central and South American communities, we cannot view the struggle of Southeast Asian refugees and migrants as separate from that of Latine and Chicane workers and families, if for no other reason than the fact that ICE does not see these communities as separate but equally deserving of deportation.

Asian American theology must not only pay attention to these struggles but in fact center these experiences and communities if we are to be serious about Asian liberation. Throughout this book I will explore various historical dimensions as they relate to Asians in the United States, but this is not to privilege a nostalgic or romantic view of the past. As Fanon wrote in the context of the struggle of Blacks and against White colonials, "Disalienation will be for those whites and blacks who have refused to let themselves be locked in the substantialized 'tower of the past.' For many other black men disalienation will come from refusing to consider their reality as definitive." Fanon also looked to Vietnamese resistance for guidance: "The Vietnamese who die in front of a firing squad don't expect their sacrifice to revive a forgotten past. They accept death for the sake of the present and the future."[40] This is about the here and now. If we are not serious about Asian liberation, then the status quo that we maintain will only perpetuate the model minority myth about Asian success and Asian American theology will play the role of an honorary-White theology supporting elite and middle-class Asians comfortable in their proximity to Whiteness and power, such as Nikki Haley and Elaine Chao who played important roles in the Trump administration and, of course, Kamala Harris in the Biden administration. Theology can cover over many sins, including class oppression, sexual violence, racism, and genocide. Or it can fight back. Liberation theology is a theology that belongs in the streets, the favelas, the ghettoes, and the slums of the world. Any theology of liberation, when confined to the academy and middle-class homes, dies of internal contradictions and sterilization. We seek instead a theology of the subaltern Asian, the migrant sex worker, the indentured laborer, the convicted refugee.

The histories of Asian Americans can be told in a multitude of ways. They are constituted by racial exclusion, migratory flows, and resistance. The views from above and below are both important, revealing different aspects of Asians in the Americas. Held together, we find a highly heterogeneous, constantly evolving community that, through the various forces of law, political economy, racial capitalism, violence, and resistance becomes racialized as Asian American. Asian American theology naturally looks to migration as a crucial source of theological reflection and, in particular, the configurations of power, mechanisms of capital, histories of colonization, and resistance. In this sense, Asian American theology as a theology of migration finds points of contact with Latine theologies, which similarly grapple with questions of racial identity, military interventionism, labor exploitation, and belonging. But it also faces a different challenge from indigeneity, which I return to in Chapter 4. The idea of Latin America, Walter Mignolo argued, is a colonial project of Europe in the way that Valentin Mudimbe argues, concerning the invention of Africa, and Sun Ge asks: "How does Asia mean?" According to Sun, Asia had for a long time not been treated as a "self-contained geographical concept, but has only been put forward ideologically in opposition to Europe." It was only when Italian Jesuit Mateo Ricci presented a world map to officials in the Ming Dynasty in the 1580s, Mignolo writes, that "the people inhabiting China and Japan 'learned' for the first time that they were living in a space called Asia, just as the Indigenous people and African slaves transported to America learned, also in the sixteenth century, that there was a continent named 'America.'"[41] It is for this reason that though this book is about so-called Asian Americans, we must but hold lightly the terms *Asian* and *American*, not to mention other identities.

Still, we press on, whatever we may be called, and whoever "we" may be. If this brief retelling in this chapter of Asian migration histories can be seen as the material construction of Asians in the United States, the next chapter then turns to their discursive construction.

3.

"WHERE ARE YOUR PEOPLE FROM?"

Deconstructing Asian American Theological Subjectivity

> *The category of Asian American sprawls: sixth-generation toddlers and undocumented teens; crazy-rich coeds chilling on Rodeo Drive or in Singapore Air first-class and couples on public assistance packing their meager belongings under eviction notices; architects and oncologists, nannies and bus drivers, seamstresses and factory bosses; class divisions that reflect the displacements of the Cold War and congressional preferences for the not so tired and not so poor; innumerable histories colliding, even in a single family. Yet here you are, the evidence of American warfare and familial risk and survival, making yourselves through panethnic coupling and an emergent culture of image, story, song, food. A tiger clan, a model fucking minority, a blueprint for multicultural democracy.*
>
> —Jeff Chang, *We Gon' Be Alright*

> *We believe the juxtaposition of the black and white races has resulted in a massive psycho-existential complex. By analyzing it we aim to destroy it.*
>
> —Frantz Fanon, *Black Skin, White Masks*

> *I'm Asian American, so I'm a 100 percent authentic fake.*
> —Corky Lee, in Ken Chen, "Corky Lee and the Work of Seeing"

"Who is us?" writer Jeff Chang asked, pondering the "impossibility of Asian Americanness." In a *New York Times* essay on the death of college student Michael Deng by hazing at an Asian American fraternity in 2013, Jay Caspian Kang declared that *Asian American* is a mostly meaningless term.[1] "Nobody grows up speaking Asian-American," Kang explains, "nobody sits down to Asian-American food with their Asian-American parents and nobody goes on pilgrimages back to their motherland of Asian-America."[2] Before embarking upon a study of Asian American theology, the problem of Asian American theological subjectivity must first be addressed. In the previous chapter, I outlined a broad history of migration of peoples from a place now called Asia; in this chapter, I turn to the discursive construction of Asia and Asian America and its subjects in the realm of theology. By *discourse* I mean conversations produced from ideology and language, describing the power to know, name, and assign meaning. Race, gender, sexuality, class, and nation are such examples of structures constituted through discourse.

According to Kang, discrimination is what really binds Asian Americans together, harkening to the accepted narrative of the establishment of Asian American identity in the late 1960s. Within theological discourses, the genealogy of Asian American theology can also be traced back to a similar era, in which Third World Liberation movements inspired the development of liberation theologies in its various forms. Asian liberation theologies, for example, agitated for a contextualization of Christianity in Asia and liberation from White Christianity, which arrived in Asia through deeply intertwined processes of missionization, colonization, and imperialism. The proliferation of liberation and contextual theologies within Asian contexts was inspired by North and South American liberation theologies, producing theologies from below, such as Dalit and Palestinian liberation theologies, minjung theology, and Pieris's Asian liberation theology.

Some argue that the emphasis of liberation theologies on "the oppressed" leaves it vulnerable to a romanticization of the poor, a critique similarly levied upon Marxism with respect to the working class. This potential flattening of oppression resembles the pitfall in intersectional politics of devolving into an "oppression Olympics." While we should certainly be wary of this, such critiques fail to appreciate the hermeneutic circle of suspicion critical to the method of liberation theology—that is, the continual reflection through praxis, being thoroughly grounded with the poor, that produces finer analyses and responses to interlocking oppressions.

One of the outgrowths of contextualized Asian feminist theology is the conception of women as the "minjung within the minjung," describing—for example, by Chung Hyun Kyung—as the multiple layers of oppression that produce a double bind, and also Wai-Ching Wong's "poor woman," interpreted as a referential locus for an Asian feminist Christology. It is possible to apply Althaus-Reid's critique of Latin American liberation theology, where "the poor" and "the poor woman" were "fetishisations, reified phenomena extrapolated from the reality of people's lives, concepts which lost any relation to the context which produced them," so that liberationists produced "a discourse of the native woman, successfully sold as 'the poor mother,' 'the poor but strong Christian woman' fitting the patriarchal romantic idea of womanhood in Latin America."[3] Perhaps more importantly, feminist theology in Latin America was critiqued for lacking a historical material analysis and offering no explanations or challenges to the "dialectical praxis between economy and genderized culture in Latin America."[4] In other words, even as we build on Asian and Asian American feminist theologies, we must also be careful to not obscure class difference or reproduce heterosexual binaries.

Asian American theology arose concurrently with Asian American identity, against the backdrop of Third World revolutions and of Asian feminist and liberation theologies. Nami Kim argues that "Asianness" in its current categorical and representational uses in theological discourse is inadequate for a pertinent and liberative feminist theology in the face of increasing globalization.[5] Tracing the genealogy of the term *Asian* reveals that it was also redeployed as an oppositional identity through the resurgence of anti-colonial nationalist movements beginning in the nineteenth century, reappropriating its representational use in orientalist discourse. According to Wong, the very history of colonialism gave rise to the conception of a contextual theology of a "vaguely unifying Asia."[6]

Nonetheless, the wide acceptance of *Asian* as a self-referential marker was registered by the time of the 1955 Bandung Conference between African and Asian nations, which indicted Western racialism and colonial exploitation. The conference, according to Franklyn Jayakumar Balasundaram, highlighted the challenges from the Asian context to theology and inspired further theological development later at the East Asian Christian Conference, the Christian Conference of Asia, and the Ecumenical Association of Third World Theologians.[7] Distinctive Asian and Asian feminist theologies were articulated by Aloysius Pieris, Virginia Fabella, Sun Ai Lee Park, and Chung Hyun Kyung, with emphases on the linguistic heterogeneity and religious plurality of the Asian context. Invoking Spivak's strategic essentialism, Kim argues for the use of *Asian* within US contexts as a political denominator based on a common history of oppression and struggle against US imperialism in Asia. Recognizing that struggle against racism is never static nor complete, an ongoing examination of the effectiveness of the use of the term *Asian* is therefore necessary, more so from the vantage point of North America where the idea of Asia is easily abstracted or caricatured.[8]

Our theological approach must move beyond a portrayal of Asian religions and cultures as relatively unchanging practices and beliefs, frozen in time and space. The imperative for such an anti-essentialist critique becomes clear when considering the works of Asian American theologians drawing from East Asian religious and cultural symbols such as Tao, Chi, Han, and Jung, as critical reflection is necessary for their theological explorations in North American contexts. These concepts are valuable in their own right, but there is no need to make caricatures of ourselves. As with Asianness, the proper use of *Asian American* in theological discourse should not be a simple racial ethnic affiliation but a "willingness to engage in a critical theological discourse that unceasingly challenges the dominant racist, nationalist, and colonial discourse, and that, simultaneously, can provide a theological vision for a better world."[9] Interrogations of the Asian lead to questions about the Asian American and, in particular, the subjects of Asian American theology.

ASIAN AMERICAN THEOLOGICAL SUBJECTIVITY

Once again, but now at a theological register, who is "us"? Asian American theology often tacitly assumes the stability of its theological subject despite elaborations on its positionality as a marginalized, liminal, or hybrid people group. This is a key contradiction that will constantly reappear. The common interpretation of Asian American theological subjectivity is as citizen-subjects who claim Asian ethnic origins.[10] The ongoing struggle to articulate an Asian American theology is often rationalized in one of two ways. First, through the failure of White theology, which maintains the self-delusion of being universal and context-free, to address the Asian American experience, and second, through the need for confronting the multiplicity and heterogeneity of Asian American identity, a theological project parallel to the political one. But simply pointing out that Asian Americans are diverse and unequal does not quite get at what Asian American *means*. Asian American theological identity is often constructed unproblematically as a historical subject and marginalized race. Decentering Whiteness from our theology requires no longer seeing ourselves as being on the margin of anything. To stand on its own two feet, Asian American theology must stake its claim as theology that is self-referential.

Many works by Asian American theologians have pivoted upon images that further entrench caricatures of Asian and Asian

American identity when viewed outside of these culturally specific frames. Doing so inadvertently reproduces stereotypes and rein-scribes Asian American theology within an orientalist framework for outsiders. In a similar vein, the Asian American imaginary is often constructed as marginal, in-between, or interstitial. While this may resonate with the emotional experiences and lived realities of certain Asian Americans, we see again how much language, the name *Asian American* itself, constrains us. Restricting attention to the marginal obscures the unequal power relations and racist hegemony by which the condition of marginality is produced. When written as "Asian-American," the hyphen is overburdened with the anxiety of being unable to conform to either of the uni-formized Asian or American subjects.

W. E. B. Du Bois famously wrote in 1903 that the problem of the twentieth century is the problem of *color line*. A term originating in racial segregation, the color line separates Black and White, a monochromatic lens through which popular US politics is inter-preted. But the Black–White dichotomy is a reductionist repre-sentation of the nation-state and its imperial history. Such binary thinking is deeply ingrained into the US psyche and manifests in many spheres of social and political life: one is only ever one of two things, having little imaginative capacity for those who are both or neither, let alone along some spectrum. The US imaginary suf-fers from not only the problem of essentialized, reified categories but also the poverty of choices produced by this ideological tunnel vision. It has material and psychic ramifications for those who do not conform to the false binary. Within this context, categories such as "Asian American," "mestizaje," and "mulatto" all disrupt the racial binary, not by simply producing a third subjectivity or even triangulating the discourse, as Claire Jean Kim argues, but more importantly by critiquing it through revealing the discursive con-structions of race itself. The problem of the twenty-first century, frankly, is much more than the color line.

The interpretation of the Asian American condition as marginal or liminal is in part a product of seeing oneself as a protagonist within the drama of immigration and assimilation along this color line. The desire of Asian immigrant parents for the success and security and prosperity of their children is a deal with the White devil. The correlation of race and class in White-dominant society requires that conventional success be constituted by a "sociological whitening" whereby socioeconomic power and class privileges are conferred by the performance of Whiteness, of which anti-Blackness and settler-colonial violence is foundational.[11] And besides the generational trauma of immigration and war, there is the disconnect between first and later generations produced by the vastly different structures of sentiment and language, a generational liminality. This whitening manifests in processes of shedding negative markers of Asianness, including inherited practices of previous generations, causing a persistent anxiety regarding this transmutation of the racial self. It surfaces in prolific narrations of this angst, a major theme in Asian American cultural production, such as the trope Kang calls the "smelly lunchbox story."[12] These racial anxieties form the basis of the diagnoses of racial melancholia and racial dissociation that I shall discuss in the next section. These experiences of not fitting in, theorized as marginality or liminality, are real and important, but they alone are not enough to produce freedom dreams.

Another key theoretical conception of Asian American subjectivity is the notion of hybridity, due to postcolonial theorist Homi Bhabha. In practice, Asian American hybridity crudely manifests almost as an "Asian fusion" in anthologies by theologians of Asian descent. Such collaborations, it should be acknowledged, have potentially inclusive and open boundaries that invite contributions from groups underrepresented in Asian American theologies. Hybridity also finds a physical basis in interracial and interethnic marriages and also transnational and transracial adoptions. But though diverse voices are put together side by side, they are not often in dialogue or debate with each other, eliding differences and disagreements.

The constant negotiation between Asian ethnicity and national origin prevents a critical negotiation of difference because of the emphases on a uniform subjectivity in Asian American theological discourse. The methodology of narrative theology in Asian American contexts, nonetheless, remains indispensable to the project of constructing Asian American theologies and contributing to writer Viet Thanh Nguyen's notion of narrative plenitude. Nguyen, commenting on the celebrated but problematic *Crazy Rich Asians* movie in 2018, observes that we "live in an economy of narrative scarcity, in which we feel deprived and must fight to tell our own stories and fight against the stories that distort or erase us." The real test of whether an economy of narrative plenitude is achieved, Nguyen writes, is when "we have the luxury of making mediocre movies. And after having made mediocre movies, we would be rewarded with the opportunity to make even more mediocre movies."[13] In Asian American theology, narrative scarcity demands that Asian-fusion anthologies be continually produced, but the luxury of producing mediocre theology is not a goal to aspire to. How should Asian American theologies move beyond narrative theological plenitude, toward generative and critical theologies?

To be Asian is meaningless in Asia. It is only outside of Asia that being Asian takes on meaning. To be Asian outside of Asia is to be othered. Kang's whimsical motherland "AsianAmerica" disrupts nationalistic approaches to Asian American identity construction: the tendency to emphasize national origin over an equally abstract Asianness reveals the dominance of nationalist discourse. Asian Americanness is an attempt at self-realization by asserting an identity that mediates between what Fumitaka Matsuoka calls the particularity of being and the commonality of being.[14] Especially with regards to people groups often rendered invisible or exterior to the Asian American category, national origin is held in tension with Asianness. One might assert their Hmongness, say, because Asian Americanness does little for them.

In what other ways have Asian American theological subjects

been conceived? The activist interpretation of Asian American identity is the operational viewpoint in the volume *Asian American Christian Ethics* edited by Ilsup Ahn and Grace Y. Kao. It seeks to establish Asian American Christian ethics as a proper subfield of Christian ethics by "invoking the social activist origins of the term Asian American in our characterization of Asian American Christian ethics as work in Christian ethics written by those who specifically adopt a pan-ethnic Asian American consciousness, identity, or set of concerns therein."[15] Their work attempts to "signal politically in a nonessentialist fashion 'Asian American' in Asian American Christian ethics," yet Kao and Ahn also choose to rely on Asian American identity defined by the US Census Bureau, carefully excluding Native Hawaiians and other Pacific Islanders who contest attempts to subsume them together with Asian Americans and those outside of South and East Asia—for example, Central and Western Asia—and the Middle East, whose exclusion "generally goes uncontested."

These seemingly contradictory assertions risk mutual negation and leave open the question of the nature of Asian American theoethical subjectivity, thus requiring a closer analysis. It is not simply the mutability of the census label that underscores the instability and therefore the inadequacy of relying on state-sanctioned definitions, but a closer look at the long history of violence perpetrated by the nation-state against Asians within its borders and colonies reveals the material risks involved in allowing the terms to be defined by empire. We must also be careful to be *only* oppositional when considering Asian American theological subjectivity in the context of liberation. The ontology of the common Asian American theological subject must be continually reexamined. To attend to the problem of subjectivity, I turn first to Eng and Han's diagnoses of racial melancholia and racial dissociation in certain Asian Americans, complemented by Fanon's psychoanalytic reflections on race, and second to Chuh's critique of Asian American uniform subjectivity within Asian Americanist discourse, which maps easily onto Asian American theological discourse. The former describes the affective dimension of one's racial identifications within the larger social structure, and the latter describes the discursive and material constructions of the racial formation itself.

RACIAL MELANCHOLIA AND RACIAL DISSOCIATION

In David Eng and Shinhee Han's study, they identify the conditions of racial melancholia in second-generation Asian immigrants come of age in a post–Cold War and civil rights era (Gen X), and racial dissociation in first-generation Asian immigrants come of age in a time of neoliberalism, globalization, and color-blindness (Gen Y/Millenials). Eng and Han build on Freud's notion of melancholia as unresolved grief, in which one knows *whom* but not *what* has been lost. They define *racial melancholia* as a series of failed and unresolved assimilations into the United States and exclusion from Whiteness. Within the context of Asian America, racial melancholia is identified in the model minority subject as the partial success and partial failure to mourn one's identification with both Whiteness and "Asian cultures." It occurs, for example, in the transnational adoptee who identifies with their White adoptive parents' race but whose White parents do not identify with the Asian adoptee's race. Racial melancholia "indexes the considerable social as well as psychological pressures associated with successfully approximating the model minority stereotype of the hard working, self-effacing, and perpetually agreeable Asian American immigrant child."[16] The ambivalence, anger, and rage produced by racial melancholia are "the internalized refractions of an institutionalized system of whiteness as property bent on the exclusion and obliteration of the racial object."[17] This nod to Whiteness as property refers to the legal structures used to delineate the borders of Whiteness, as theorized by Cheryl Harris.[18] Institutional oppression and exclusion are introjected within to produce what W. E. B. Du Bois called a "double consciousness," "this sense of always looking at one's self through the eyes of others, of measuring one's soul by the tape of a world that looks on in amused contempt and pity."[19]

In an attempt to depathologize racial melancholia, Eng and Han adapt psychoanalyst D. W. Winnicott's theory of transition to conceive of race as a transitional space. Winnicott refers to the "first possession" of an infant, such as the thumb or doll, as a transitional object that opens up a transitional space, an intermediate area between the subjective and that which is objectively perceived. Transitional space exists between internal and external, between subjective and objective, and provides a third space between inner and outer worlds, making negotiable what was thought to be mutually exclusive categories. And unlike the lost object in racial melancholia that is mourned, the transitional object is never lost but instead undergoes a gradual decathexis, meaning that emotional investment is withdrawn from it. As Winnicott writes, it loses meaning as the transitional phenomena diffuse and spread out over the whole intermediate territory between inner psychic reality and the external world as perceived by two persons in common.[20] This negotiation between inner psychic reality and external world captures the process of racial formation as *both* an intersubjective and intrasubjective experience. I am formed by both how I view myself and how you view me. Eng and Han use racial melancholia to describe the intergenerational transference between immigrant parents and child—what it means to carry the trauma, dreams, and hopes of one's parents without quite knowing what they are. In place of Winnicott's notion of object relations, it is in the field of racial relations—relations through which race is constituted—that "racial transitional objects" function. Conceptualizing race as a transitional space opens to the possibility of racial reparations, in which the psychic splitting of differently racialized objects into either good or bad objects can be healed: both good and bad are allowed to inhabit and transit across once segregated racial divides, where White is purely good and Asian is purely evil.

Racial dissociation, on the other hand, draws on Phillip Bromberg's notion of adaptive and pathological forms of dissociation shaped by early infantile experiences. Dissociation is the loss of the capacity for self-reflection and the ability to process emotionally charged mental conflicts. It acts as a defense to preserve a sense of selfhood and self-continuity, becoming pathological to the degree that it limits and forecloses one's ability to hold and reflect upon different states of mind with a single experience of "me-ness." Adaptive dissociation, on the other hand, is the ability to "feel like one self while being many" and the psychic capacity to "stand in the spaces between opposing realities without losing any of them." Importantly, this psychic stability is not predicated on a seamless integration but rather on the adaptive "illusion of cohesive personal identity."[21] Existing contradictions are not resolved but rather allowed to be in dialectic relationship with one another. The connection to Asian American identity is clear: within the field of racial relations, the question is how competing racial realities, such as W. E. B. Du Bois's notion of double consciousness and Fanon's *Black Skin, White Masks* can be balanced in "a society in which it is often difficult, if not impossible, to reconcile the ways in which others see you with the ways in which you see yourself."[22] Individual racial formation negotiates between looking versus feeling, skin versus flesh, intersubjectivity versus intrasubjectivity.

While various transnational accounts celebrate cosmopolitanism and globalization as being "at home in the world," or as the poet Nima Yushij declared, "The world is my home," Eng and Han identify in transnational Asian subjects like parachute children who are sent to be educated abroad at an early age while their parents remain in their home country, a pathological racial dissociation that produces a psychic nowhere. Psychic nowhere is a condition that correlates with "the absence of a clear geographic belonging or destination."[23] In contrast to racial melancholia, which projects its racial discontents onto one's parents—whether biological and Asian or adoptive and transracial—that exist nearby, the psychic nowhere of racial dissociation arises from the physical dislocation and collective unconscious of a color-blind or "post-racial" US society, even if emotional attachments to faraway family persist. Racial melancholia follows Freud's hysteric model of condensation, wherein hysteria arises from repressed identifications and desires, and the lost object demands to be analyzed and interpreted. Racial dissociation, on the other hand, follows Freud's paranoid model of dispersion, where what is repressed is disavowed and then projected outward into multiple spaces, thus more difficult to locate: I will not admit it, even to myself, even as I obsess over it.[24] In Eng and Han's work, race appears as the political unconscious of sexuality and sexuality the political unconscious of race. The one arises as a conscious manifestation of the unconscious prohibitions and taboos of the other.[25] Intersectionality in critical race theory suggests attending to both aspects in legal theory; Eng and Han suggest doing the same for psychoanalysis.

In order to move from a pathological to healthy form of racial dissociation, they adapt Winnicott's notion of the good-enough mother in psychoanalytic theory to a good-enough interpretation of race. The concept of the good-enough seeks to mediate the extreme dialectics of love and hate, self and other, White and Black, allowing for different racial self-states, feelings, and experiences instead of forcing frozen and intransigent states of racial division and dissonance. It makes us okay with the in-between, the not-quite, and the somewhat. A good-enough racial formation would "avoid creating a binary of absolute victims and perpetrators that render individual agency and responsibility of the racial subject moot in the face of larger historical and political shifts."[26] Together, the notions of racial melancholia and racial dissociation, answered by race as a transitional space and the good-enough race, offer useful descriptions of the Asian American psyche. Yet, while Eng and Han's work provide an important convergence of critical race theory and psychoanalysis, they acknowledge that their study is limited to the setting of "comparatively privileged class of Asian American adolescents and young adults in private and public US institutions of higher education"—namely, Columbia University and New York University, thus predominantly East Asian students in majority White elite spaces. The class dimension of their study is necessarily obscured, even if it is acknowledged, by the subjectivities of their anonymized students and patients. Indeed, modern psychotherapy itself is a highly lucrative practice and unaffordable option for most. Secondly, despite the emphasis on psychoanalysis, Eng and Han's work is largely asexual, affording few insights into the sexual unconscious of race and leaving open the sexual nature of Asian American construction, let alone Asian American theology.

Fanon's psychiatric work that included "students, workers, and the pimps of Pigalle and Marseille" offers something of a corrective. His aim in *Black Skin, White Masks* was to "liberate the black man from the arsenal of complexes that germinated in a colonial situation" and "from himself."[27] Among these complexes is the alienation arising from the desire to become White, or "lactification," as "it is commonplace in Martinique to dream of whitening oneself magically as a way of salvation."[28] The failure of resolving one's alienation through lactification produces racial melancholia. Writing in the context of the Antilles, Fanon describes the attempt at identification as follows: "The black child subjectively adopts a white man's attitude" and gradually "a way of thinking and seeing that is basically white forms and crystallizes in the young Antillean. Whenever he reads stories of savages in his white schoolbook he always thinks of the Senegalese." The collective unconscious, according to Fanon, is the repository of prejudices, myths, and collective attitudes of a particular group.[29] Moral consciousness implies a splitting, a fracture of the consciousness between a dark and a light side: "Moral standards require the black, the dark, and the black man to be eliminated from this consciousness. A black man, therefore, is constantly struggling against his own image."[30] So within this collective unconscious, the Antillean seeks to become White. Moreover, "in the collective unconscious of *Homo occidentalis* the black man—or, if you prefer, the color black—symbolizes evil, sin, wretchedness, death, war, and famine." Thus, Fanon writes, the Antillean shares the same collective unconscious as the European, and it is normal for the Antillean to be a negrophobe: "Unconsciously, then, I distrust what is black in me, in other words, the totality of my being."[31] Much of this easily transposes onto Asian aspirations for Whiteness and revulsions toward Blackness and also Asianness.

Another complex of the colonial condition is the self-withdrawal of the ego as a defense mechanism in response to pain, wherein the only way out is the White world: "From black to white—that is the only way to go. One is white, so one is rich, so one is handsome, so one is intelligent."[32] Related to this self-withdrawal, which is also indexed by racial dissociation, is an abandonment neurotic or "Cinderella complex" based on "the *anxiety* aroused by any abandonment, the *aggressivity* to which it gives rise, and the resultant *devaluation of self*," leading one "not to love so as not to be abandoned."[33] The way out through the White world is not simply in becoming White but also being loved by and having sex with White people. By loving me, Fanon writes as a Black man, the White woman "proves to me that I am worthy of a white love. I am loved like a white man. I am a white man. . . . I espouse white culture, white beauty, white whiteness. Between these white breasts that my wandering hands fondle, white civilization and worthiness become mine."[34] Similarly, the Black woman "has only one way open to her and one preoccupation—to whiten the race. The mulatto woman wants not only to become white but also to avoid slipping back . . . it's a question of saving the race."[35] In both cases it is White love, the White body, that gives value to the non-White, a perversion of Rowan Williams's notion of the body's grace, which I discuss in the final chapter. To an extent, this also resonates with the racial unconscious of Asian American sexual anxieties, though we will uncover some significant differences later.

According to Fanon, the Black self in White society is both a phobic and phobogenic object, provoking anxiety in both itself and others. It is surrounded by a fearsome world of anti-Black violence, itself inducing irrational fear in non-Blacks. Negrophobes do not have the guts to hate the Black man, Fanon writes: "Hatred is not a given; it is a struggle to acquire hatred, which has to be dragged into being, clashing with acknowledged guilt complexes. . . . In a sense he must embody *hatred*. This is why Americans have replaced lynching by discrimination."[36] The phobic object is over-determined; it "need not be there, it is enough that somewhere the object *exists*: is a possibility. Such an object is endowed with evil intentions and with all the attributes of a malefic power."[37] The Black man is both "genital" and the "symbol of evil and ugliness," and together "whoever says rape says black man," at the same time embodying genital power out of reach of morals and taboos. Conversely, White women "see the black man at the intangible gate leading to the realm of mystic rites and orgies, bacchanals and hallucinating sexual sensations."[38]

In this respect the Asian body is a departure from the Black body in a White society: the Asian is a robotic and erotic object. Robotic in the sense of beliefs about Asian hyperproductivity and academic accomplishment, just as Iyko Day draws parallels between Moishe Postone's analysis whereby Jews become the personification of "the tangible, destructive, immensely powerful, and international domination of capital as a social form" and Colleen Lye's discussion of pre-1942 expressions of anti-Japanese sentiment in California agriculture, wherein the "inorganic quality of the Asiatic body" manifests the threat of finance capital[39]—in other words, the economic identification of Asians as the "new Jews."[40] Building on Lisa Lowe's argument that capitalism profits through producing racialized difference in labor forms, Day proposes that within this difference, Asians personify the abstract dimension of capitalism through labor time. That is, whereas Jews in nineteenth-century Europe personified the destructive nature and abstract domination of capital, confined to financial sectors of the economy, the Chinese workers of the transcontinental railroad in the United States personified a robotic efficiency and the quantitative sphere of abstract labor, measured in time.[41] Furthermore, Day triangulates the settler/native binary with a third "alien" category, wherein the African American represents an indisposable alien labor force and the Asian American a disposable one, made possible through immigration and deportation.

The Asian body is also an erotic object, highly sexualized through the White male gaze. In the Asian woman it is both exotic sex object and evil temptress, capable of untold sexual mechanics, while the Asian man is *also* feminized, through emasculating caricatures of effeminate disposition and small penises. In Edward Said's study of the West and the Middle East in *Orientalism*, he shows that the Orient was seen as exuding "dangerous sex" that threatened hygiene and domestic seemliness with freedom of intercourse yet containing "unimaginable antiquity, inhuman beauty, boundless distance," concealing a "deep, rich fund of female sexuality."[42] And to state the obvious connection between sexual dominance and colonialism, "the space of weaker or underdeveloped regions like the Orient was viewed as something inviting French interest, penetration, insemination—in short, colonization."[43]

Again, here the problem of desire makes trouble: the White male gaze that dreams an orientalist sexual fantasy desires the Asian female body—whether consciously or unconsciously. It is unfortunately compatible with the desire of the non-White person for lactification. In Fanon's critique of Octave Mannoni's dependency and inferiority complexes in the colonized, he quotes Mannoni: "Wherever Europeans have founded colonies of the type we are considering, it can be safely said that their coming was unconsciously expected—even desired—by the future subject peoples. Everywhere there existed legends foretelling the arrival of strangers form the sea, bearing wondrous gifts with them." Fanon mocks this: "The white man is governed by a complex of authority, a complex of leadership, whereas the Malagasy is governed by a complex of dependency. Everyone is happy." The job of psychoanalysts in response to this inferiority complex, Fanon prescribes, is to "consciousnessize" the unconscious of the patient, to "no longer be tempted by a hallucinatory lactification, but also to act along the lines of a change in social structure." The social structure here is one that makes the inferiority complex possible, a society that "draws its strength by maintaining this complex" and "proclaims the superiority of one race over another."[44]

Whereas in the libidinal nature of anti-Black violence, where there exists an unconscious fear that Black people will do unto White people what the White person imagines they would do to Whites if they were Black, in anti-Asian violence and Asian fetishism there is only the unconscious gratification or sadism from the expectation that this dominance by the White man—whether sexual, economic, or physical—is desired, asked for, fantasized about. What all of this suggests to us is that to identify the Asian as both a robotic and erotic object in White society is to implicate the violence embedded in the structure of racial capitalism in ways that diagnoses of racial melancholia and racial dissociation alone cannot. Fanon's analysis reveals more clearly race and sex operating as the political unconsciousness of the other: sexual desires are also racial ones, and racial relations are also sexual ones. Racial and sexual violence contain each other.

A dramatic example of this is the case of Daniel Holtzclaw, born in Guam to a White male police officer from Oklahoma and a Japanese mother. Holtzclaw, also an Oklahoma City police officer, was convicted in 2015 for sexually assaulting eight Black women, most of whom were sex workers, ex-offenders, and current or recovering drug addicts between 2013 and 2014. The trial took place in the height of the Black Lives Matter movement and fueled much public outrage. Racially, Holtzclaw was coded as simply White rather than biracial, though some Asian American activists pointed out this fact, leading both to calls for collective introspection and suspicion that Holtzclaw was yet another "fall guy" like New York Police Department officer Peter Liang who was convicted for the murder of Akai Gurley earlier that year.

While it is not known how Holtzclaw identifies racially, one might speculate whether a stronger identification with his Whiteness over his Asianness—or indeed a need to overcompensate for his *un*erotic, Asian heritage through playing football in high school and college and becoming a police officer after failing to get drafted into the National Football League—produced a libidinal drive for sexual dominance over and gratuitous violence toward vulnerable Black women. With regards to Holtzclaw's position at the intersection of Whiteness, carcerality, and heteropatriarchy, Fanon's notion of the "racial allocation of guilt" is helpful, wherein "every time there was a rebellion, the military authorities sent only the colored soldiers to the front line. It is 'peoples of color' who annihilated the attempts at liberation by other 'peoples of color,' proof that there no grounds for universalizing the process."[45] Elsewhere:

> In no way must my color be felt as a stain. From the moment the black man accepts the split imposed by the Europeans, there is no longer any respite, and from that moment on, isn't it understandable that he will try to elevate himself to the white man's level? To elevate himself into the range of colors to which he has attributed a kind of hierarchy? We shall see that another solution is possible. It implies restructuring the world.[46]

In summary, psychoanalytic considerations reveal that what structures the Asian American theological subject, both racially and sexually, is particular to the Asian American experience. Pathologies such as the racial melancholia of loss and psychic nowhere of racial dissociation arise from the dislocation of migration and generational difference or trauma. Similarly, objectifications as robotic or erotic nonhumans are everyday occurrences within a White supremacist racial capitalist order. These together begin to point to the cracks in what we pretend is the stability of Asian American identity. Liberation thus requires in part interpreting race as a transitional space, a good-enough race. But most of all, liberation requires restructuring of the world. But before we begin this restructuring, we turn to a final deconstruction of Asian American subjectivity.

AGAINST UNIFORM SUBJECTIVITY

Asian American studies, Kandace Chuh proposes, ought to be reconceived as a subjectless discourse, one that creates a conceptual space to prioritize difference by foregrounding the discursive constructedness of Asian American subjectivity. The need for this arises as Asian American studies—and, as I argue, Asian American theology—has mounted sophisticated interrogations of representational objectifications of Asians but has not paid equally critical attention to the ways in which the Asian American subject is conceived. In other words, Asian American theological discourse often essentializes Asian American subjectivity, taking for granted that its epistemological boundaries are static and neatly circumscribed.[47]

For example, in pursuing the construction of Asian American identity alongside biblical interpretation, Mary Foskett and Jeffrey Kah-Jin Kuan refer to *Asian American* as the experience of living in North America as a member of a constellation of racial or ethnic minority communities, "more a social and political designation than a cultural identifier."[48] Elsewhere, Matsuoka introduces an anthology of Asian North American theological voices written from the perspectives of "those who claim themselves to be Americans of Asian ancestry who reside in Canada and the United States."[49] Assertions of the heterogeneity must be further pushed toward interrogations of Asian American theological subjectivity itself. Ahn and Kao, as I have described above, ground their Asian American theo-ethical subject in political activism. But to stop there avoids confrontation with the later historical processes that have afforded relative privilege to Asian American immigrants who live up to the model-minority myth.

Following Chuh, we are led to ask: What does it mean to practitioners of Asian American theologies when the anchoring terms *Asian* and *American* seem so fatally unstable? What motivates *Asian American* in the face of infinite heterogeneity among its referents?[50] The 1965 Act introduced a managerial class of professionals whose migrations may be multilateral and disinterested in formal identification with the United States through citizenship, calling into question reliance on solely immigrant or refugee narratives. This problematizes discourses on marginalization and resistance in Asian American theologies, requiring an investigation of the "scattered hegemonies" that characterize the present and a materialist critique of the complicity with oppressive economic systems through narratives of upward mobility, corporate representation, and immigrant success.[51]

The notion of subjectlessness allows us to attend to the constraints on the liberatory potential of the achievement of subjectivity, manufactured by the powerful demands of the US nation-state through identity and citizenship. Again recalling Spivak, Chuh describes subjectlessness as ethical grounds for the political practice of "strategic anti-essentialism" whereby *Asian American* is manufactured situationally and enables critiques of the configurations of power and knowledge through which the term comes to have meaning.[52] Reconstituting Asian American theology through difference allows for a consistent theological critique of US nationalism and its apparatuses of power, particularly as it implicates theological institutions, and also of analytic frameworks that privilege identity over difference.

Viewed thus, *Asian American* as a discursive structure provides an entry point into histories of resistance and racism. It transfers properties of a racialized and gendered nation onto bodies—of people, of literatures, of fields of study. Far from being a transparent, objective description of a knowable identity, the term becomes a mediating presence that links bodies to the knowledge regimes of the US nation. *Asian American*, in this sense, is a metaphor for resistance and racism.[53] In the following, I summarize Chuh's analyses of legal and literary texts, examining their consequences for Asian American theological discourse.

First, the colonial relations of Filipine America calls for a twofold critique: of US nationalism and its promise of subjective equality and of Asian Americanist reliance on paradigms that require uniform subjectivity for coherence that, like US nationalism, equate subjectivity with justice achieved.[54] Chuh reads through Carlos Bulosan's and Bienvenido Santos's fiction an image of US militarism in the Philippines as "feminized and infantilized burdens of the white man, simultaneously to be uplifted and mastered, and the heteronormative dimensions of migration and assimilation."[55] Racial difference in this register "alibis the reaffirmation of patriarchal heteronormativity" in anti-miscegenation laws and popular discourse surrounding Filipinos while sexuality "instruments the regulation of the racialized identity of the nation."[56] These intersections problematize one-dimensional conceptions of Asian American theology as racial difference, which feminist theologians have also sought to dismantle.

Secondly, the Japanese incarceration required the imagination of a "nikkei transnation" to which Japanese Americans belonged, regardless of citizenship, out of a belief in the essential and delocalized sameness of all Japanese people in order to justify their incarceration. That is, the fact of US citizenship of Japanese Americans was rejected in favor of allying them with the Japanese nation, thereby producing a "foreigner within" and rendering Japanese Americans vulnerable to the alleged exigencies of war. This state production of transnationality raises the necessity of contesting both US nationalism and Asian American theological dependence on nation-based paradigms that "functionally rely on a seemingly stable and knowable prediscursive identity for objective coherence."[57] Naive notions of transnationality such as through the heterogeneity of Asian American demographics must therefore give way to more nuanced understandings of how the transnational is constituted, keeping in view racialization as a technology of state power.

Thirdly, the conception of Asian American studies and Asian American theologies in part through the distinction between, as Sau-ling Wong has put it, "Asians in America" and "Asians in Asia" reproduces the territorial logic of US nationalism.[58] Within the context of Asian American theological discourse, a critical transnational focus disrupts received conceptions of Asia as "someplace and something that happens somewhere over there." It challenges us to identify the material consequences of the imagined yet militarized boundaries of the United States and what interests are served by maintaining this distance between *Asia* and *America*.[59] Following Chuh, *Asian America* ought to be conceived of as a "heterotopic formation" that contains multiple and dissimilar spaces and places of discourse and history. This has critical implications for Asian American theological approaches to ecclesiastical practice, such as missiological projects at home or abroad that reproduce the spatial logic of "us" versus "them" through the "here" and "there."

It is the absence of a unified identity, the meaninglessness of *Asian American*, that collectivizes Asian American theologies, undecidability rather than identity that "provides the grounds for unity, and identifying and contesting the forces that control intelligibility, that affiliate meanings."[60] Similarly, Lowe calls for rethinking racialized ethnic identity in terms of differences of national origin, class, gender, and sexuality rather than presuming similarities and erasing particularity for the sake of unity.[61] Yet, a subjectless approach to Asian American theology is insufficient if only the discursive and not material relations are held in view. In proposing that Asian American theologies be reconceived through subjectlessness, I do not mean to throw out meaning but rather call for an explicitly political approach to Asian Americanness through both the constitutive *discursive* and *material* relations, recognizing the inherent instability of its definition. These unstable relations are inscribed on the Asian body, dehumanized as robotic and exoticized as erotic, producing affective complexes such as racial melancholia, racial dissociation, inferiority, and dependency. Subjectlessnes as a theoretical and theological approach dovetails with the psychoanalytic approach to race as a transitional space and good-enough race to depathologize the sense of psychic nowhere.

Having opened the way for an unbounded approach to Asian American theology, it is imperative from the point of view of liberation that deconstruction cannot be an end in itself but a means of rendering visible the racial, sexual, and nationalist discourses that produce Asian Americanness, particularly those consistent with the projects of empire and capital. Rendered visible, we see where we must strike unhesitatingly. Crucially, it is from this vantage point that solidarity not only with marginalized persons in North America can be built but also with those in post and neocolonial societies throughout the world. In other words, the abstractness of deconstruction remains an academic exercise unless it transcends the desire for institutionalization, which has become an end rather than the means through which liberation and conscientization is achieved, and is perhaps symptomatic of broader aspirations to Whiteness that Asian American theology must be prepared to relentlessly critique in self-reflection.[62]

The will to Whiteness, or lactification, is further problematized in its inherent connection to empire, which brings to mind Kuan-Hsing Chen's critique of East Asian imperialist desires and, more pointedly, historian Gary Okihiro's argument that the establishment of ethnic studies post-1968 rather than Third World studies as the Third World Liberation Front demanded, was a capitulation because of its narrow focus on national subjectivity. Ethnic studies as such domesticated an international alliance and struggle and reduced its revolutionary power.[63] In place of what might have been an internationalist and multiracial field of Third World studies, we were given a fractured and siloed pacification in the form of African American studies, Native American studies, Latin American studies, and, yes, Asian American studies. Okihiro's critique also implicates Asian American theologies insofar as they are conceived as "ethnic theologies" confined to struggles of identity and inclusion within institutional and national frames. The constructive next step of an Asian American theology liberation then is to rebuild these severed connections. It begins with the land beneath our feet.

LAND

4.

"GO BACK TO WHERE YOU CAME FROM"

Unsettling Asian American Theology

If to help us is your wish then stand behind us.
Not to the side
And not in front.

—'Imaikalani Kalahele, *Kalahele*

As a mestiza I have no country, my homeland cast me out, yet all
countries are mine because I am every woman's sister or potential lover.
—Gloria Anzaldúa, *Borderlands / La Frontera*

Annakilli! Annakilli! Parrot sitting in the banyan tree
Blessing to lead a good life, our ancestors have bequeathed us this soil
Across the river banks and on the fertile fields
Our forefathers have sung through their life
The lakes and ponds belong to the dogs, foxes, and cats too . . .
I planted five trees, nurtured a beautiful garden
My garden is flourishing. Yet my throat remains dry
My sea, bank, forest, people, lands, clan, place, and track
Enjoy, my dear. Come together as one
Ride on the elephants—shower in the rains.

—Arivu Dee, *Enjoy Enjaami*[1]

In 2021, Asian Americans made up 6.1 percent of the population in the United States, in contrast to Indigenous Americans (1.3 percent) and Black or African Americans (13.6 percent).[2] Yet in 2019 a discrimination lawsuit was brought against Harvard by a group of Asian Americans, who made up almost 26 percent of Harvard's domestic undergraduate student population, represented by Edward Blum, a "longtime crusader against affirmative action."[3] The suit was intended as a clear challenge by right-wing Republicans to affirmative-action policy.[4] While arguments about representation or diversity, equity, and inclusion often center around racial demographics relative to US population data, this form of reasoning through proportional representation is inherently flawed considering that Indigenous Americans tend to make up less than 2 percent in any statistic of this kind. As a matter of fact, it happens that Indigenous Americans can be easily over-represented in some cases. Harvard eventually won the case and neoliberal critiques of the lawsuit were readily supplied by other Asian Americans, rehearsing arguments about the model minority myth and anti-Blackness, the fact of Asians being weaponized by White supremacy remains, while aspiring Asian American teenagers downplayed aspects of their identity in order to appear "less Asian" to college admissions committees.[5]

Of the thousands of higher education institutions in the United States, the singular focus on Harvard is telling. This episode can be placed in the larger context of Asian settler colonialism in the United States and the complicity of Asians in violence against communities of color through racial technologies such as, yes, model-minority aspirations and color-blindness. *Settler colonialism* describes the ongoing occupation of Indigenous land, such as the Americas, Israel, Australia, and elsewhere, by non-Indigenous people. Often used to describe European settlers, the populations that arrive later in the settler colony are typically referred to instead as immigrants. In the United States, for example, the early British and French settlers are referred to as such, whereas the later arrivals from the Italians and Irish to the Filipine and Japanese and Chinese are coded as immigrants, regardless of legal status. Anti-immigrant rhetoric in the Trump era was met with the counterclaim that the United States is a "nation of immigrants" and that "immigrants make America great," an equally nostalgic response to the slogan "Make America Great Again." Yet, Native Americans—and similarly Indigenous populations in settler colonies elsewhere—continue to be annexed, their land occupied and treaties broken.

The history of violence of early settler colonizers in the Americas is tragic but relatively straightforward, such as told in the works of Tzvetan Todorov, Eduardo Galeano, and Roxanne Dunbar-Ortiz. But what about the histories of oppression and exclusion of Black people and other people of color who did not establish the settler colony, arriving instead through more complicated functions of slavery, indentured labor, asylum, or economic migration? While interlocking forms of oppression exist and maintain heteropatriarchal White supremacy and racial capitalism, and while there is a key distinction to be made between forced and intentional migrations, the fact remains that all of us non-Indigenous persons live and move and have our being on occupied land. This question is increasingly relevant as extreme climate events increase in frequency, leading to a growing number of climate refugees and forced migrations.[6] For reasons such as this, a robust theology that accounts for the complexities of diaspora populations, fraught with both the inherent trauma of displacement and the potential to displace others or maintain the settler-colonial order, becomes increasingly necessary. Continuing from the psychic nowhere of the previous chapter, I turn to a geographic nowhere and its relation to settler colonialism and indigeneity.

Asian Americans are settlers of color, in the words of Haunani-Kay Trask, the late leader of the Hawaiian Sovereignty Movement. This label properly positions non-Indigenous people of color within the settler-colonial power structure: though systematically oppressed, the struggles of non-Indigenous people of color against racism and discrimination is predicated upon the void created by the continuing genocide of Native populations and cultures.[7] The rhetoric of multiculturalism and immigrant rights weaponizes notions of equality, eliding this crucial difference that sets apart Natives from settlers. For settlers of color, the routine disavowal of White supremacy, including its settler coloniality, is a convenient one: relegating Native populations to the past, casting them as an essentially extinct or mythical people, allows for the settler-colonial society to legitimate itself as the natural heir to the land while settlers of color are allowed to inherit a selective amnesia as they seek legitimacy from the settler-colonial power, the right to reside within the settler colony and to be productive citizens thereof. Under this erasure, the oppression experienced by exogenous non-White persons come to the fore, drowning out Indigenous struggles for land and sovereignty. I contend that any proper theology of liberation, particularly any one developed on North American soil, must first reckon with the Indigenous struggles for self-determination anywhere. From an Asian diasporic perspective, it is necessary to negotiate between theologies of migration and indigeneity. Asian American liberation will be incomplete if it does not destroy the settler colony.

Asian American settler colonialism is mediated by the relationship between Asian migrations and United States imperialism. While the West may have produced arguably the most hegemonic forms of domination, it does not have a monopoly on enacting oppressive systems. Blaming Whiteness alone is too easy. Not confining our analysis of power to Whiteness makes it possible to conceive of people of color, including Asian Americans, as existing beyond the oppressor-oppressed dialectic, as the concept of a good-enough race leads toward.

Several distinct aspects of settler colonialism emerge, some of which involve complex histories within Asia. First is the experience of colonization and neocolonialism by the West in Asia. Following decolonization, rather than returning the land and reins of power to the native population, some colonies became the inheritance of intermediary Asians, non-Indigenous peoples brought over by their colonial masters such as the Mindanao in the Philippines and the Chinese in Singapore. The second is settler colonialism carried out by Asian countries within their own borders such as China, Israel, India, and Vietnam, sometimes called internal colonialism, independent of Western interference. Third is the Asian experience of settler colonialism. Many Palestinians, Kashmiris, Tibetans, and Uyghurs have sought asylum in the United States as a result of conflicts with settler-colonial forces. Together, these bring us to a key theological reflection of this chapter—namely, the capability of being both oppressor and oppressed.[8] The dynamic potential for either reflects the resistance of the category "Asian American" to an easy definition. There is no tenable blanket characterization of Asians as being either oppressor or oppressed.

This sets the stage for Asian American settler colonialism. This has been explored mainly by Native American scholars and Asian settler scholars in the context of Hawaii, where Asians have become the majority racial group. The struggle of Hawaiians against first White and later Asian settlers, against militarization, incarceration, and domination, provides a particularly useful framework for interpreting Asian American settler colonialism at large. The subjugation of Native American populations is a continuing project of the settler state at large, so successful as to render the Native American nearly invisible, transformed into a mythological person who exists only in history books and racist holidays, never fully humanized.

A theology of liberation requires the humanization of the non-humans in settler society, whereby Indigenous people must be seen not as a population to be evangelized rather than exterminated, as Bartolomé De La Casas argued, but as the rightful stewards of the land, who deeply understand the ways of the earth, wind, water, and trees in this continent. The concept of land as property is a feature of capitalism, foreign to Indigenous traditions. The earth belongs to no man: it is the Lord's and the fulness thereof; the world and they who dwell therein. Before turning to the specificity of Asian settler colonialism and Asian American theology, I first begin with the broad contours of settler colonialism and Native American liberation theology.

SETTLER COLONIALISM: THEORY AND THEOLOGY

Patrick Wolfe introduced a structural distinction between settler-colonial and colonial formations: settler colonialism is not a master-servant relationship "marked by ethnic difference," an important aspect of post-colonial criticism, but a relationship characterized by the dispensability of the Indigenous person. "The primary object of settler-colonization," Wolfe writes, "is the land itself rather than the surplus value to be derived from mixing Native labour with it. Though, in practice, Indigenous labour was indispensable to Europeans, settler-colonization is not exploitation but replacement. The logic of this project, a sustained institutional tendency to eliminate the Indigenous population, informs a range of historical practices that might otherwise appear distinct— invasion is a structure, not an event."[9] Settlers are colonists who come to stay. Their primary aim is to dispossess, displace, and destroy Indigenous peoples rather than to exploit them for their labor. Settler social orders are established through complementary logics of elimination and exclusion, dispossessing natives and then attempting to police the racial, gender, and class boundaries of the settler polity.[10] Nonetheless, Wolfe points out that though the settler-colonial logic of elimination has manifested as genocidal, such as in the Americas, settler colonialism is inherently eliminatory but not invariably genocidal, as in Jammu, Kashmir, and Palestine.[11] This is a crucial distinction when seeking an understanding of settlers of color who do not themselves participate in the genocidal founding of settler society yet remain complicit in its maintenance, thus in the elimination of the Native.

According to Lorenzo Veracini, "Settler projects are inevitably premised on the traumatic, that is, *violent*, replacement and/or displacement of Indigenous Other" and at the same time "needs to disavow any foundational violence."[12] In the case of European settler societies, the disavowal of violence is aided by myths produced through biblical narratives. This problematizes straightforward applications of the Exodus story in liberation theological frameworks: the freedom that Israel had gained from Egyptian slavery ended in the genocide and occupation of Canaan. The deliberate forgetting of the second half of the Exodus narrative resonates with what Eiko Kosasa calls the production of blankness, whereby "acts of erasure produce an American imaginary where concepts and images of 'blankness' and blank spaces proliferate." [13] This production of blankness and disavowal of settler violence underscore the fantasy of the terra nullius during the "discovery" of the Americas and the settler colonization of Australia, not only at the level of physical place but also representational space. These European discoveries were sanctioned by the Doctrine of Discovery established in the 1494 Treaty of Tordesillas, which declared that only non-Christian lands could (and, implicitly, should) be colonized. The imperial Christian theologies that underwrote European colonization of the Americas, Africa, and Asia continue to function in the settler colony of the United States and cannot ultimately coexist with liberation theologies.

Even Christian ethicists ignore this fact. In *Resident Aliens*, Christian ethicist Stanley Hauerwas, declared "America's Best Theologian" in 2001 by *Time* magazine, and William Willimon proposed a conception of Christians in the United States as resident aliens, members of a colony. Rather than recognizing the settler-colonial structure, they define a colony to be "a beachhead, an outpost, an island of one culture in the middle of another, a place where the values of home are reiterated and passed on to the young, a place where the distinctive language and life-style of the resident aliens are lovingly nurtured and reinforced."[14] This romantic view of colonialism is problematic in two ways: first, the term *resident alien* is a play on the non-US citizen category, though the authors make no explicit reference to it. The notion of being a resident alien as a means of separating the US Christian from nationalist aspirations is, at best, naive, failing to interrogate the actual condition of Christians living within a settler colony, and, at worst, perpetuating the dispossession of Native Americans.

Second, there is no way of using the term *colony* in a positive manner with regards to humans, especially in a Christian context and in the presence of ongoing settler colonialism. They write, "We believe that the designations of the church as a colony and Christians as resident aliens are not too strong for the modern American church—indeed, we believe it is the nature of the church, at any time and in any situation, to be a colony." The modern American church certainly *is* a colony—a colony within a colony, we might say—founded on genocidal violence and maintained through the logic of elimination. Settler invasion is the structural foundation upon which the White church in the United States was built. As Walter Hixson wrote concerning American settler colonialism, "Born of settler colonialism, indiscriminate violence against savage foes forged an American way of war and a pathway first to continental and then to global empire."[15] That is, warfare against Indigenous Americans was formative in how the US military wages its wars abroad, a connection that must not be lost on us. From this brief examination, it already becomes painfully apparent that it is impossible to take the lead from White settler theologians with regards to constructing a theology of freedom (or, frankly, any theology that does not do violence to others). Such naive Christian ethics has little value to Asian American theology that wrestles with colonialism, imperialism, and displacement, or to Indigenous Americans whose continuing survival is only despite settler-colonial elimination, or to Black and Latine Americans who understand their position in the United States as one of internal colonialism.[16]

Now, any discussion on the relation between Indigenous Americans, settler colonialism, and liberation theology must face head-on the challenges posed by Vine Deloria Jr., whose work forms the foundation for most Indigenous scholars in the field of religion or theology. Deloria contends that liberation theology assumes that the common experience of oppression is sufficient ground for solidarity and indiscriminately classifies all minorities in a single category of people seeking liberation, eliding the specificity of various forms of oppression and violence into a single, undifferentiated binary of oppressed/oppressor. [17] This sentiment is echoed by Elaine Kim, who reflects in "At Least You're Not Black," that coalition work requires specific issues of concern such as workers' rights or educational opportunity rather than some vague notion of oppression.[18] Moreover, Deloria argues that liberation theology was "an absolute necessity if the establishment was going to continue to control the minds of minorities. If a person of a minority group had not invented it, the liberal establishment most certainly would have created it."

Thus a direct challenge is posed to liberation theology: in developing a liberation theology that is comprehensive but not reductive, we must avoid falling into the trap of participating in a hierarchy of oppression. We must also be constantly vigilant so as not to allow liberation theology to be co-opted by the so-called liberal establishment. Identifying liberation theology as a solely liberal or leftist ideology is to misunderstand the aims of liberation theology. At the same time, it must be acknowledged that liberation theology at large has already capitulated in this exact manner, to the extent that its relevance today must be argued for and cannot be taken for granted. Keeping Deloria's critiques in sight, I propose that there remains a theology of liberation that can be productively used as a unifying principle and that it is in fact the only viable candidate for a theology for the revolution.

Arguably the most notable work of Deloria in the field of religious studies is the book *God Is Red*, which launched an unflinching critique of Western thought and Christianity in the United States.[19] In it, Deloria singles out Western Christianity as the root cause of the inability of the United States to "win peace" in its entire history of war-making. Christianity, along with Judaism and Islam, religions of the Near East, are qualitatively different from other religions in terms of their anthropology of man and creation, sharing the view that the planet is "not our natural home and is, in fact, ours for total exploitation."[20]

Deloria points to theologians such as Paul Tillich who argue that the corrupted state of nature is inextricably linked to the sinfulness of mankind, which inadvertently leads to the conclusion that nature cannot be redeemed by human means.[21] Moreover, in the 1992 edition, the ecological crisis that Deloria earlier foresaw had grown to the point that he was able to write, "We are today reaching the 'nth' term in this sequence of exploitation and face ecological disasters of such complete planetary scope as to surpass our wildest imagination."[22] Three decades later, we are farther along than ever along this track toward ecological collapse. Revolution is more urgent than ever. Certainly, Deloria writes with this in mind in his original conclusion: "As the long-forgotten peoples of the respective continents rise and begin to reclaim their ancient heritage, they will discover the meaning of the lands of their ancestors. That is when the invaders of the North American continent will finally discover that for this land, God is red."[23]

Native American theologian George Tinker, on the other hand, while building on the foundation laid by Deloria, is more optimistic about the possibility of Christianity and Native American theology despite their first encounter. Tinker argues that, as with other advocates of liberation theology, "American Indians must also see liberation, or freedom, as our principal goal." Tinker drew a distinction between any Native American theology of liberation and other liberation theologies, writing that "as Indigenous communities, our notions of freedom and liberation will be necessarily different from the expressions of Christianity that have emerged, for example, from Latin American liberation theologians during the last thirty or more years."[24] Similarly, we must also ask what constitutes Asian notions of freedom and liberation, distinct from other theologies of liberation. This is a crucial point because of the genocidal role that Christian doctrine has played in the Americas.

Moreover, the denominational doctrine, according to Tinker, requires a particular form of erasure in seeking to replicate itself in the convert—an erasure of Indigenous identity. This assimilation is another feature of settler colonialism, whereby the "vanishing native" is produced through various modes of elimination that are still genocidal, as more information about residential schools come to light. "Denominations seem to have deeply invested themselves in a politics of replicating themselves in the colonized. The missionaries want nothing more than to themselves reflected back in the faith and language of their Indian wards,"[25] a sentiment not unfamiliar to Asians subject to evangelizing missions. In 1551, Bartolomé de Las Casas engaged in a public debate before the Spanish court, arguing that the Indigenous Americans were also human beings, a position not patently obvious to the Spanish conquistadores. Instead, he promulgated a "gentler conquest," hoping to destroy Indigenous cultural structures by replacing them with a European value system and cultural patterns of behavior.[26] This process became the predominant structure used by Roman Catholics in the Americas and later reproduced by Protestants in North America, captured by the famous saying of Captain Richard Henry Pratt in 1892 Colorado: "Kill the Indian in him, and save the man."[27] This missionizing assimilation produced political divisions within the Indigenous American communities. Forcing the choice between Indigenous traditions and the settler religious traditions was so successful in dividing communities and coercing compliance that missionization was adopted as a colonial political strategy.[28]

The goals of other liberation theologies in the United States, while important, come second to the need to decolonize the foundational settler-colonial structure. Part of the work of Asian American liberation is imagining such Indigenous futures. Freedom must be for all peoples. Liberation theology must not only humanize the nonhuman, as Gutiérrez contended, but also privilege and render visible the erased Native, giving primacy to the ones whose land upon which we are theologizing. More than just rendering human or visible, we must join in the fight for Indigenous sovereignty and resurgence.[29] Any liberation theology developed in settler societies that does not explicitly address the settler-colonial order is already complicit in the logic of elimination and on its own cannot be a theology of freedom for all.

What sort of theology of liberation emerges when taking seriously the task of decolonization? As a start, radical reinterpretations of Jesus in the tradition of other liberation theologies, Tinker argued, are counterproductive because "the first proclamation of Jesus among any Indian community came as the beginning of a colonial conquest," replacing Native religious traditions with "the imposition of a one-size-fits-all euro-western Jesus."[30] Furthermore, moves to correct Jesus's ethnicity "helps little to obviate our historical experience of the way missionary preaching about Jesus was used to destroy our cultures and legitimate the theft of our property." Race remains a social construct, as Wolfe also emphasizes, in the context of settler-colonial society. The dialectic of race underwrites sociohistorical arguments about the racial identity of Jesus, through which very different theologies emerge. Thus, while it may be important for Christian doctrines to have Jesus at their core, any naive setting of Jesus as the cornerstone of liberation theology runs afoul of committing ahistorical violence, ignoring the physical, social, and psychological damage that continues to be done in the name of Jesus throughout Asia, Africa, and the Americas.

ASIAN AND ASIAN AMERICAN SETTLER COLONIALISM

With the broad contours of (mostly European) settler colonialism and its relation to Native American liberation theology in place, we can now turn to Asian and Asian American settler colonialism. A first examination of Asian American complicity in settler colonialism in Hawaii opens the way for thinking through the idea of Asian American immigrants as participants in settler colonialism in the Americas, the United States mainland, and its colonies. It is worth quoting Trask at length:

> Our native people and territories have been overrun by non-natives, including Asians. Calling themselves "local," the children of Asian settlers greatly outnumber us. They claim Hawai'i as their own, denying Indigenous history, their long collaboration in our continued dispossession, and the benefits therefrom. Part of this denial is the substitution of the term "local" for "immigrant," which is, itself, a particularly celebrated American gloss for "settler." As on the continent, so in our island home. Settlers and their children recast the American tale of nationhood: Hawai'i, like the continent, is naturalized as but another telling illustration of the uniqueness of America's "nation of immigrants.[31]

Here, the signifier *local* is deployed in opposition to the term *immigrant* as a means of legitimating the presence of multigenerational Asian settlers in Hawaii, viewing themselves as locals while not being indigenous to the land. This belies the contention that settlers ultimately desire to having or belonging to the land as they imagine an Indigenous person would, and in doing so indigenize. Once in possession of the land, settlers deny the logic of possession and dispossession that enabled them to acquire it in the first place.[32] In Hawaii, where the Asian population now represents the largest racial demographic and has effectively inherited the colonial order, the problem of settler colonialism is particularly pertinent. Filipines, Japanese, Koreans, and Chinese migrants arrived in Hawaii as *haole*, or persons who are not descendants of the ethnic native Hawaiians, especially White people, and became laborers in the sugarcane plantations set up on the lands taken by overthrowing the Hawaiian kingdom. The immigrant narrative in which one arrives, both seeking economic prosperity and fleeing unrest, working hard while enduring racism and cultural loss, and finally achieving success and assimilation into White normativity, is a hallmark of the immigrant hegemony that Trask describes. How can we negotiate the hardship of Asian migration and the desire for belonging with Native American struggles against settler colonialism?

Iyko Day critiques the notion of Asian settler colonialism as a blanket attempt to enforce a settler/native binary, arguing that it is unclear whether settler identity in Hawaii is generalizable to Asian immigrant formations elsewhere. Day acknowledges, as did Fujikane, that the initial political and economic subjugation does not exempt Asian ethnic groups from participating as settlers in a colonial system, but goes on to argue that the fact that Asian settlers have attained demographic majority, political represen-tation, and economic power in Hawaii distinguishes them from Asian migrant settlers elsewhere. The history of Black people used as Buffalo Soldiers in the wars against Indigenous people in the western United States and during the Philippine–American War, according to Day, is an example of "an oppressed group's unwitting (and sometimes unwilling) participation in settler colonialism and imperial invasion, yet the continued economic and political sub-jugation of African Americans seems to exempt them from most theorizing on settler colonialism, as a 'third space' or otherwise."[33]

But does this let us off the hook? The lack of theorizing about settlers of color does not mean that non-Indigenous people of color do not cooperate and administer the settler-colonial order, regardless of who invaded in the first place. While Day insightfully argues that a core logic of the settler-colonial mode of produc-tion centers on the systematic exploitation of a racialized, gen-dered, and sexualized alien labor force, her insistence on this third space, which she calls "the alien," is at the same time inadequate and superfluous.[34] Superfluous because it evades the central claim of Indigenous peoples against settlers and does not address the fact of Asian settler-colonial violence; inadequate because Day triangulates between native, settler, and alien, placing African Americans and Asian Americans in the same category of analysis while acknowledging the heterogeneity contained within an alien position given the divergent historical and economic contexts of Asian and African labor.[35] As I shall contend in the next chapter, the particular experiences of Asian Americans and African Americans are not only differentiated under racial capitalism but are often at odds with one another.

Wolfe, on the other hand, maintains that "the opposition between native and settler is a structural relationship rather than an effect of the will. . . . Neither I nor other settlers can will our way out of it, whether we want to or not."[36] Wolfe compared the Australian context in which unfree White convict labor was imported from Britain, who did not pass on the condition of their criminality to their offspring, with the American context in which enslaved African were trafficked to the Americas and where the particularity of the Black experience lies in the exclusive and transferable condition of racial slavery. Against this backdrop, Day rightly argues for proper boundaries that distinguish between voluntary and forced migrations, that "folding them into a generalized settler position through voluntaristic assumptions constrains our ability to understand how their racialized vulnerability and disposability supports a settler colonial project."[37] But the solution is not so much to create a third "alien" space that is *neither* settler nor native that evades Indigenous claims but rather to attend to the complexities *within* the settler populace, including settlers of color. The will of non-White, non-Indigenous peoples to indigenize, to possess land, must not be underestimated. Race alone cannot play the role of the transitional space for Indigenous liberation, as the structure of invasion exceeds it.

That said, in each category of analysis a different binary is set up with respect to a given power relation, such as native/settler,

East/West, rich/poor, Black/White, male/female, and so on. In United States racial discourse, the Asian American is invoked—as one might with Latine Americans, say—to disrupt the Black and White binary, or in this case the native and settler binary, producing settlers of color that disavow their settler-colonial inheritance through more complex formations such as divergent histories of slavery and oppression. Triangulating between a binary and a third space produces a ternary relationship that can be productive and yet insufficient. Andrea Smith's framework of the three pillars of White supremacy—slavery/capitalism, genocide/capitalism, and orientalism/war—with heteropatriarchy as its base attempts to go further, "constituted by separate and distinct, but still interrelated, logics."[38] Regardless of the model used, the key to solidarity is to be able to hold the larger picture in constant view while maintaining a granular perspective on the particularities of each form of oppression without easily dismissing others.

Asian American settler colonialism is a corollary of White settler colonialism, located in the nexus of the transatlantic and transpacific slave trades, proxy wars in East Asia, the afterlife of European colonization, the expansion of global finance capitalism, and the "war on terror." Indeed, to write about the beginnings of Asian and Asian American church history requires a reckoning with the history of White missionary expeditions and their cooperation with colonial expansion. These expeditions brought not only the Gospel and civilization to the natives by colonization and reeducation but also extracted wealth in the form of natural resources and human labor, or what David Harvey calls accumulation by dispossession. Many flows of Asian migration into the United States are inextricably linked to US military involvement in Asia, whether through the "mixing" of US troops with the local populace, refugees seeking asylum, or international adoption.

Asian Christians, as with Indigenous Americans, must negotiate their relationship to Christianity and the violence it has visited upon the world in a way that does not deny the agency of our communities in developing their own spiritual practices that are often syncretic and hybrid. Under the umbrella of Asian American Christianity are vibrant South Korean, Taiwanese, and Filipine church communities, for example, immigrant churches that serve as immigrant community centers, places to gather when all else is foreign and unwelcoming. They provide strong networks of social support, and in this way both immigrant religious practices and home cultures are passed on to the next generation.

At the same time, we must also interrogate the aspects of the White man's religion that have been internalized and reproduced in Christian communities of color. For example, missions to Native American reservations and Caribbean and Central American countries such as Haiti and Guatemala often reproduce an honorary White savior complex and feel-good voluntourism. Asian American missions tend to target poorer countries in the Global South or "urban" areas in much the same manner as White missionary work, reproducing a benevolent racism toward people who are seen as backward or undeveloped. One tragic case is John Allen Chau, a twenty-six-year-old from Alabama, killed in 2018 in an attempt to evangelize the Sentinalese people in the Adaman and Nicobar Islands, a self-isolated group that Chau referred to as "Satan's last stronghold."[39] The brand of Christianity brought to Asia by White missionaries carries White systematic and biblical theologies, whose hermeneutics study deeply the historical contexts of biblical texts and figures but have little to say about the application of the texts to racial injustice, gender oppression, and class difference in the present day. This is deeply symptomatic of a White mythology that narrates specific facts about itself and forgets others, such as in the US support of Israeli settler colonialism in Palestine through cultural exchange, direct investment, and military backing. This narrative is particularly pertinent as it is intertwined with the biblical narrative of Israel's right to inheritance and the conquest of Canaan.[40]

Another crucial dimension of Asian settler colonialism that I will not be able to describe in any satisfactory manner here is the fact of settler colonialism within Asia itself. To mention but a few examples, there are the Taiwanese Indigenous Gaushan people who in the recent past were occupied by the Chinese Nationalist Party, retreating after their defeat by the Communist Party of China in 1949. This underscores the complexities of settler colonialism, whereby the arriving population does not necessarily arrive by choice or with intent of domination yet eventually does come to dominate the Indigenous populace.[41] Jammu and Kashmir, nearby, remain caught between the land claims of India and Pakistan, all of whom were partitioned by the British. In 2019, Article 370 in India, which granted Jammu and Kashmir special status as autonomous administrative regions, was revoked in the midst of a lockdown, Internet blackout, and military occupation that continued into the COVID-19 pandemic. In particular, the article had prevented Indian citizens from other states from purchasing land or property there. This move angered Pakistan and drew sympathy from the international community, but their present reality remains the same: an Indian scramble for Kashmiri land ensued. A final example is the Muslim Moro and animist Lumad people in the Mindanao region in the Philippines: following the successive colonization by the Spanish, the Americans, and the Japanese, Christian Filipines from neighboring regions took over the reins from the colonial administration and perpetuated the marginalization of the Moro and Lumad in their native land, similar to the present dominance of ethnic Chinese in Singapore. These vignettes serve as reminders of the real potential for Asians themselves to inherit power in the form of imperialism and settler colonialism, that the will to power (and settle) is not an exclusive feature of Whiteness, and also of the possibilities of transnational solidarity in struggles against settler colonialism.

UNSETTLING ASIAN AMERICAN THEOLOGY:
TOWARD A THEOLOGY OF LANDLESSNESS

Settler colonialism describes the occupation of Indigenous land, including the United States. Settlers of color maintain the settler colonial structure, and their struggles against racism and discrimination are predicated on the "blank space" that is created out of the continuing genocide and suppression of Indigenous Americans. As Fujikane wrote, the rhetoric of multiculturalism and immigrant rights weaponizes notions of equality but elides the crucial difference that sets Indigenous Americans apart from settlers. As Asian American settler colonizers, it is necessary to actively fight against the amnesia of immigrant communities surrounding the centuries of pillage, subjugation, and extermination in the Americas, reproducing settler-colonial domination. Asian Americans also straddle the economic divide as the most economically unequal racial groups in the nation. In the struggle for upward mobility, Asian Americans perpetuate the dispossession of Indigenous people with lukewarmness, something in between capitalist calculating and stability seeking. It is simply the best we could do to survive. Or is it?

Here liberation theology becomes useful: the class analysis in theologizing from the viewpoint of the poor and the oppressed is a rebuke to Asian Americans who have succeeded far too well at achieving the Asian American dream. The model-minority myth of hard work and conformity encourages us to be comfortable with wealth, especially wealth earned through perceived merit. The myth that one can succeed in the Americas solely through hard work hides the systematic disenfranchisement of poor people of color, especially Black and Indigenous communities. Landholding is a crucial means by which generational wealth is passed down in capitalist societies, not least where land was stolen from Indigenous people and withheld from Black people,[42] so that the common wisdom to buy land or property does not come without moral strings attached.

But more is necessary. Just as we must fight the tendency to become weaponized as model minorities against others, we must also resist the comfortable urge to occupy Native land unproblematically and to imagine Indigenous Americans as people of the past. Tinker criticized the shortcomings of Black and Latin American theologies of liberation, arguing that their class analyses inadequately address the Native American condition. The visions of socialism or Marxism that have influenced these liberation theologies alone do not offer compelling futures for Indigenous Americans any more than racial capitalism does. As such, we must look to Native American liberation theology not as just another addition to the multiculturalist project but rather as the foundation upon which to build our theology in the Americas. Just as James Cone argued that any Christology in the Americas must reckon with the historical fact of lynching, so must any theology in the Americas account for Native American liberation. [43]

Native American theology challenges settlers to think of ourselves as never being only unto ourselves but interconnected to community and land and creation, to consider our freedom not as an individual but as a *collective* spiritual condition. As in James, "If a brother or sister is naked and lacks daily food, and one of you says to them, 'Go in peace; keep warm and eat your fill,' and yet you do not supply their bodily needs, what is the good of that? So faith by itself, if it has no works, is dead."[44] Solidarity with other communities of color in their struggles is an exercise in demonstrating our faith through works. For Asian Americans, repentance requires the conviction of our own complicity before we can even begin working toward the freedom first of all of Indigenous peoples, then of Black people, and, finally, the rest of us. Christians more than anyone must believe that another world is possible.

It is time to return to Wolfe's phrase "invasion is a structure, not an event." Much has been written on the structural nature of settler-colonial invasion, how settler society is built upon and sustained by the logics of elimination and exclusion. The structural analysis of settler colonialism allows us to distinguish it from colonialism, which seeks to extract value from the land, oftentimes through the subjugation of the Indigenous population and exploitation of imported, enslaved, or trafficked alien labor. Settler colonialism invades to take over the land, to replace the Indigenous population and thus indigenize. Liberation theology—and liberation at large—is the *affirmative* aspect of decolonization and a decolonized theology. That is, decolonization, as both a process and analytical tool in the post-colony and settler colony, is an emancipatory move that leads to liberation. But as with invasion, liberation is a structure, not an event. Liberation must come to stay. Liberation must be understood as a structure to be sustained, not an event that occurs once as a rupture in historical time. As such, theologies of liberation must be worked out both in theory and in practice, as it occurs in historical processes and also in dialectical relations, in ideology.

Arguably, this is the first place to start working through what Reverend Duke Kwon calls "ecclesiastical reparations"—reparations owed by the church as an institution and its members to communities whose oppression it has been complicit in. Reparations is typically discussed in the context of what is due to African Americans for the centuries of enslavement and subjugation, most recently popularized by Ta-Nehisi Coates.[45] Reparations for slavery is a crucial topic in its own right that the church needs to reckon with, but reparations for settler colonialism, I argue, has been largely ignored in conversations about justice even though the "Land Back" claim is far more tangible than reparations for enslavement. Christians of color have begun to come to terms with the complicity of Christianity in the conquest of the Americas through the Doctrine of Discovery, which also justified the colonization of the Third World. Yet this continues today in the form of legal uses of eminent domain as a means of seizing land, as was used, for example, for the construction of Trump's border wall along the Mexico–US border.[46] Additionally, the evangelistic missions by Christians of color to Native American reservations reproduce the colonial mentality, without being critical of the history that has produced the present conditions faced by Native Americans. As J. Sakai wrote, "It is the absolute characteristic of settler society to be parasitic, dependent upon the super-exploitation of oppressed peoples for its style of life."[47]

We already know enough about the settler-colonial situation. The challenge to all settlers has been, still is, and will be the question of land and self-determination—in other words, to "desettlerize" the colony. According to Sakai, "Euro-Amerikan liberals and radicals have rarely dealt with the Land question; we could say that they don't have to deal with it, since their people already have all the land."[48] The same could be said of settlers of color, including Asian Americans, inasmuch as they are able to prosper into landholding homeowners. Some might object, saying that giving control to a vanishingly small Indigenous population would simply lead to a kind of oligarchic rule. But the near extinction of Indigenous populations is not a coincidence, as obvious as this may seem, and if desettlerization is being taken in conjunction with deimperialization, demilitarization, and the dismantling of capitalism, it is worth remembering that "everyone could live here who lives here, quite well, with a lot of autonomy, a lot of justice, a lot of room for expression and development."[49] From a theological standpoint, Kwon invoked the encounter between Jesus and Zacchaeus, who in repentance offered to give half his possessions to the poor and repay four times what he had stolen from others.[50] Paying ecclesiastical reparations is not conditional upon the moral character of the one who has been stolen from but rather an imperative on the part of the thief. Land Back does not need to know how the Indigenous nations will steward the land.

Decolonization is not a metaphor, Tuck and Yang insist.[51] Calls to decolonize too often metaphorize decolonization in the context of a settler colony. Doing so kills the very possibility of decolonization and recenters Whiteness; it is yet another form of settler appropriation. What would it mean to actually decolonize something like theology, such as Asian American theology? I want to suggest that decolonizing Asian American theology requires *giving up the search for physical belonging*, the mythical land of AsianAmerica, replacing it with a theology of landlessness, and being in solidarity with Indigenous struggles for sovereignty. To talk about decolonizing anything on Turtle Island, we have to start with settler colonialism. At least up until 1965, most Asians arrived in the United States through US military and colonial interests in Asia. We are here because you were there, the saying goes. But we often forget or, worse, ignore the fact the United States is a settler colony that sits atop of stolen land. The geographic nowhere, the in-betweenness, the homelessness of Asian American identity should not be viewed as a deficit but rather as a complement to Indigenous struggles.

Decolonizing requires understanding ourselves as settlers of color. Trask implicated Asians who reject the label "haole" in favor of terms like "local" or "immigrant," through which Asians tell a model minority fairy tale of success, of overcoming hardship and exploitation and racism. To Native people, Asian success is "but the latest elaboration of foreign hegemony."[52] Immigration foregrounds movement across state borders, whereas migration points to the geographies of labor and capitalism. Settlers are not immigrants. Immigrants have permission to enter and stay; settlers squat on land they pretend is uninhabited. Asian American theology today is a theology of hybridity, marginality, and liminality.[53] It looks for the possibility of becoming settled in a place that has viewed Asians as perpetually foreign, of becoming comfortable in one's own skin. In a sense, Asians in the United States have always been looking for a home that was never there, from the 1882 Chinese Exclusion Act to the 1935 Filipino Repatriation Act to the 1942 Japanese internment to the 2017 Muslim Ban. The wrong kind of Asians have never been welcomed by the United States.

An Asian American theology of liberation, on the other hand, is a theology from the viewpoint of migrant, undocumented, refugee, and working-class Asians, Asians who fall below the poverty line or who struggle to stay in school. Asian American theologies are by necessity *landless* theologies, for Asian America is a country that has no soil. But if we are to decolonize our theology, or properly liberate it, we cannot be hoping to settle on stolen land. That is to say, Asian American theology cannot become yet another settler theology. Indigeneity and struggles for sovereignty are not foreign to Asians: Palestine, Jammu, Kashmir, Ladakh, Taiwan, Hong Kong, Tibet, Hawaii, and Mindanao are all fighting to be free. At the same time, decolonization in Asia has almost always led to the transfer of power to new post-colonial masters. The ongoing oppression and colonization of Indigenous peoples and minority groups are made possible only by the collaboration of our own people, the colonized intellectuals and petite bourgeoisie. Narrow-minded nationalisms and tribalisms led to conflict and bloodshed that the West conveniently washed their hands of as the liberal world order came into being.[54] They divided and conquered us, and we continue to pay the price for being so divided.

The struggles of Indigenous peoples everywhere are deeply connected because water does not separate land but instead joins it together as Okihiro's ocean worlds show. Rather than simply look to the Third World, the first secretary of the Tanzanian High Commission, Mbuto Milando, declared that "when Native peoples come into their own, on the basis of their own cultures and traditions, that will be the Fourth World."[55] We cannot support the freedom struggles in the Third World such as Hong Kong and Palestine without also fighting to dismantle the settler colony that is the United States. "Indian country" is a term used by the US military to refer to enemy or foreign territory.[56] That is what they called Vietnam, Afghanistan, and Iraq. The United States as an imperial force does to Asia what it does to Turtle Island as a settler colony. Conversely, the same counterinsurgency tactics used in Iraq were also deployed against water protectors in Standing Rock, Dakota, and Ferguson, Missouri, and Israeli suppression of Palestinians was taught to anti-riot police in response to Black Lives Matters protesters in the United States. If we were to truly attempt to decolonize, we would be called terrorists. The United States has been in a state of perpetual war from the very beginning of its founding: against Native Americans, Africans, and all over the Third World. To set ourselves against imperial violence in North America, we must continuously hold in view the ongoing war—and resistance—that began here over five hundred years ago. If the military views all these disparate geographies as "Indian country," how dare we not see our struggles as interconnected?

In articulating a Palestinian liberation theology, Palestinian theologian Naim Ateek turns to the historical Jesus who lived in Rome-occupied Palestine as the hermeneutic key to connect with the present-day, Israel-occupied Palestine.[57] Tinker's critique of Jesus notwithstanding, Ateek reads the metaphor of Jesus as Temple as signaling a move away from an attachment to the land of Palestine, Jerusalem, and the Second Temple, which itself was destroyed in 70 CE by the Roman military.[58] But rather than relieve the land of its holiness, through the immanence of the Messiah it reminds us that *all* land is sacred and we must live in right relation to it. A proper theology of land that calls for the liberation of occupied lands such as Palestine directly conflicts with settler theologies such as Christian Zionism in the United States that justifies the taking of that land. Most visibly, Trump's border wall along the Mexico–US border—which is of course Native land—was built in part by an Israeli-owned defense manufacturer, also tear gas manufactured in the United States was found to be used against Hong Kong protesters between 2019 and 2020. Once again, the capitalists sure know that these business opportunities are connected. Indeed, the locus of Palestine as a means of connecting struggles reenters in the next chapter through abolitionism that connects the prison industrial complex, the military industrial complex, and policing assemblage at large as various means of preserving state power.

To unsettle Asian American theology is to joyfully accept our landlessness here as we fight for Indigenous sovereignty everywhere. Decolonizing the Americas means all land is repatriated and all settlers become landless, Tuck and Yang write.[59] As some Indigenous activists and scholars will argue, this does not mean that all non-Native persons are repatriated to their ancestral lands, but rather that the First Nations will be sovereign and settlers will live in a new relation to the land and to their hosts.[60] Only then can Asian Americans begin to repair their relationship to the land. The reorganization of material realities goes hand in hand with the transformation of not only social but also ecological relations. In practice, this means fighting for the rights of Indigenous communities such as in Standing Rock, honoring the treaties that continue to be broken as the Trail of Broken Treaties demanded in 1972, and working toward the resurgence of Indigenous peoples and the return of stolen land.

This is not a theoretical exercise. Many small but significant instances of land return have been initiated such as the nonprofit groups Planting Justice and the women-led Sogorea Tè Land Trust, which, in 2018, facilitated the return of a quarter acre of Ohlone land in East Oakland, California, to Ohlone stewardship. One and a half acres of land was returned to the Nimíipuu by the Wallowa Lake Camp in Oregon, facilitated in part by the United Methodist Church. While symbolic and important, we must put this in the perspective that the coalition of American Indian and First Nation organizations, which participated in the Trail of Broken Treaties caravan protest to Washington, DC, included in their demands that the United States federal government restore a permanent Native American land area of no less than 110 million acres by July 4, 1976. Still, as we strive to build a coalitional politics through Asian American organizing and with other people of color, there will be an incommensurability to decolonizing our theology as irreducible differences arise in the process of struggling together if, for example, advocating for civil rights only means inclusion into the settler state. To unsettle ourselves requires giving up our immigrant identity as a purely virtuous one—not to mention mortgages—and to risk a coalitional politics that is sometimes unfriendly as we reckon with Asian settler colonialism.

Such unsettling can be violent as well. Those who prefer the metaphor must remember that "decolonization is always a violent event," as one translation of Fanon's *The Wretched of the Earth* paraphrased.[61] It "fundamentally alters being, and transforms the spectator crushed to a nonessential state into a privileged actor."[62] It is the verification of Jesus's proclamation that "the last shall be first." There is no way the land will be given back, the prison system abolished, and the military disarmed without a fight. Fanon continues: "In its bare reality, decolonization reeks of red-hot cannonballs and bloody knives. For the last can be the first only after a murderous and decisive confrontation between the two protagonists."[63]

A theology of landlessness does not ask for undocumented migrants to remain undocumented, nor for those with multiple passports, but no sense of belonging, to feel superior. But it should trouble those who desire to possess land unproblematically, to own property as a means of individual wealth accumulation. Listen to the earth as the blood of Indigenous people cry out. Consider as you pass through the open landscape where tens of millions of buffalo roamed. Watch what seeds grow and trees bloom whenever spring comes, and ask what they know of this land. A theology of landlessness is an invitation to become grounded, rooted, related to the land without needing to possess it or entirely give ourselves up to the settler-colonial structure. It is also a call to war—the settler-colonial war that continues to be quietly fought across a rampant yet haunted landscape.

As Psalm 137 asks, How can we sing the songs of the Lord while in a foreign land? Under the captivity of Babylon, the psalmist concludes: "Daughter Babylon, doomed to destruction, happy is the one who repays you according to what you have done to us. Happy is the one who seizes your infants and dashes them against the rocks." If Christians prefer to skip over the cursing Psalms, perhaps it is because they simply have not suffered the same. To begin to decolonize Asian America requires that we hold the complexity of being both oppressed and oppressor, victims of racial discrimination and still complicit in systems of domination. Psalm 137 is both directed by us and against us. To conclude, let us return again to Trask, who puts the challenge to settlers of color thus:

> Non-Natives need to examine and re-examine their many and continuing benefits from Hawaiian dispossession. Those benefits do not end when non-Natives begin supporting Hawaiians, just as our dispossession as Natives does not end when we become active nationalists. Equations of Native exploitation and of settler benefit continue. For non-Natives, the question that needs to be answered every day is simply the one posed in the old union song, "which side are you on?"[64]

Blessed are the damned, for they shall inherit the earth.[65]

BEING

5.

SEARCHING FOR AN ASIAN RADICAL TRADITION

Asian American Liberation, Dalit Theology, and the Black Radical Tradition

So don't follow me up and down your market or your little chop suey ass'll be a target of a nationwide boycott / Juice with the people, that's what the boy got
So pay respect to the Black fist or we'll burn your store right down to a crisp and then we'll see ya / Cause you can't turn the ghetto into Black Korea

—Ice Cube, *Black Korea*

If we are to be honest with ourselves, we must admit that the "Negro" has been inviting whites, as well as civil society's junior partners, to the dance of social death for hundreds of years, but few have wanted to learn the steps. They have been, and remain today—even in the most anti-racist movements, like the prison abolition movement—invested elsewhere. This is not to say that all oppositional political desire today is pro-white, but it is usually anti-Black, meaning it will not dance with death.

—Frank Wilderson, "The Prison Slave as Hegemony's (Silent) Scandal"

The Martinican is a crucified man. The environment which has shaped him (but which he has not shaped) has torn him apart, and he nurtures this cultural milieu with his blood and his humors. The blood of a black man, however, is a fertilizer much appreciated by the experts.
　　　　　　　　　　　—Frantz Fanon, *Black Skin, White Masks*

In 2015, Chinese American NYPD officer Peter Liang shot and killed Akai Gurley, a Black man in New York City. Convicted of manslaughter, thousands of protesters, the vast majority of whom were of Chinese descent, rallied in protest. They claimed that Liang was a scapegoat in a time of heightened opposition to the police, because Liang was Chinese and not White. At around the same time, a smaller and younger group of Asian Americans cowrote a "Letter for Black Lives" after the police shooting of another Black man named Philando Castile during a traffic stop in Minnesota, explaining to their Asian American families their support for the Movement for Black Lives. The overwhelming numbers of protesters against Liang's conviction are in stark contrast to the relatively few letter signatories.

The Liang protests mark one of the most pivotal moments in the Asian American community since the Los Angeles riots. As Kang's *New York Times* coverage of the Liang protests points out, even if one believes that Liang was rightly convicted, to ignore the question of "Why only Liang?" is intellectually dishonest. The protesters, according to Kang, were trying in their way to create a new political language for Asian Americans, "but this language comes without any edifying history—no amount of nuance or qualification or appeal to Martin Luther King will change the fact that the first massive, nationwide Asian-American protest in years was held in defense of a police officer who shot and killed an innocent Black man."[1] Kang also described the "cultural aphasia" that comes from "decades of political silence" registering a growing anger at the lack of "Asian faces" among the marchers throughout Kang's coverage of Black Lives Matter protests across the country as a reporter. "I had long lost faith in storybook solidarity," Kang wrote, "but I had never expected to see the divide between Blacks and Asian-Americans laid out so starkly."[2]

The Movement for Black lives, first begun in 2013, came roaring back at the end of May 2020, at the height of the coronavirus lockdown in the United States and following the murders of George Floyd, Breonna Taylor, Ahmaud Arbery, and Tony McDade. What began as protests about police brutality against Black people in the United States exploded into a worldwide movement expressing solidarity with the protests while calling attention to local cases of police brutality and anti-Black racism. Asians in the United States again spoke out in solidarity, building on the Letters for Black Lives initiative from 2016.[3] This new wave of activism and introspection was fueled in no small part by the fact that Hmong American Tou Thao was among the officers involved in Floyd's killing, his face captured on video and spread widely on social media. Thao's complicity, in holding the crowd back as Derek Chauvin held his knee to Floyd's neck, turned into a metaphor for Asian America keeping watch as White America crushed the life out of Black America.[4] Many explainers on Asian anti-Blackness in the United States appeared, connecting this moment to the 1992 LA riots and the model-minority myth, first used in 1966 to describe Japanese immigrants and denigrate African Americans, and more broadly couched in the context of the racial logic of the Cold War.[5]

At first glance, this broader engagement might be seen as an improvement from when the Black Lives Matter movement first began, which saw not only a lack of Asian participation in protests but also counterprotests such as in support for Peter Liang.[6] At the same time, the latest moves to critique Asian anti-Blackness and the model-minority myth suggest a collective amnesia about the history of Asians in the Americas, its connection with Black struggle, and a deep-seated anxiety about the place of Asian Americans within the US racial hierarchy.[7] As African American Studies scholar Seulghee Lee argues, these repetitions naturalize the notion that Asian Americans and African Americans are inherently in opposition and "is simply a neoliberal update to the American racial project devised to divide people of color and ultimately all of us."[8] To be clear, the ground truth is far from a tale of storybook solidarity but a long history full of tensions and alliances. The responsibility of Asians in this revolutionary moment is not only to address anti-Blackness but to reinsert ourselves into the long history of Afro-Asia, which, according to scholar Bill Mullen, signifies "the imperative to imagine a 'new world' grounded upon two great ancient worlds as well as a radical and revolutionary anti-imperialist tradition."[9]

Whereas the transatlantic slave trade triangulated Africa, Europe, and the Americas since as early as 1501, the slave trade was a more general international phenomenon. European colonization of Asia began around the time the transatlantic slave trade began: even as Christopher Columbus "discovered" the Caribbean in search of India, by the 1600s Manila had become the center of the transpacific slave trade.[10] Ships arrived not only with enslaved Africans but also enslaved peoples from Macao, India, Myanmar, Malacca, Java, and other European colonies. From there, ships carried these slaves to the Americas, along with the Filipino and Chinese sailors. While Asian slaves were emancipated in New Spain in 1672, and in 1700 a Spanish royal order prohibited the Asian slave trade, slavery in the United States only ended in 1865, and even then, it evolved into racial segregation for a hundred years, then into mass incarceration under the Thirteenth Amendment that allows for enslavement and involuntary servitude as a punishment for crime.

As slavery formally ended in the 1800s, settler colonizers throughout the Americas found a replacement for enslaved Africans in Chinese labor, indentured and free. Among these grew maroon Chinese communities such as in the Mississippi Delta, living in Black neighborhoods during segregation and intermarrying with local Indigenous and Black people.[11] Later, in the wake of Chinese exclusion, South Asians immigrated to New Orleans and also moved into Black neighborhoods, becoming a part of the community there. During the era of racial segregation, Asians were seen as neither Black nor White but racial middlemen. It was not long until the Chinese grew into the Yellow Peril, leading to a string of exclusionary laws. The anti-Chinese sentiment was not limited to the United States, and the exclusion acts inspired similar bans on Chinese immigration throughout the rest of the Americas. As Chinese labor began to dry up, they were replaced with influxes of Japanese, then Korean, then Indian labor, which altogether led to the Asian Exclusion Act in 1924 that banned all immigration from Asia.

The civil rights era, spanning the 1950s and the 1960s, culminated in the Civil Rights Act in 1964, outlawing discrimination based on race, color, religion, sex, or national origin. This opened the way for the 1965 Immigration Act, which repealed previous restrictions on immigration. This was also a time that saw the most prominent alliances between Black and Asian radicals that form the basis of considerable nostalgia in the present moment. Malcolm X argued that no African American movement would flourish unless it was "tied in with the overall international struggle," himself visiting Palestine in 1964.[12] At a meeting of representatives from twenty-nine African and Asian nations, then prime minister of India Jawaharlal Nehru foregrounded the transatlantic slave trade and the moral duty of those not directly responsible for it:

> When I think of it, everything else pales into insignificance; that infinite tragedy of Africa ever since the days when millions of them were carried away in galleys as slaves to America and elsewhere, the way they were treated, the way they were taken away, 50 percent dying in the galleys. We have to bear that burden, all of us. We did not do it ourselves, but the world has to bear it.[13]

The Black Panther Party was also famously internationalist in their work, visiting China, North Vietnam, and North Korea, opposing the Vietnam war, and promoting "survival programs" inspired by Mao's Little Red Book. Several Asians also joined the Panthers, such as Richard Aoki, Lee Lew-Lee, and Guy Kurose.[14] Among the organizations that the Panthers inspired were the Dalit Panthers in India, who fought against caste-based oppression. The Dalit Panther manifesto directly connected United States imperialism, the Black struggle, and Dalit oppression:

> Due to the hideous plot of American imperialism, the Third World, that is, oppressed nations, and Dalit people are suffering. Even in America, a handful of reactionary Whites are exploiting Blacks. To meet the force of reaction and remove this exploitation, the Black Panther movement grew. From the Black Panthers, Black Power emerged. The fire of the struggles has thrown out sparks into the country. We claim a close relationship with this struggle. We have before our eyes the examples of Vietnam, Cambodia, Africa and the like.[15]

Around that time, the Third World Liberation Front was formed in 1968 in San Francisco and Berkeley when Asian American identity first coalesced. This was also a time when prominent activists such as Yuri Kochiyama, a close associate of Malcolm X, and Grace Lee Boggs, who worked with activists James Boggs and C. L. R. James, were active. The Black Power movement also directly inspired Asian Americans, as Amy Umeyatsu wrote in 1969:

> Asian Americans can no longer afford to watch the black-and-white struggle from the sidelines. They have their own cause to fight, since they are also victims—with less visible scars—of the white institutionalized racism. A yellow movement has been set into motion by the black power movement. Addressing itself to the unique problems of Asian Americans, this "yellow power" move-

ment is relevant to the black power movement in that both are part of the Third World struggle to liberate all colored people.[16]

These vignettes offer a historical picture of Asians and Africans who saw the struggles of the Third World as one of social and not geographic location.

The global movements of the last decade have ushered in a new era of global protest. These intersecting histories show just how the struggles of Asia and Africa at home and abroad are connected, and that Asian liberation is tied up in Black liberation. There are deep conflicts that prevent any easy form of solidarity, but this shared history of international struggle against empire, racism, colonization, and capitalism suggests that the Third World may be able to come into focus again—or better yet, the Fourth World—following the Third World studies curriculum that the Third World Liberation Front envisioned, which "subscribes to that species of positivism for the imperative of pointing to privilege and poverty, exploitation and oppression, revolution and liberation."[17]

The subjectlessness and landlessness of Asian American identity are not ends in themselves but means of realizing a coalitional politics and broader critiques of the power relations through which Asian Americanness is constituted. Interrogating the racial formation, whether of Asian Americanness or Blackness, pushes against the reification of racial categories that have contributed to the degeneration of discourses around race into shallow forms of identity politics. Put differently, an Asian American theology of liberation, as with any other form of liberation theology, is not about speaking only *to* a specific racial group but rather speaking *from* a specific social location to all who have ears to hear. The historical sketch above reveals the possibilities of excavating an Asian radical tradition that will serve such a purpose, whereby racial identity has neither inherent value nor meaning but is a socially constructed vessel, able to be weaponized for the work of justice. At the same time, the history of Black–Asian relations is complex, with as much betrayal as there is solidarity. Attempts to narrate this history are often either romantic and optimistic or suspicious and pessimistic.

The most prominent Black–Asian conflict in the United States are the LA riots in 1992. While the rioters and looters were made up of White, Black, Latine, and Asian people, the media characterized it as a Black–Korean conflict, as the LAPD left the Korean community to fend for itself. According to one account, it was a "media-fanned minority vs. minority bogus race war" in which the Black residents of South Central Los Angeles were portrayed as unproductive citizens living off welfare while the Koreans were hardworking immigrants trying to achieve the American Dream.[18] Regardless of the role of the media, the controversial song *Black Korea* by Ice Cube captures an undeniable sentiment within the Black community in relation to Korean businesses, only to be matched by the suspicion of Asian business owners of Black clientele. Released a year before the riots, it opens with the lines:

> Every time I wanna go get a fuckin' brew
> I gotta go down to the store with the two
> Oriental one penny countin' motherfuckers
> That make a nigga mad enough to cause a little ruckus

Perhaps most importantly, the killing of Latasha Harlins by Soon Ja Du remains an incontrovertible fact of Black death at the hands of a petite bourgeois Korean shopkeeper, echoed in the killing of George Floyd in 2020, where the police were called by an employee at Palestinian American grocery store Cup Foods on suspicion of a counterfeit bill. On the other side, the trauma of the LA riots—a day known as Sa-I-Gu in Korean, meaning April 15th—and its aftermath has left an indelible scar on the Korean community.[19]

The specter of anti-Asian violence committed by the Black community looms as something of a taboo in liberal and left discourses, an uneasiness and unwillingness to confront the questions raised not only in the LA riots but also in the wake of the

COVID-19 pandemic. For example, in January 2021, a viral video circulated on social media showing an eighty-four-year-old Thai man, Vicha Ratnapakdee, being shoved violently onto the ground in San Francisco by a Black assailant and succumbing to his injuries days later. Many similar attacks were widely reported around the same time, particularly given the heightened awareness due to the political moment, such as sixty-one-year-old Yao Pan Ma, who was attacked while collecting used cans and bottles, his head stomped on multiple times, while thirty-one-year-old Chinese woman was struck on the head with a hammer.

This suggests that not only has the animus between the Black and Asian communities never been properly resolved but that it continues to be reproduced as anti-Asian violence also took place in the intervening years, such as in 2010 when eighty-three-year-old Huan Chen was beaten up by Black teenagers in San Francisco and fifty-nine-year-old Tian Sheng Yu in Oakland a few months later. Both died from their injuries. According to Kang, the suppression of these events, for upwardly mobile second-generation Asian Americans, "metastasize, not quite into a reactionary politics but into an abiding resentment that makes you question your place within the multicultural, liberal elite."[20] At the same time, Kang identifies this aphasia as a "class-bound affliction," an identity crisis that the working Asian poor and elderly do not necessarily concern themselves with—a collective psychic dissonance generated by the choice to see oneself as no longer oppressed and the desire to be counted among the oppressed and not the oppressors. This is often attempted through the careful arrangement of trauma narratives, which Kang describes as ultimately a nation-building project that elides class difference, presumably in the hope of constructing an abject subjectivity parallel to Black and Indigenous claims.

So where does this all leave us? Rather than seeking an alternative Asian American historiography of oppression, the fact of Black anti-Asianness and Asian anti-Blackness underscores the complexity and nonlinearity of the racial order, calling for more careful attention to the contradictions and complements arising in the intertwined racial formations. To build Asian American theology of liberation on a solid foundation requires not only addressing Asian settler-colonial desires but also Asian pro- *and* anti-Blackness, the latter being the racial register in which dialectical materialism operates in the United States. In this chapter, I turn to the Afro-pessimist critique of anti-Blackness stretching from the curse of Noah to the present afterlife of slavery, finding resonances with Cone's Black theology of liberation, and placing it in dialogue with Dalit theology and Dalit liberation, finding points of connection in the separate invitations to social death—to Blackness and to Dalitness—and shared horizons of the abolition of prisons and police with the annihilation of caste. Taking seriously the enjoinment to social death, or nonbeing, this charts a path forward for Asian Americans and others in an anti-Black world.

AFRO-PESSIMISM, BLACK THEOLOGY, AND THE HUMAN

In reflecting on the future of Black theology, Cone emphasized the need for Black theology to be in dialogue with Third World theologians and with other minorities in the United States.[21] According to Cone, serious dialogue between the theology of the Black poor and with the theologies of the marginalized people of the Third World can help to liberate churches from enslavement to White theology.[22] Cone also lamented the lack of coalition among "oppressed minorities" in the United States, who seemed not to be able to talk to each other or with Third World peoples except through structures "controlled and financed by whites."[23] Rather than staying within the limits of each one's particularities, Cone argued that every theology ought to move toward the concrete experiences of others, that encountering of the God of biblical faith should draw us outside of ourselves and to the poor of the world, where God is to be found.

These reflections are noteworthy, for the inclusivity of Black theology and Black radicalism, the willingness to work in coalition with other oppressed peoples in a collective struggle for liberation is often lost in contemporary discourse. In a social media era, hot takes and uncompromising oppositional stances are valued more than careful discussions of complexities. The Combahee River Collective, an important group of Black feminists, issued a statement in 1977 declaring that "the inclusiveness of our politics makes us concerned with any situation that impinges upon the lives of women, Third World and working people."[24] Inasmuch as such forms of radical theology and politics emanate from a thoroughly Black embodiment and experience, they often fight with open hands, welcoming whomever is also willing to lay their lives down and be transformed in the service of the work. The latter is particularly resonant with the hermeneutic circle of liberation theology, the principle of *preguntando caminamos*.

At the same time, while such platitudes and invitations exist, there remains the unavoidable work of examining and exorcising anti-Blackness in non-Black theologies, particularly as they might be inherited in Asian and Asian American theologies. Sylvia Wynter argues that in the European renaissance "Man" was overdetermined by secular racial ideology and its break from Judeo-Christian thought. Race was the "non-supernatural but no less extrahuman ground" for the secularizing West's answer to the question "as to the who, and the what we are."[25] In other words, whether through race science or theological anthropology, it is the European man who is considered human. As it were, the colonization of the Americas and the enslavement of Africa were both legitimated through such terms, eventually replacing a "Christian/Enemies-of-Christ" or "Spirit/Flesh" narrative with a biological law of "natural masters/ natural slaves." Both biology *and* theology can power anti-Black thought. The colonial world, according to Fanon, is a Manichean world that dehumanizes or, rather, animalizes the native, and the church in the colonies calls the native not to God's way but to the ways of the White man.[26] While Manicheanism itself—a religion of dualism—found a formidable adversary in Augustine of Hippo, the same dualistic thinking persists in evangelical doctrine to this day and, according to Martinot and Sexton, manifests as a "Manichean delirium" in the United States in a dichotomy between White ethics or civil society and Black life.[27]

Wynter traces a genealogy of anti-Blackness in Abrahamic religions to the biblical tradition that the descendants of Ham were cursed by Noah with Blackness and condemned to slavery.[28] As Felipe Fernández-Arnesto noted, in as early as the fourteenth century of European expansion into the Mediterranean, Black Africans were already placed in a category "not far removed from the apes, as man made degenerate by sin."[29] This resonates with Edward Said's reading of Joseph Conrad's usage of contrasts that leads to a chain of equivalences connecting White to good and Black to evil, which Said uses to mount a broader critique of Western colonial imagination and orientalism.[30] Western Judeo-Christian theological enterprises are thus deeply implicated in the genealogy of global anti-Black racism and orientalism. What Wynter's work encourages us to do here, as a whole, is to be able to think through the cross-pollinations of anti-Blackness via coloniality, theology, and biology, and in connecting this to the specificity of Asian Americanness, I hope to expand and deepen the view through a comparison with Afro-pessimism and Black liberation theology.

Afro-pessimism is a critique of the persistence of anti-Blackness and the afterlife of slavery, primarily in the context of the United States. Its challenge is one of ontology, which might be traced back to Fanon, who wrote that "there is a zone of nonbeing, an extraordinarily sterile and arid region, an incline stripped bare of every essential form which a genuine new departure can emerge. . . . We are aiming at nothing less than to liberate the black man from himself."[31] Building on Orlando Patterson's notion of social death, Afro-pessimism interprets the condition of slavery and its afterlife as not being defined by a labor relation but a *property* relation:

the slave is a commodified object, socially dead, hence "1) open to gratuitous violence, as opposed to violence contingent upon some transgression or crime; 2) natally alienated, their ties of birth not recognized and familial structures intentionally broken apart; and 3) generally dishonored, or disgraced before any thought or action is considered."[32] In an interview with C. S. Soong, Frank Wilderson asserted that "violence against the slave sustains a kind of psychic stability for all others who are not slaves." This gratuitous violence "sustains the psychic health of the people in the first ontological instance. In the second instance, it gets good sugar cane production out of them—and that could even be questioned"—that is, anti-Black violence is dealt for both psychic and economic purposes.[33]

Indeed, in Ida B. Well's work on Black criminalization, she used data analysis to show that lynching had no consistent and hence coherent justification, though its central pretext was as the punishment for the Black man who raped a White woman.[34] Similarly, as Fanon quoted a friend from the United States in his time, "The Blacks represent a kind of insurance for humanity in the eyes of the Whites. When the Whites feel they have become too mechanized, they turn to the Coloreds and request a little human sustenance."[35] Afro-pessimism would argue that it is the non-Whites more generally who turn to the Blacks to request this human sustenance. The ontological argument rests in part on what Fanon called an "epidermal racial schema," in contrast to, say, the "Jewishness of the Jew" that can pass undetected: "I am overdetermined from the outside. I am a slave not to the 'idea' others have of me, but to my appearance."[36] For this reason, it is a "paradigm of oppression that does not offer some type of way out."[37]

The question of being, of the human, is one shared by Afro-pessimism, post-colonialism, and liberation theology.[38] Blackness, according to Wilderson, is understood as being not only exterior to the concept of humanity but in fact the "dark matter surrounding and holding together the categories of non-Black;" the ontology of non-Blacks is underwritten by the violence of anti-Black violence, the slave/non-slave or Black/human relation.[39] Against the backdrop of police brutality, medical and environmental racism, redlining, segregation, and, of course, slavery so deeply woven into the fabric of the United States, Afro-pessimism and Black theology question the premise of racial capitalism by reminding us that anti-Blackness also exists outside of capitalism.

Second, in connection to post-colonialism or anti-colonialism more accurately, to overcome anti-Blackness requires a program of complete disorder such as Fanon had described of decolonization, and moreover a "fundamental reorientation of the social coordinates of the human relation."[40] According to Fanon, in the struggle for liberation and decolonization, not only does colonialism disappear but so does the colonial subject. A new humanity emerges. The systematic negation and denial of the humanity of the colonial subject forces the colonized to continually question: "In reality, who am I?"[41]

Thirdly, from the point of view of liberation theology, Gustavo Guttièrez saw the liberation of Latin America as not only overcoming economic, social, and political dependence but, in a deeper sense, the building up of a new humanity, a qualitatively different society in which humanity is free from all servitude.[42] The prophetic task of the church, according to Guttièrez, is to identify elements within a "revolutionary process" that are humanizing and dehumanizing, acting in both constructive and critical functions.[43] Fanon concludes, and Wynter reasserts, at the end of both *Black Skin, White Masks* and the *Wretched of the Earth*, that beyond the horizon of decolonization and at the end of anti-Blackness is the invention and discovery of a new humanity, a new Adam.

Liberation theology is a theological reflection through praxis, and indeed we find the question of the human posed more forcefully still among mass movements. Besides the simple assertion of the value of Black life through the Black Lives Matter movement, we can detect resonances in the 2020 Thai protests against the monarchy, in which the People's Party 2020 or Khana Ratsadon 2563 directly posed the question "Are you still human?" in an attempt to question those condemning the prodemocracy movement in the name of protecting Thainess. According to scholar Saichol Sattayanurak, Thainess is a discourse that enforces a hierarchical social and political order, insisting that Thai people are naturally unequal and that each should know their place and behave accordingly, from the family to the monarchy.[44] This question played on the earlier question "Are you Thai?" popular among right-wing Thai protesters around 2005 and the People's Democratic Reform Committee around 2013. The epistemic shift toward a broader conception of the Thai imaginary creates space for Malay Muslims, sex workers, trans and queer people, and other marginalized groups not typically welcomed in Thainess. A popular hashtag at the time, translating to "decrease Thainess, increase humanness," signaled a delinking of the Thai ethnoclass with belonging and a move toward a broader humanity, compatible with that envisioned by Fanon, and a signal to Asian American liberation theology to remain guarded against tribalism and the limits of identity politics.

At the same time, there are crucial differences in emphases between these schools of thought. Whereas post-colonial and anti-colonial theorists draw from Fanon's *Wretched of the Earth*, Afro-pessimist theorists look to *Black Skin, White Masks*. Fanon writes in the latter,

> For not only must the black man be black; he must be black in relation to the white man. Some will argue that the situation has a double meaning. Not at all. The black man has no ontological resistance in the eyes of the white man. From one day to the next, the blacks have had to deal with two systems of reference. Their metaphysics, or less pretentiously their customs and the agencies to which they refer, were abolished because they were in contradiction with a new civilization that imposed its own.[45]

But if, as Sylvia Wynter and others have pointed out, anti-Blackness today has theological roots, then religious traditions offer a critical response not found in Afro-pessimist theory.[46] Indeed, within the study of Christian ethics, Vincent Lloyd and Andrew Prevot argued that genealogies of anti-Blackness provide useful analytic frameworks, but less so as guides for ethical and political action. Studying the practices of Black communities struggling against injustice instead produces better insights than studying European theologians alone.

Also necessary, I would add, is study accompanied by participating in struggle, which represents Cone's imperative to become Black.[47] Wilderson makes a similar assertion, which I recall at length to contextualize the guiding quote of this chapter:

> Indeed, [Blackness] means all those things: a phobogenic object, a past without a heritage, the map of gratuitous violence, and a program of complete disorder. Whereas this realization is, and should be, cause for alarm, it should not be cause for lament, or worse, disavowal—not at least, for a true revolutionary, or for a truly revolutionary movement such as prison abolition. If a social movement is to be neither social democratic nor Marxist, in terms of structure of political desire, then it should grasp the invitation to assume the positionality of subjects of social death. If we are to be honest with ourselves, we must admit that the "Negro" has been inviting whites, as well as civil society's junior partners, to the dance of social death for hundreds of years, but few have wanted to learn the steps. They have been, and remain today—even in the most anti-racist movements, like the prison abolition movement— invested elsewhere. This is not to say that all oppositional political desire today is pro-white, but it is usually anti-Black, meaning it will not dance with death.[48]

So Afro-pessimism is not as pessimistic as is often presumed! The way out, according to Wilderson, is a kind of violence "so magnificent and so comprehensive that it scares the hell out of even radical revolutionaries," a violence "against the generic categories of life, agency being one of them," a Black revolution that "blows the lid off the unconscious and relations writ large."[49]

Similar ideas are already found in Cone's Black theology of liberation, which preceded Afro-pessimist theory by decades: "By white definitions, whiteness is 'being' and blackness is 'nonbeing.'. . . 'To be or not to be' is thus a dilemma for the black community: to assert one's humanity and be killed, or to cling to life and sink into nonhumanity." Furthermore, that White Americans "decreed that blacks were outside the realm of humanity, that blacks were animals and that their enslavement was best both for them and for society as a whole," and in an indication of the afterlife of slavery, "when black labor was no longer needed, blacks were issued their 'freedom.' The freedom to live in a society which attempted to destroy them physically and spiritually."[50] All these can be anachronistically read as Afro-pessimist themes.

Yet again, Cone invites everyone to become Black with God, just as in the invitation to social death. Blackness here stands for "all victims of oppression who realize that the survival of their humanity is bound up with liberation from whiteness," and to be Black is to be "committed to destroying everything this country loves and adores."[51] The Black experience, according to Cone, is "the feeling one has when attacking the enemy of black humanity by throwing a Molotov cocktail into a white-owned building and watching it go up in flames. We know of course, that getting rid of evil takes something more than burning down buildings, but one must start somewhere." The urgency of Cone's Black theology of liberation is spelled out in no uncertain terms: "White appeals to 'wait and talk it over' are irrelevant when children are dying and men and women are tortured. We will not let whitey cool this one with his pious love ethic but will seek to enhance our hostility, bringing it to its full manifestation."[52]

Black theology came into being when "the black clergy realized that killing slave masters was doing the work of God," when they "refused to accept the racist white church as consistent with the gospel of God."[53] God's revelation is "what happens in a black ghetto when the ghettoized decide to strike against their enemies. In a word, God's revelation means *liberation*—nothing more, nothing less."[54] Faith is "the existential element in revelation—that is, the community's perception of its being and the willingness to fight against nonbeing." The sin of the oppressed is not that they are responsible from their own enslavement but rather that of trying to "understand" enslavers, to "love" them on their own terms: "As the oppressed now recognize their situation in the light of God's revelation, they know that they should have killed their oppressors instead of trying to 'love' them."[55] Asian American theology can only dream of operating with such prophetic clarity. But no matter. Cone has already laid out so clearly for us exactly what it means for Asians to become Black, to embrace social death.

INTERACTIONS WITH DALIT THEOLOGY

That the Black struggle and the Dalit struggle are connected has already been gestured at, with the Dalit Panthers and expressions of solidarity among leaders of the respective movements. Another such example is the brief correspondence between Du Bois and B. R. Ambedkar in 1946, where Ambedkar expressed that there is "so much similarity between the position of the Untouchables in India and of the position of the Negroes in America that the study of the latter is not only natural but necessary," to which Du Bois in response expressed "every sympathy with the Untouchables of India."[56] Despite continuing expressions of solidarity, the valences of these struggles remain distinct despite continuing attempts to collapse the two notions of caste and race.

Most recently Isabel Wilkerson's book *Caste: The Origins of Our Discontents* has been properly criticized for repeating old arguments that have been long refuted, beginning with Oliver Cromwell Cox's 1948 work *Caste, Class, and Race*. Reasoning by analogy does not require the two be identified, as Wilkerson attempted in suggesting that "in the process of defining Negro caste we have defined Negro race, and the final accomplishment is a substitution of words only." Wilkerson points to Martin Luther King Jr. and his wife Coretta's 1959 visit to India, where he was introduced at a Dalit high school as a "a fellow untouchable from the United States of America," and after the initial shock at such an assertion, agreed, "Yes, I am an untouchable, and every negro in the United States of America is an untouchable."[57] Echoing Cox's critique of his contemporary Gunnar Myrdal, Charisse Burden-Stelly argues that Wilkerson "recapitulates the representational function of the Black elite, whereby their political and social agenda stands in for the Black community as a whole," obscuring class difference in favor of racial difference, engendering a "desire for empathy, acceptance, and meritocracy as the generalizable solution for the structural and material violence of modern U.S. racial capitalism."[58] In other words, for Wilkerson, caste is race and race trumps class.

But Ambedkar himself had asserted long before that the caste system is *not* a racial division—rather, it is a social division of people of the same race.[59] Pseudo-scientific theories such as the one invoked by dominant caste Bhagat Singh Thind, that North Indians were in fact descended from Aryans, suggest a logic of difference that intertwines caste and race in complex ways. With this difference in mind, let us consider Dalit theology more closely, its relation to Black theology, and how it can inform an Asian American theology of liberation. The significant attention devoted to the Dalit struggle here is quite intentional: I offer it as a corrective to the dominance of Northeast Asian figures in Asian American politics, not to mention the rich interconnections between caste and race.

What is commonly referred to as caste in India conflates the distinct concepts of *jati* and *varna*, while other countries in South Asia such as Nepal, Pakistan, and Bangladesh possess their own configurations throughout their diasporas.[60] The vedas divide society into four varnas according to function: brahmins, kshatriyas, vaishyas, and shudras, corresponding to the priestly, warrior, trader, and servant classes, respectively, arranged from highest to lowest. Outside of this social stratification are the avarnas or atishudras, the subhuman and casteless ones, arranged in hierarchies of their own: the untouchables, unseeables, and unapproachables, whose very presence and shadow are considered polluting to privilege-caste Hindus. Also outcaste are the Indigenous or Adivasi people.

Jati, on the other hand, describes a social division according to birth and can be thought of as subcastes. The approximately four thousand endogamous jatis determine hereditary occupation and are divided among the four varnas.[61] Each region of India, and indeed South Asia, Arundhati Roy writes, has "lovingly perfected" its own unique version of caste-based cruelty based on an unwritten code much worse than the Jim Crow laws.[62] The Marathi word *Dalit* now most commonly refers to avarnas as a whole, where in Sanskrit the term *dal* refers to the state of being broken and downtrodden. It is worth noting that *Dalit* operates as a coalitional identity, bringing together a large number of subcastes across geographical and linguistic divides in common struggle against caste oppression, an act of self-naming that brings to mind the forging of Asian American identity.

Untouchability is marked by religious and cultural notions of pollution, in contrast to the touchability of Jesus. Dalit feminist theologian Prasuna Gnana Nelavala explores this relation in the Gospel account of the woman with the "flow of blood," also considered ritually unclean according to Jewish law, who in touching the hem of Jesus's robe is healed rather than corrupting him.[63] Healing rather than uncleanness is transmitted. Similarly, as another Dalit feminist theologian Surekha Nelavala points out, we find Jesus's encounter with the "sinful woman," by some readings a sex worker who anoints his feet, open to Dalit feminist readings. Sinfulness and womanhood are correlated in the text, and pollution is identified with Dalitness.[64] The struggle of Dalit women has been described as that of the Dalit within the Dalit, the way Chung Hyun-Kyung described the struggle of Asian women as that of the minjung within the minjung.

The root of Dalit oppression, according to Ambedkar, is Brahminism. Brahminism makes it impossible to draw a clear line between victims and oppressors, because of what Ambedkar called the "infection of imitation" that produces a hierarchy of "graded inequality" so that "every class is interested in maintaining the system" due to the relative privilege of every caste, except for the one at the base of the social pyramid. Each caste fights for the scraps that fall off the table of the one above it. Casteism precludes the possibility of social or political solidarity across caste lines.[65] Though caste is distinct from race and class, caste oppression blends only too easily with racial oppression. In Mohandas K. Gandhi's early years in South Africa (1893–1914), he served as the "stretcher bearer of empire" and developed his strategy of nonviolent protest there—namely, satyagraha or "soul-force"—through fighting for the rights of Indians to be segregated *from* Black Africans.[66] Indeed, Gandhi, as did Thind in 1923, invoked the Aryan invasion theory to argue for common cause with the British colonizers in South Africa and against identification with Africans. Gandhi's method of satyagraha, while deeply resonant in nonviolent movements across the world (most notably Martin Luther King Jr.'s involvement in the civil rights era), was a moral appeal to authority and thus had no interest in abolishing the prevailing power structures. Notably, Gandhi prescribed such methods to the Jews of Germany and discouraged Dalits from it.[67]

Yet, inasmuch as caste oppression may be rooted in Brahminism, it is not confined to it. It is certainly not limited to what is now called Hinduism, where, as Ambedkar notes, "the name Hindu itself is a foreign name" imposed by the British who conveniently co-opted caste as a tool of colonization in India. The problem of caste arises in other communities, most notably in Christian, Sikh, and Muslim communities in India, but also Muslim-majority Pakistan and South Asian diaspora in the United States. For example, between 2005 and 2009, the Texas-based Vedic Foundation and the Hindu Education Foundation complained about the coverage of Hinduism in California's sixth-grade textbooks, including its mention of the caste system. The Hindu American Foundation sued the state board of education over the procedures used for reviewing the textbooks. As a result, revisions were made largely to the satisfaction of the dominant caste organizations, but the matter arose again in 2016 when advocacy groups on either side of the issue submitted proposals for the routine update of history and social science curricula in California. In 2017, a final decision was made to include teaching about caste, using the word Dalit, among other changes. Opposing the Hindu American Foundation's agenda was the intercaste and multifaith group South Asian Histories for All, founded by Dalit American activist Thenmozi Soundararajan. In 2022, the University of California system added caste as a protected category after over two years of campaigning led by Nepali Dalit student Prem Pariyar. The campaign cited a 2016 survey by Equality Labs, an Ambedkarite organization founded by Soundararajan, where 26 percent of Dalits reported having faced verbal or physical assaults based on their caste.[68] The same report also found that 52 percent of Dalits and 25 percent of Shudras feared being outed as such.

The problem of caste finds resonances in other forms of oppression and social stratification—for example, according to Ambedkar, the problem between Catholics in Ulster and Protestants in Southern Ireland during his time was also a "problem of caste."[69] Ambedkar questioned Indian socialists who sought a proletariat revolution that did not also seek the annihilation of caste. The assurance of socialists that they do not believe in caste was insufficient, according to Ambedkar, as the social order prevalent in India is one that must be dealt with, whether before or after any socialist revolution. More strikingly, "turn in any direction you like, caste is the monster that crosses your path," and this monster must be killed before any political or economic reform is to take place.[70] In contrast to Marx's exhortation to the proletariat that they have nothing to lose but their chains, Ambedkar argued that the same call is useless against the caste system because of the graded hierarchy it produces, preventing any easy form of class solidarity. Caste and capitalism, as Roy puts it, have "blended into a disquieting, uniquely Indian alloy" and is exported along with its diaspora. The same question continues to be debated between race and class struggles. Class, caste, and race, therefore, are inter-locking forms of oppression and must all be dealt with without compromise or conflation.

Here is one high-profile incident. Lakireddy Bali Reddy arrived in the United States in 1960 to study engineering at the University of California, Berkeley. He later opened a successful Indian restaurant in downtown Berkeley and used its profits to acquire property, that by 2000 he was the second largest landlord in the city, after the University of California. While not a Brahmin, Reddy was from a dominant caste in Andhra Pradesh. Between 1986 and 2000, he trafficked close to a hundred Dalit and other caste-oppressed people from his village through fraudulent visas and fake marriages, both as workers and sex slaves. While living in one of Reddy's run-down buildings, seventeen-year-old Sitha Vemireddy died and her fifteen-year-old sister Lalitha fainted from carbon monoxide poisoning caused by a blocked heating vent. Reddy and several other men rolled Lalitha's body inside a carpet and were moving it into a van as their other roommate, eighteen-year-old Laxmi Patati, was crying and pleading with bystanders, unable to communicate well in English and resisting going into the van. As the carpet was placed in the van, a bystander noticed a leg protrude from the carpet and alerted 911. Sitha's body was found at the bottom of the apartment building's stairwell.[71] The incident launched a larger investigation into Reddy's trafficking, but many of Reddy's victims were afraid to testify. He was eventually convicted and served an eight-year prison term.[72]

The abolition of caste that Ambedkar calls for means conversion, or new life: "The old body must die before a new body can come into existence and a new life can enter into it."[73] The authority and the religion of the shastras and the vedas must be destroyed. It is not Hindusim itself but the legalism, the blind adherence to the rules and religiosity rather than the principles of Hinduism that Ambedkar found issue with. Much the same can be said of Christianity. Instead, Amebdkar writes that "the idea of law is associated with the idea of change," as should Dalit theology and any theology of liberation continuously evolve. That is, as often as it becomes decent or intellectually respectable, it must be continuously indecented, queered, and reshaped according to the ground truth of the communities of faith that it purports to speak from, of, and to. Indeed, Ambedkar was India's first minister of law and justice, widely considered the chief architect of the Constitution of India, lending serious weight to his understanding of law and legal ethics. According to him, the worst evil of the code of ordinances in the Hindu religion is its unchanging nature, iniquitous for its unequal treatment, made perpetual for all generations. Such religion, Ambedkar writes, must be destroyed.[74] Dalit theologians have also drawn connections from Ambedkar's critique of Brahminism with Jesus's temple cleansing and broader critique of Pharisaism and capitalist oppression.[75]

Let us turn from the broader struggle for Dalit liberation to Dalit Christian theology. The beginnings of Dalit theology can be traced to a 1981 address in Bangalore, where Dalit theologian Arvind P. Nirmal cautioned Dalits against contributing to the monolithic project of Indian Christian theology that was driven by nationalistic ideas of unity, and advocated for the project of Dalit theology instead. Dalit theology has since developed so deeply and broadly that it is impossible to properly summarize, so I will only offer snapshots here.

The first generation of Dalit theologians, so to speak, dealt with constructing Dalit theology from various perspectives: methodological, historical, Christological, cultural, and along the inter-sections of gender, class, and religion. As Dalit theology gradually grew into an accepted form of theology, parallel to the acceptance of liberation theologies in North American academies, the issues and questions raised by Dalit theologians shifted, including recon-siderations of what in fact constitutes Dalit identity. It constructed Dalitness as intrinsic and not inherently oppositional and Dalit theology as not merely a "counter-theology," again reminiscent of how Black liberation theology grew beyond a critique of White theology. Plus transnational reflections as caste discrimination follows the Indian diaspora. Indeed, the present reconfigurations of Dalit theology reflect the demands of liberation theology at large: the pressing need to close the widening rift between activist and academic theologians, or what Gramsci saw as the difference between organic and traditional intellectuals, and a recognition of the limits of identity politics.

Dalit theology, according to Sathiananthan Clarke, is a school of Indian contextual thinking that collectively reflects on the ongoing Christian vocation of resisting oppression and advancing libera-tion. Included in it are reflections of "liberation-identified Dalits and Dalit-identified liberationists" on the interlocking divine and human matters that generate life now and reimagine future life for "communities pushed towards physical, social, and economic death."[76] Dalit theology is grounded in the methodological exclu-sivism originating from Dalit subjectivity and balanced with theo-logical inclusiveness as all particular theological expressions offer trajectories to the universality of God. Nirmal describes this ten-sion through the differences in pathetic, empathetic, and sympa-thetic knowing, allowing for the possibility of non-Dalits doing Dalit theology from a sympathetic standpoint.

This sentiment continues to hold, for example, in the statement of the Global Ecumenical Conference on Justice for Dalits held in Bangkok in 2009, which brought together Dalit activists and theologians together with church leaders from around the world.

It stated that "today, regardless of where we come from, which church we represent, we all become Dalits. Not only for today and during this conference, but also for our life until Dalits are liberated, we all become Dalits."[77] This move away from biologically or ontologically determined identity politics not only invites others into identification with Dalits but also frees Dalits in joining other subjugated identities in solidarity.[78] At around the same time, an international conference on Dalit theology held in Kolkata in 2008, called "Dalit Theology in the Twenty-First Century," recognized the need for Dalit theology to reinvent itself in order to become a theology of life for all, as some believed that there was a real danger that "even if caste is annihilated in Hindu society, it might continue to flourish among Indian Christians."[79]

This expansiveness of Dalit theology resonates with the invitation of Afro-pessimism and Black theology, all a priori built on identity politics but in fact highly aware of their limits and welcoming those outside of their immediate interlocuters to partake in the suffering and social death that define them. How we define an inclusive theology based upon particular identities can take notes from the insistence of both Black and Dalit communities on the specificity of their struggle balanced with an open invitation to partake in their suffering. For non-Black, non-Dalit Asians, accepting the invitation to become Black and Dalit is a call to become race and caste traitors, rejecting the privileges afforded to us by the coincidence of birth and finding solidarity with those who have been made nonhuman—dehumanized. At the risk of stating the obvious, these calls to die to oneself can be viewed as very Christian in nature (also Buddhist).

TOWARD ABOLITION OF CASTE, POLICE, AND PRISON

So this is where this all leads us to: In attempting to construct a theology of Asian American liberation beyond the contours of East Asian diaspora, we can look toward Dalit theology as a creative and robust source of theological reflection, not least with its deep historical connections with the Black struggle in the United States, which, as Cone has pointed out, any theology in the United States must reckon with in its self-understanding. Importantly, the recent movement for Black lives has found points of solidarity—not only with Dalit struggles against caste oppression but also with Palestinian struggles against the Israeli apartheid state and the Hong Kong prodemocracy movement that is firmly anti-police. These solidarities were built through international campaigns expressing solidarity with each other, often connected through their respective diaspora and refugee communities in the United States and the present-day empires that link these struggles together.

At the same time, moving beyond expressions of solidarity and toward collective power has proven to be an immensely difficult task. We have seen this time again through the rise and fall of radical movements from the very beginning of Asian America, and this tentative nature of organizing for collective power should give us pause. For the non-Dalits and non-Blacks among us, perhaps the proper theoretical intervention is to advance Ambedkarite and abolitionist theologies as direct descendants of Dalit and Black theologies, as necessary constituents of any comprehensive theology of liberation. By Ambedkarite theology here I mean a militant, anti-caste theology that sees God as both Dalit and the liberator of Dalits and grasps the theological roots of caste oppression, its complexity, invisibility, and transnationality.

Looking to the contemporary United States, the murder of George Floyd in Minneapolis ignited riots in June 2020, which saw the burning of the Third Precinct of the Minneapolis Police Department, the commandeering of a Sheraton hotel by activists for houseless people, and the temporary establishment of autonomous police-free zones that practiced community defense. Minneapolis inspired other riots and protests internationally and marked the largest protest historically in the United States. While the riots and lootings polarized political opinion regarding the legitimacy of the protests as observers condemned the destruction of private property as a response to the annihilation of Black lives, a broader call for defunding and abolishing the police began to take root.

In the Capitol Hill neighborhood of Seattle, after weeks of protests and clashes with riot police involving tear gas and water cannons, police abandoned their East Precinct building, leaving activists free to establish an area covering six city blocks called the Capitol Hill Occupied Protest (CHOP) and later the Capitol Hill Autonomous Zone (CHAZ).[80] Community control of the area lasted over three weeks, maintaining itself as a self-organized and leaderless space with daily community meetings, protests, demands to the state, community gardens, and food distribution. In the end, the Seattle Police Department regained control and cleared out the area following a series of shootings that had occurred and reports of sexual assault.

It is important to note here the difficult but necessary questions that abolition of policing and the prison industrial complex poses to pragmatic visions of the future. While we mustn't shy away from these questions of how exactly we hope to keep our people safe in an abolitionist world, neither must we stop trying to build such a world to come. From a liberationist perspective, or even a plain Christian perspective, it must be that our eschatology is abolitionist. How could there possibly be police in any heaven? What happens when people inevitably hurt each other? What implications does this have for a prefigurative politics of the here and now? Of course, abolitionism also raises deep and important questions about hell and divine justice, but I will not venture them here. What lessons and visions can we glean from the riots of 2020?

More than solidarity, contemporary abolitionist movements within Black radicalism and Black theology complement the anti-imperialist and anti-colonial dimensions of Asian and Asian American theology; they deepen each other, and in the final analysis they are inextricably connected through the transatlantic and transpacific slave trades, extractive colonialism, empire, and their joint invitations to social death. While their geographic scales and racial registers differ at first sight, with abolition being concerned with policing and prisons domestically and anti-imperialism with imperial powers globally, their interrelatedness is revealed through careful considerations such as the prison-to-deportation pipeline that affects Southeast Asian refugees and undocumented peoples and the long history of conscription of communities of color into fighting the forever wars waged by the United States.

The George Floyd uprising that involved the decapitation and vandalism of confederate monuments in the United States also inspired renewed efforts in the United Kingdom and post-colonial nations against statues and other forms of memorialization of colonizers, one of the most prominent being the Rhodes Must Fall movement that began in Cape Town in 2015, which later, in 2020, inspired the Raffles Must Fall movement in Singapore. These rebellions against national memory are linked not only to struggles of once oppressed peoples against the glorification of their oppressors' past but on a deeper level they are connected by shared colonial legacies and global configurations of race, capital, and empire. Conversely, the transnational nature of Dalit struggles is readily seen in the perpetuation of caste oppression in immigrant South Asian populations in the United States, many of whom work in tech companies, which constitute the most advanced layer of the present carceral system.

Another prominent example of the intersection between abolition of carcerality and caste is the rise of Kamala Harris as the vice president of the United States, the first Black and South Asian woman to hold such a high office. There are several points of observation here: the first being Harris's Tamil background—and not to mention Brahmin—was raised to prominence only after her nomination to vice presidency, before which she was read racially as just Black. Harris's mother, Shaymala Gopalan, the daughter of a colonial bureaucrat, pursued post-graduate studies at the University of California, Berkeley, and as the South Asian aspect of Harris's racial identity became highlighted so too did Harris become popular in Tamil Brahmin circles. Indeed, due to the embeddedness of anti-Blackness within South Asian communities, it is safe to say that Harris's acceptance by the latter is despite her shared ancestry through her Jamaican American father and qualified by her rise to power. The second point is Harris's earlier work as the district attorney of San Francisco and later attorney general of California, where she played an active and important role in maintaining the carceral system, styling herself as a "top cop" and "progressive prosecutor."[81] Harris's genealogies and vice presidency are a sharp reminder of the limits of identity politics and points directly to the complicated fusion of race and caste politics.

On the other hand, Soundararajan insists on the notion of caste apartheid and the appropriateness of the terms *genocide* and *slavery* in describing the horrors of caste. The term *caste apartheid* was first used by Dalits who visited Durban in South Africa, but South African apartheid itself was a British institution modeled on the Indian caste system. As Cecil Rhodes declared in Cape Town, "The native is to be treated as a child and denied the franchise. We must adopt a system of despotism, such as works in India, in our relations with the barbarism of South Africa."[82] The many forms of abuse that the Dalit and Shudra were subjected to over millennia constitute slavery by any other name. Anti-caste reformer Jyotirao Phule's important books titled *Gulamgiri* (1873) and *Shetkaryaca Asud* (1881) can be translated as "slavery" and "the farmer's whip," respectively. His work was in part a tribute to the slave abolition movement in the United States, from which he and his wife, Savitribai Phule, an activist in her own right, drew inspiration. In fact, India today has the highest absolute number of people living in modern slavery worldwide.[83] Thus even as Black studies may talk about the afterlife of slavery, how it continues to live on despite being outlawed, the same goes for the caste system despite being outlawed by the 1950 Constitution of India.

Still, the vision that abolitionism puts forward is far more expansive than the focus on police and prisons often portrayed in the media. Abolitionist futures seek a world beyond carceral systems and surveillance capitalism, calling for alternative visions of justice, community care, and defense—in others words, a complete transformation of the relations of production and social reproduction. Moreover, an abolitionist future is necessarily one without empire: militarized police forces, state borders, and the military industrial complex all perform the disciplining functions that maintain state power, whether it is vulnerable communities or Third World countries that are being policed. As such, the role of policing—and hence the demands of abolition—carry us across oceans, from US settler colonialism to the Black Lives Matter movement to Israeli apartheid to the Uyghur genocide in Xinjiang to the Hong Kong resistance, which I shall return to in the next chapter. On the other hand, the anti-caste movement is no less complex than abolition, as it is constituted by theological, social, and legal apparatuses, and unlike race, it has no phrenological aspect except perhaps through the brand of Brahmin supremacy grounded in Aryan invasion theory. Casteism is so foreign that it is largely illegible to the blunt instrument of US racial logic, though the anti-Black racism that South Asians are accused of is often aligned with Brahminism through class structures and colorism.

Yet the parallels remain: the well-known Indian author and activist Arundhati Roy's book-length introduction to an annotated 2014 edition of Ambedkar's *Annihilation of Caste* was criticized by Dalit anti-caste activists for Roy's failure as a Brahmin to grasp Ambedkar's work and for presuming the authority to introduce the foundational text. Telugu poet and activist Joopaka Subhadra insists that Roy does not know the pain of caste, yet Subhadra does not foreclose the possibility of non-Dalits writing faithfully about caste pain, saying, "Tell the whole world about the caste system in this country. Write about caste discrimination, tell the whole world, but, engage with the pain, empathize with it and then talk about it. Talk about the intensity of the pain."[84] The pain that the Dalit body inhabits in the caste system, as with the abjection of Blackness in an anti-Black world, is precisely the difference between the pathetic, empathetic, and sympathetic knowing that Nirmal describes. And yet, as Subhadra and Dalit theologians have noted, this chasm can also be bridged. "Caste has to go," she goes on to say, "Work with the Dalit intellectuals, the pain has to be expressed through them in their own voices."

Worse still, in 2020 Roy disavowed her Brahmin identity, becoming the latest high-profile upper-caste person to view themselves as casteless, which is as much nonsense as White people who are "color-blind" or "do not see race." As much as we may argue that race and caste are social constructs, which Asian Americanness certainly helps to reveal, we can by no means disavow their very real and material consequences. Roy's failure to properly reckon with her own privilege is far more serious than the problems that Harris's intersectional identity raises, as Roy is major figure of what views itself as the international Left whereas Harris is simply the latest "diverse" addition to the liberal establishment. Just as Amilcar Cabral warned to claim no easy victories, so must we claim no easy solidarities. The only way out is through. The abolition of carceral systems, the annihilation of caste, and solving the problem of the color line can only be carried out with an unwavering commitment to not only dismantling systems and internalized behaviors that perpetuate them, but also building nurturing and joyful alternative ecologies that fundamentally transform the ways we relate to and care for each other.

The annihilation of caste that Ambedkar called for is a call to abolish caste, and with it the social relations that maintain caste oppression. In total, abolition requires a world where not only racial capitalism is destroyed but also caste and any other oppression like it. Abolition requires the structure of liberation. We can also draw lessons from Dalit theology, its rich history and deep reflection on the nature of oppression rooted in one's birth, complexion, and occupation, and also God's identification with the poor, the broken, the outcaste, the nonhuman, and the unclean. As such, we can see more clearly the pathways to liberation that theological reflection illuminates for us, regardless of the particularity of the oppressed.

While Black theology and Dalit theology speak to very different communities, both have found liberative elements in Christian theological sources that speak to the pain of oppression and offer comfort through the possibility of a God who weeps and suffers in incarnation. These shared sources of theological reflection for both Black and Dalit communities suggests points of solidarity from which a coalitional political theology can grow. This important link that Dalit theology provides us with, then, represents another touchstone alongside other Asian liberation theologies: Palestinian liberation theology of the previous chapter and minjung theology of the next, not to mention other grassroots Asian and Asian American theologies that have not found the need to name themselves. Whether or not such attempts at building solidarity and perhaps even a coalitional theology can survive remain to be seen, but it remains that the task required of us is to keep our hands on the plow and set our faces like flint toward the liberation of all.

THE INVITATION OF THE CROSS TO SOCIAL DEATH

In *Black Marxism*, Cedric Robinson weaves together a historical Black radical tradition through the lens of the African diaspora, the Atlantic slave trade, various Black resistances, and the works of W. E. B. Du Bois, C. L. R. James, and Richard Wright. At the heart of the text is chapter 7, titled "The Nature of the Black Radical Tradition," which frustrates certain leftists concerned only with material and not metaphysical realities. Having recounted a history of the Black movement, Robinson seeks to understand its "ideological, philosophical, and epistemological natures."[85] The question of what is the metaphysical nature of the Black radical tradition might seem strange to a historical materialist or Marxist, but it is entirely natural to a liberation theologian. From a theological perspective, the metaphysical is at least as important as the physical. Robinson points to a violence "turned inward"—a jihad or dharma one might say—the "renunciation of actual being for historical being" and the "preservation of the ontological totality granted by a metaphysical system."[86] This revolutionary consciousness that Robinson saw as proceeding from the Black historical experience was a collective consciousness informed by historical struggles for liberation grounded in African tradition. This harkening to an African tradition resonates, in fact, with later developments in Black theology. Here, notably, Robinson invokes the Black slave preacher Nat Turner who read the Bible and, following an encounter with the Holy Spirit in 1831, led the only sustained slave rebellion in all of US history.

What might an Asian radical tradition look like, and what would its relation to liberation theologies be? While its intellectual and historical debt to the Black radical tradition will be evident, any Asian radical tradition must be able to stand on its own two feet. Otherwise, we would only be parasites trying to join and co-opt other movements rather than being able to lend power to others even as we build it. In seeking touchstones for an Asian American theology of liberation, we can turn not only to the coalitional work of Yuri Kochiyama and Grace Lee Boggs but also the many labor strikes carried out by Asian garment workers and farmers and the desertion of the first Filipino sailors when the Spanish colonizers first arrived on American land.[87]

I would argue that Afro-Asian solidarity is also a feature of the Black radical tradition going back to even before the first Bandung conference in 1955. Recall that Du Bois had offered every sympathy with the untouchables of India. Martin Luther King Jr.'s nonviolent strategies were famously inspired by those of Gandhi, despite Gandhi's own anti-Black racism. And in more recent times, we have the solidarity between Palestinians, Black lives, and Indigenous people; Hong Kong's Umbrella Movement in 2014, chanting "Hands up, don't shoot," which began at protests for Michael Brown; and the explicitly anti-police nature of Hong Kong's protesters in 2019, who in turn offered practical advice for protesters in the 2020 George Floyd rebellion. Such internationalism is not a new thing. It is only often forgotten, suppressed, or perhaps too much to hold altogether at once. But if we are to seek an Asian radical tradition, one that is properly nuanced and held up against capitalism, anti-Blackness, settler colonialism, and heteropatriarchy, this is what is required of us; we must see all these dimensions, intersections, and contradictions together and articulate an Asian radical tradition on its own terms. Any Asian radical tradition would necessarily be one that is carefully and socially constructed—not born out of anachronistic historical determinism but one that weaponizes Asian American history in the precise sense that Asian American identity was intended to be a political and coalitional strategy. This therefore represents a crucial step in laying the foundation for a renewed Asian American theology of liberation.

But liberation does not come easy. "Power concedes nothing without a demand,"[88] Frederick Douglass tells us. Cone understood the contradictions inherent in "the conspicuous absence of the lynching tree in American theological discourse and preaching," as the crucifixion was "clearly a first-century lynching."[89] Of course, the parallels were already clear from Billie Holiday's 1937 song "Strange Fruit." And if it wasn't clear enough, even the UN Working Group of Experts on People of African Descent connected the police killings of Black people in the United States in 2016 and "the past racial terror of lynching."[90] In my years of attending majority White or multiethnic churches in the United States, the connection between the cross and the lynching tree was never made and only became obvious after reading Cone. It is imperative for any Asian American theology to recognize the cross not only in the lynching tree but also in police killings today.

The Cross of Jesus is a fixture of evangelical theology and Christianity at large. The call of Christ requires a dying to self. "Take up your cross and follow me," he said.[91] Or, in the words of Dietrich Bonhoeffer, a German pastor imprisoned and killed for his resistance to Nazi rule, "When Christ calls a man, he bids him come and die."[92] At the same time, Wilderson's charge should be cause for many a repentance, for "if we are to be honest with ourselves, we must admit that the 'Negro' has been inviting whites, as well as civil society's junior partners, to the dance of social death for hundreds of years, but few have wanted to learn the steps."[93] So, too, the call to join into Dalitness. It must be, then, that the call of Christ to come and die must in fact include the invitation to join the dance of social death.

The resonance between these three invitations is striking. Asians in the United States are most certainly civil society's junior partners: we can either be for Black lives or Black death; there is no third option in this country. So even as we build an Asian radical tradition, we must live a revolutionary praxis that requires us to die many deaths. How hard is it for us to die the kind of social death that is the foundation of anti-Black society, yet all the time in churches we hear preaching about dying to self? And what about the invitation of Dalit theology to enter into untouchability?

What even does Asian social death look like? Does it mean the abolition of carceral logics or the annihilation of casteism? Does it mean the repatriation of Native land? Does it mean trading our embedded anti-Blackness and honorary Whiteness for nothingness? Does it mean becoming willing to allow our bodies to "magnetize bullets" the way that Black bodies do, as Wilderson writes? Perhaps it is all these things and more. In the least, it is but one aspect of a faithful attempt to heed the call to die to self. We must certainly also be about the liberation of Asians everywhere: so many Asians are hidden in poverty, in community colleges, in houselessness, in prison and in detention, at risk of deportation and travel bans. The coronavirus pandemic has revealed not only our interconnectedness on a global scale but also the deep-seated racism and xenophobia under the pretense of fear and safety. There is no way that the liberation of all will come at no personal cost.

Indeed, the invitation of Afro-pessimism to non-Blacks—in the United States, at least—is a kenotic call, the emptying of oneself as Christ also did. In one translation of Paul in Philippians, the Messiah "became nothing," or, as John the Baptist declared, "He must increase, and I must decrease"—to go outside the camp, to become outcaste.[94] The idea of kenosis as Christian ethic is deeply embedded within many Christian traditions, so the invitation of Blackness to ontological surrender is not, in fact, too much to ask: Christ has already demanded it and more also. Indeed, Wilderson points out that captivity does not constitute the being of Latine and Asian people the way it does Black people, and so offers to non-Black people that "we [Black people] will be in coalitions with you" but at the same time "while we are in these coalitions, we will ridicule you for the impoverishment of your demands, even while we are fighting against white people on [the coalition's] behalf, and we will do so until you surrender your agency and authority to the end of the world."[95] The world is ending. To practice a broader and deeper coalitional politics that characterizes Asian American political identity, we must be willing to embrace the social death of Blackness and Dalitness that we have been invited to, and from which perhaps a new humanity will spring eternal.

So we must be dreadfully careful of what we wish for, including when we talk about liberation. Jesus said that whoever the Son sets free is free indeed. But Saidiya Hartman insists that "a Black revolution makes everyone freer than they actually want to be" and "no one in the world who suffers and who says they want to be free, wants to be as free as Blackness will make them."[96] How rightfully damning. As Eleazar Fernandez writes, "Only those who are comfortable can stay at the level of abstract ontological analysis. For someone who is worried about the next day's meal, eviction, or massacre, a discussion of anthropology at the level of ontological categories is highly irrelevant."[97]

Do we dare to live in the dreams of the oppressed? Latin American liberation theology was concerned with the nonhuman, or the dehumanized, but would we be willing to join them, to become them, to empty ourselves and incarnate into nothingness? Would we truly welcome capitalism's destruction, patriarchy's dismantling, and settler society's decolonization? What if workers actually owned the means of production or women the means of social reproduction? What if we were really as free as the Son sets free? As free as Blackness and Dalitness will make us?

The history of Afro-Asia is full of solidarities and betrayals. Anti-Blackness plagues Asian communities and Western thought, influenced first by Judeo-Christian ideas and then by scientific racism. The problem of the (non)human, of being itself, is one shared by liberation theology, Afro-pessimism, and post-colonialism. While Afro-pessimism offers an invitation to "the dance of social death," Dalit theology and Black theology also invite those on the outside into Dalitness and Blackness, to partake in the pain of caste and racial oppression. For non-Dalits and non-Blacks, the liberative horizon of abolition is not one in which we are magnanimous saviors, lifting others from nonbeing to being, but one in which the call of the cross to die to ourselves is faithfully answered in radical identification with others, to incarnate, to become undead Black flesh and pitch our tents with the outcaste, the dehumanized, the dispossessed. For some this may look like the surrendering of dreams of upward mobility, betraying the dreams of our parents, living in underfunded districts and food deserts, being on the receiving end of environmental racism and over-policing, relying on public transit and broken infrastructure—in short, the preferential option for the poor. Such choices are as much material as they are ontological, as the next chapter will show. At the same time, as Ruth Wilson Gilmore writes, abolition is not about absence but the presence of life-affirming institutions, a commitment to be with rather than to do for is what makes of us true *compañeres* and faithful disciples.[98] Only through love and struggle is our liberation theology lived. Thus, to a subjectless and landless Asian American theology of liberation we must also add beinglessness, but these absences should in fact point us to a deeper faithful presence upon which we may build an Asian radical tradition for the world to come.

HAVING

6.

"LET IT END IN OUR GENERATION"

Minjung Theology, Racial Capitalism, and Struggle in a Post-pandemic World

Having said this, I must deal immediately and at some length with the question of violence. Some of the things so far told to the Court are true and some are untrue. I do not, however, deny that I planned sabotage. I did not plan it in a spirit of recklessness, nor because I have any love of violence. I planned it as a result of a calm and sober assessment of the political situation that had arisen after many years of tyranny, exploitation, and oppression of my people by the Whites.
—Nelson Mandela, "'I Am Prepared to Die.'"

Now when Yeshua heard this, he said unto him, "You still lack one thing: sell all that you have, and distribute unto the poor, and you shall have treasure in heaven: and come, follow me."
—Luke 18:22

And seeing the multitude, he was moved with compassion for them, because they were wearied and downcast.
—Matthew 9:36

By faith Moses, having become grown, refused to be called Pharoah's daughter's son, rather having chosen to suffer with the people of God than to have the passing pleasure of sin, having regarded the Messiah's reproach greater wealth than Egypt's treasures, he was looking toward the compensation.
—Hebrews 11:24-26

On March 16, 2021, fifty-three years after the Mỹ Lai massacre in Vietnam, a White man walked into several massage parlors in Atlanta, Georgia, operated by East Asian women, shooting and killing eight people. Six of the victims were women of Korean and Chinese descent, many of whom were employees and immigrants. The event was a crescendo in the wave of anti-East Asian violence that had been on the rise, particularly within the United States, in the wake of the COVID-19 pandemic that had set in a little over a year ago. In the beginning, then president Donald Trump referred to it as the China virus, Wuhan virus, or Kung Flu, an act criticized by many for exacerbating latent xenophobia and renewing anti-Asian sentiment.[1] Indeed, violent attacks, including stabbing, spitting, beating, and more subtle forms of discrimination against East Asians in the United States, appeared to be on the rise as reports emerged and efforts were made to document these actions as hate crimes.

What followed were protests to "Stop Asian hate" and discussions on anti-Asian racism, in part following the zeitgeist set in place by the public discourse on anti-racism, anti-Blackness, and abolition from the previous year.[2] The contrast between Black people dying at the hands of the police and Asian women dying by a White shooter who frequented massage parlors simply drives home the ways in which the configurations of race, gender, and nationality not only structure the lives but also the deaths of individuals differently.[3] Crucial to any consideration of the Atlanta shootings is not only the pointed intersection of fetishistic orientalism, migrant labor, sex work, empire, and White supremacy but also the fact that the shooter was raised in a conservative evangelical church and claimed the attack was "not racially motivated" but rather because of a "sexual addiction." Two points of qualification are important here: first, that the leading Korean newspaper *Chosun Ilbo* reported an eyewitness who claimed that the shooter had said, "Kill all Asians,"[4] and second, it is not known—nor is it of utmost importance—that the employees murdered were indeed also sex workers.

Our reflections on Asian American theologies reveal themselves to be unfortunately pertinent and urgent in the present political moment. They must also be able to rise to the occasion. Political scientist Claire Kim argues that anti-Blackness is structural while anti-Asian racism is contingent, but as I argue, it is the inclusion of Asians within the United States' White-supremacist, settler-colonial structure that is contingent, and although what has been called anti-Asian violence appears acute, its roots are indeed structural. To see anti-Blackness and anti-Asian violence as separate is a failure to properly grasp the comprehensiveness with which racial violence structures our daily life.

Considering the Atlanta shootings within a theological framework, the problematic of sexual repression within conservative theologies—not least those inherited by many Asian American churches—and its interactions with the fetishization of Asian women and imperial conquest all come into sharp relief. The discourse in the aftermath quickly turned to generic notions of "Asian hate" and the suffering of Asian American women at large. We do the victims a disservice by shifting too quickly away from the specific site of their vulnerability—namely, that of migrant labor and, often enough, sex work. The disavowal of gendered labor under capitalism and the discursive move toward more palatable forms of discrimination, such as violent attacks against elderly Asians, replays entrenched notions of shame and pollution around sex and migrant work. Indeed, within the world of migrant labor—and Northeast Asian flows to the United States in particular—there is much circulation and little differentiation between work in grocery stores, nail salons, dry cleaners, restaurants, massage parlors, and, of course, sex work. These pathways of migrant labor, whether trafficked or freely willed by some measure, are highly porous and interdependent as they are built on communal networks and personal connections. They are very much gendered and classed. As such, this falls squarely within the concerns of Asian American liberation theology, our task being to reflect on and struggle with these communities.

While undeniably tragic, the Atlanta shootings come as no surprise. The incident is perfectly located within the narrative of Asian exclusion from the very beginning of the US empire and its many wars in East Asia, not to mention the ongoing power struggle with China for global dominance. The historical convergences that have led to this moment raise no new questions about how such a horror could have occurred. More surprising, perhaps, is the rise to prominence of the sex worker collective Red Canary Song as a representative voice speaking on behalf of massage parlor workers. One of its members, Wu, pointed to the combinations of whore-phobia, homophobia, xenophobia, racism, and sexism at work, both in how the women were murdered and how certain Asians choose to discuss the issue at hand.[5] Moreover, Wu's analysis delivers a devastating critique to calls for increased policing and the prosecution of hate crimes as the key response to the rise in anti-East Asian violence. Increased policing does not protect sex workers from the many forms of violence that they face on a daily basis. Instead, it makes things worse because the police themselves are often the perpetrators of violence against sex workers and often raid massage parlors regardless of any reliable information about possible sex work there.

What about the characterization of such attacks as hate crimes? Sociologist Tamara Nopper has noted that attempts to address anti-East Asian violence as hate crimes run counter to an abolitionist framework, as police departments benefit from the perception of increased hate crimes as a crime wave, lending legitimacy and leading to increased funding.[6] But what is a hate crime, anyway? Within the US legal framework, a hate crime is deemed as such if there is provable bias or motivation on the basis of the victim's identity, most often on the basis of race, though itself blind to the unequal racial dynamics.[7] A crime that is prosecuted as a hate crime allows for an increase in the severity of the punishment, so the notion of a "hate crime" is a carceral mechanism: in prosecuting a case as a hate crime, we just want to punish the person *more*.

As both transformative justice advocates and prison abolitionists have long pointed out, the current criminal justice system is built on *punitive* justice: when someone commits a crime, we want to see them suffer, with no expectation or pathway to reform or reconciliation.[8] Red Canary Song's statement in response to the Atlanta shooting, cosigned by 323 allied organizations, flatly rejected calls for increased policing:

> The impulse to call for increased policing is even greater in the midst of rising anti-Asian violence calling for carceral punishment. We understand the pain that motivates our Asian and Asian-American community members' call for increased policing, but we nevertheless stand against it. Policing has never been an effective response to violence because the police are agents of white supremacy. Policing has never kept sex workers or massage workers or immigrants safe. Due to sexist racialized perceptions of Asian women, especially those engaged in vulnerable, low-wage work, Asian massage workers are harmed by the criminalization of sex work, regardless of whether they engage in it themselves. Decriminalization of sex work is the only way that sex workers, massage workers, sex trafficking survivors, and anyone criminalized for their survival and/or livelihood will ever be safe.
>
> Media coverage that examines the racist or sexist motivations of the killings as independent of each other fail to grasp the deeply connected histories of racialized violence and paternalistic rescue complexes that inform the violence experienced by Asian massage workers. We see the effort to invisibilize these women's gender, labor, class, and immigration status as a refusal to reckon with the legacy of United States imperialism, and as a desire to collapse the identities of migrant Asian women, sex workers, massage workers, and trafficking survivors.[9]

In two short paragraphs, Red Canary Song connects police abolition, labor, sexism, imperialism, and racism. From a theological standpoint, this carceral system built to deliver mass suffering without redemption can be traced to bad ideas about hell and purgatory. Moreover, calls for prosecuting such acts as hate crimes suggest a misplaced optimism that the US judiciary system has been and will be able to deliver justice and punishment in a satisfactory manner, particularly through the mechanism of hate crime laws. The criminal justice system does not even perform well according to its own punitive goals! If any Asian American theology is also to be abolitionist, it must have the capacity to think beyond carceral solutions, an imperative that has highly concrete implications for the here and now. Now more than ever it is necessary to develop theologies and frameworks of care informed by intersectional feminisms and transformational justice.

With these preliminary considerations in mind, this chapter attempts to consider in earnest the various reconfigurations of Asian and Asian American identity in the wake of the coronavirus pandemic on the competing levels of identity as racial subjects operating within the confines of nation-states, and of the collective organizing in resistance to state power and in relation to international geopolitics. To name but a few protest movements that occurred throughout Asia between 2019 and 2020: in Hong Kong against the security law in 2019, which can be viewed as a continuation of the Umbrella Movement in 2014; in India against the Citizenship Amendment Act beginning in 2019, denationalizing Muslims and Northeast Indians, and later against a series of farming laws beginning in 2020; in Indonesia against an omnibus law amending more than seventy-five laws, whose effects included the erosion of workers' rights and environmental protections, following smaller student protests a year earlier in response to another series of laws that were passed; in Thailand against the monarchy and in support of democracy; in Myanmar against the military junta's coup. How should these resistances inform Asian organizing and theologizing in the United States? What lessons can be gained toward cooperation between radical movements within and between the United States and Asia, even as the contours of a new Cold War began to form? Why do we need a theology of protest?

The urgent answer to the latter question lies in observing the increasing number of protests worldwide over the last decade. Moreover, major climate reports from scientific experts suggest that the increasingly uninhabitable Earth will only destabilize societies further and scientists warn that global suffering is set to increase exponentially with the irruption of climate refugees, faced with ethnonationalism and xenophobia. This all points to the growing unrest of the global 99 percent whose backs are breaking under an unsustainable system produced by the capitalist world order.[10] Protest is the oppressed crying out and, in the absence of change, revolting through direct actions such as blockades, occupations, strikes, and riots. Jesus's cleansing of the temple has much to teach us. In the Gospel of John's account, Jesus made a whip of cords and drove out the merchants and moneychangers inside the Temple in Jerusalem, overturning tables and chairs. A theology of protest leads us straight to theologies of liberation: theologies that are produced from the consciousness of those marching and bleeding on the streets, rendered invisible in slums, favelas, ghettos, and prisons. The agitation of protest is best understood not as simply calls for democratic choice or economic equality but for freedom from exploitative and oppressive forces of all kinds.

With regards to the recent social and political unrest in Asia, one might ask what any of it has to do with Asian Americans. One answer lies in the simple fact that migrant labor and immigration patterns continue to flow from Asia into the United States. The lived experiences of the Asian proletariat that our theology is built upon directly connects to these flows, and thus the social and political unrest in Asia reverberate among diasporic networks and form bases for solidarity and coalition-building.[11] After all, how could a theology claim to be from below if it had no understanding of the concern of the people for their loved ones? Asian movements in US history organized domestically around issues such as labor justice and political recognition while also being allied with struggles abroad in Asia such as against the Park Chung Hee dictatorship in Korea, the authoritarianism of Ferdinand Marcos in the Philippines, and of course the US wars in Vietnam, Laos, and Cambodia in the mid- to late-twentieth century.

Cone taught us that the Cross of Christ can only be understood in view of the lynching tree. Rather than the Cross that evangelicals wish to elevate, perhaps it is the whip of Jesus that must inform our praxis. The Black experience, once again, is "the feeling one has when attacking the enemy of black humanity by throwing a Molotov cocktail into a white-owned building and watching it go up in flames."[12] The slave bibles from the 1800s, which omitted passages that could have incited rebellion, also come to mind. Maybe what is required of us is a holy insurrection, a willingness to put our own bodies and jobs on the line. Some observers have praised protests like the ones in Hong Kong for their lack of violent encounters—before they eventually turned violent—contrasting them with conflicts in places like Ferguson or Minneapolis, Minnesota, where Black uprisings were deemed riots from the very beginning, as a kind of transnational model-minority myth. Concerns over destruction of property are a value of capitalism and Whiteness, which tell the oppressed that they should protest nonviolently. Cheryl Harris's notion of Whiteness as property reminds us that race is entangled within an economic logic, so the protection of property against violence extends also to a defense of Whiteness itself.[13] The world as we know it is ending. The time is short. It is time to get righteously angry.

HONG KONG: THEOLOGIES OF THE MINJUNG AND THE MULTITUDE

On June 16, 2019, the song "Sing Hallelujah to the Lord" became a popular anthem of the Hong Kong protests against the extradition to China bill.[14] The bill, it was widely believed, would provide the Chinese Communist Party unchecked power in detaining political

dissidents in Hong Kong. To many, it represented China's authoritarian rule and a breakdown in the "one-country, two systems"
governance that has placed Hong Kong at an arm's length from
Beijing since the British handed it over in 1997. The first major
anti-extradition protests occurred on June 9—not long after
the thirtieth anniversary of the Tiananmen Square Massacre in
Beijing—with around a million participants out of a seven million
population in Hong Kong. The annual July 1 prodemocracy demonstrations in Hong Kong that year also saw a massive turnout. The
largely peaceful protesters were met with violent anti-riot police,
water guns, tear gas, and batons. The decision to use force was
a preemptive strike on the part of the police, after the Umbrella
Movement five years prior. The anti-extradition protests in Hong
Kong should be situated alongside other protest movements that
preceded it: the Umbrella Movement, Occupy Wall Street, the Arab
Spring, and Black Lives Matter. While each one of these demonstrations differed in their goals, they shared a method of mass protest and largely peaceful occupation of public space, sublimating
a collective anger and frustration at the lack of democratic power,
whether it be against dictatorial regimes or financial overlords.

The Hong Kong protests continued to escalate. Numerous
Hong Kongers committed suicide in protest of the bill and police
brutality; also out of despair over Hong Kong's future. On July 1,
2019, a group of protesters stormed the Legislative Council while
it was empty and vandalized it. Other actions include a general
strike supported by the Confederate of Trade Unions, a three-day
sit-in at the Hong Kong International Airport, and clashes with
police and pro-China counter-protesters on the street and underground in subway stations. On September 4, 2019, the chief executive of Hong Kong Carrie Lam announced that the bill would be
withdrawn, but protesters continued to press their five demands:
A full withdrawal of the bill, retraction of the characterization of
the protests as riots, the release of arrested protesters, an inquiry
into police brutality, and the resignation of Carrie Lam.

In early November, police clashed with student protesters at the Hong Kong University of Science and Technology, the Chinese University of Hong Kong, and Hong Kong Polytechnic University (PolyU). In particular, what became known as the siege of PolyU lasted almost two weeks, with the university under complete lockdown by the police and over a thousand students arrested over the course of the siege. During the siege, the District Council election on November 24 saw a historic voter turnout, and the pro-Beijing camp suffered its greatest electoral defeat in Hong Kong's history. Despite this, the COVID-19 outbreak that soon followed prevented protesters from gathering, allowing police to disperse or detain protesters under the cover of the health emergency. Finally, despite the protesters' efforts and international attention, the National Security Law was passed on June 30, 2021 and had an immediate chilling effect on free speech and protests. Subsequently, the law has been used to crack down on and detain hundreds of prodemocracy activists, businesspeople, and lawmakers, and the present future of Hong Kong remains uncertain.

The sustained protest saw a range of tactics develop on both sides. The use of violence by protesters, such as Molotov cocktails, arson, vandalism, and physical attacks against progovernment counter-protesters in the 2019–2020 protests, represented a break from a general consensus on nonviolent tactics since the 1967 Hong Kong riots. Bombing and arson attacks were carried out by local leftists against colonial police and communist sympathizers, following which the British colonial government invoked an Emergency Regulations Ordinance leading to aggressive crackdowns and later introduced social reforms supported by local elites.[15] Besides the physical casualties and property damage caused during the latest protests, the mental strain and anguish of the struggle can be glimpsed through the many suicides committed, the notes that activists left for their families in the event of their detention or death, and the flight of Hong Kongers to the United Kingdom and Canada as political refugees. The movement's greatest champions were Hong Kong students, who had grown up in the recent era of independence from British rule.[16]

The earlier Umbrella Movement of 2014 finds its roots both in the Occupy Wall Street movement and in the church—namely, the Occupy Central with Love and Peace protests in 2013 whose leaders included law professor and evangelical Christian Benny Tai Yiu-ting—eventually arrested under the security law—and Baptist minister Reverend Chiu Yiuming. As geographer Justin Tse writes, the Umbrella Movement can be seen as the birth of a kind of liberation theology in Hong Kong, albeit not in the genealogy of earlier forms of liberation theologies, in relation to mainland China rather than, say, explicitly capitalist regimes.[17] Further, Tse argues that if the theology that is produced out of the Hong Kong movement is to be understood as a liberation theology, it must be understood in its own terms and not as an Asian liberation theology (presumably in the sense of Pieris) nor as an inculturation project. Indeed, while direct connections can be made to Rieger and Kwok's recent reflections on the Occupy movement from the lens of minjung theology, or a theology of the multitude, as they call it, Hong Kong theologians have themselves differed on the theological interpretation of the movement.[18]

For example, Rose Wu reads the Umbrella Movement as a new Pentecostal experience and a form of practical eschatology, but at the same time she also deploys feminist theology to declare that redemption includes both reconciliation with God and liberation from bondage and oppression, having in mind not only the struggle against the state but the gendered violence toward female protesters, from both police and fellow protesters.[19] Female protesters were told that since they came out to protest, they should expect to be sexually assaulted.

On the other hand, theologian Sam Tsang applies liberation hermeneutics in the sense of Edward Said to point to ruptures in liberation theology's interactions with the Hong Kong theological landscape. In the first case, Tsang addresses the earlier work of theologian Lap Yan Kung on liberation theology and Hong Kong's "predicament" in 1999, drawing from Latin American liberation theologians.[20] As Hong Kong's most prominent liberation theologian, Kung argued that Hong Kongers should stand up to the powerful corporate hegemony in Hong Kong and be a church *among* the poor instead of *for* the poor, primarily constituting of upper-middle-class people.[21] In the second place, Tsang describes the Anglican Primate, the senior bishop Reverend Paul Kwong, who opposed Hong Kong democratic reform, as an "anti-liberation liberation interpreter." Kwong drew upon Croatian American theologian Miroslav Volf's work on exclusion and embrace in the wake of the Bosnian genocide to argue that Hong Kong should remain loyal to the People's Republic of China. While Volf dramatically argues that Christian theology demands that victims embrace rather than exclude their oppressors to break the cycle of violence, Tsang points out that Kwong perversely constructs China as the other that needs to be embraced while in Volf's paradigm it is the oppressed and powerless who are othered. More importantly, Volf asserts that reconciliation is not possible without justice first. Thus, Kwong's criticism of the Umbrella Movement presents no liberative horizon for Hong Kongers. Tsang, in conclusion, asks whether liberation is an adequate vision for Hong Kong's theology, suggesting debate about liberation as an effort to contextualize power relationships, asking who the occupier and the occupied are.[22]

While it may not be best to describe these theological reflections on the Hong Kong protest as a theology of liberation, it can certainly be said that the Hong Kong church, as far as it identified with the struggles of ordinary Hong Kongers and migrant workers, indeed produced a theology from below. Moreover, the recent struggles of Hong Kong might be interpreted as the first skirmish in a new Cold War between Western powers and China. Crucial to our consideration here is the need to forge an anti-imperialist coalitional theology that resists all forms of imperialism and that is also careful that any critique of one does not implicitly endorse the other. In anticipation of these and future developments, it will be helpful to step back and reflect on past contributions of theologies from below. In particular, I turn to minjung theology.

Developed in Korea, minjung theology views itself as a contextual theology. The word *minjung* can be translated as "the people," or multitude, while minjung theology can be translated simply as "the people's theology." According to minjung theologian Tong H. Moon, the term *minjung* itself first described those under the ruling Yangban class in the Yi dynasty (1392–1910), after which the Japanese occupation reduced almost all Koreans to a minjung status. After independence, it came to generally describe anyone who did not belong to the elite class. The status of minjung is thus characterized by both class and social oppression.[23]

At the core of minjung theology is the broader Korean concept of *han*. According to minjung poet Chia-Ha Kim, it is the anger and sadness of the minjung "turned inward, hardened, and stuck to their hearts."[24] It is accumulated, transmitted, and inherited, thus internalized within a collective subconscious. According to Kim, it is also "the emotional core of anti-regime action."[25] Yet, while the sublimation of han has revolutionary potential, it is also destructive and therefore requires the dialectic tension of *dan*, meaning to "cut off," which minjung theologians view as both self-denial and the severing of the cycle of violence that han produces. That is, inasmuch as han allows for the articulation of collective and vicarious trauma, if the accumulated suffering of oneself, one's ancestors, and community is sublimated only as pure violence, then the liberation that it provides is only partial.[26] This, we shall see, resonates with the negating work of divine violence in the next chapter.

Indeed, the anti-Asian attacks during the COVID-19 pandemic, many of which were reportedly perpetrated by people with mental health conditions,[27] and the 2021 Atlanta, Georgia, massacre can both be read as involuntary expressions of a collective subconscious within the United States regarding the place of East

Asians during the pandemic in particular and in the long durée of US colonial history at large. As it were, the psychodynamic interplay between these two forms of collective subconscious begs further reflection. The Atlanta massacre, in particular, highlights the hypersexualization and fetishization of Asian women within the Western imagination as the site of forbidden desire and foreign conquest.

The layered suffering of Asian women under racialized and gendered forms of violence, in particular, calls to mind Chung's "minjung within the minjung" with whom Christ identifies.[28] To Chung, the minjung are "the oppressed, exploited, dominated, discriminated against, alienated and suppressed politically, economically, socially, culturally, and intellectually, like women, ethnic groups, the poor, workers and farmers." Thus, Christ is identified most strongly with racialized, poor women workers. As theologians of the streets, we must not theologize too quickly away from the specificity of the shooting deaths of migrant working-class Asian women, many mothers and possibly sex workers, to a broader feminist framework. More to the point, the theologies and theories that emanate from the academy too often have nothing to say directly to the plight of such women and do nothing to change their material conditions.

The basic hermeneutical task of minjung theology is to interpret the suffering of the minjung in light of scripture. And at the risk of pressing it into the framework of liberation theology, which minjung theologians resist, it also enters into the hermeneutic circle of reflection and praxis: it must be able to interpret and act. In the wake of the Atlanta massacre, many solidarity statements were published condemning "anti-Asian hate," sometimes even supporting the decriminalization of sex work and the rejection of carceral solutions, and many panel discussions were hosted around the topic of anti-Asian violence. What material or even spiritual difference did these panels make in the lives of those like the victims?

New Testament scholar Ahn Byung Mu identified the *laos* and the *ochlos*, often translated from Greek as the crowd or multitude in the Gospels and writings of Paul, as the minjung—the minjung whom Jesus had compassion for, who followed Jesus during his ministry. Kwok and Rieger, writing in the wake of Occupy Wall Street and borrowing from minjung theology, propose a theology of the multitude, in which the preferential option of the poor is brought to the fore, as God favors the poor, the proletariat, the working-class, the 99 percent. Within such a theological framework, they draw on theologian Althaus-Reid's chaotic God who stands against the order of dominant systems and Mayra Rivera's link between the otherness of God and the otherness of humans, locating the activity of God in the struggles of the Occupy movement against finance capitalism.[29] Kwok and Rieger further argue that any theology of the multitude is unfinished in nature, unlike the finished character of theologies of the empire, because it "unfolds in the movements of people encountering the movements of the divine along the way, no one person or group can ever be in control of it, no theologian can ever exhaust it."[30] It is just as well that it is so, as we can see a decade after the Occupy movement, itself born in part from the Arab Spring, that the global minjung have been continuously on the move, and so has the capitalist order along with it. All told, we must learn to sustain our reflection and praxis at both the local level of migrant Asian workers to transnational anti-capitalist and anti-imperial mass movements, which brings us to the consideration of Asian American class struggle.

ASIAN AMERICAN CLASS STRUGGLE: RACIAL CAPITALIST AFTERMARKETS AND THE RETURN TO THE SOURCE

While there is no room here for a proper treatment of the subject, it is important to note the inextricable link between race and capitalism. The racial configurations of Asian American identity and the migration flows of Asian labor are all tied to the development of the political economy. The thesis of racial capitalism, developed by Cedric Robinson, suggests that not only is capitalism racial in the sense that racial difference was produced for the purpose of capitalist accumulation, but that it in fact produced the structures of race and racialization as we know it.[31] This concept undergirds Robinson's construction of the Black radical tradition and also informs theologian Jonathan Tran's recent study of Asian Americans.

As a nod to Saidiya Hartman's notion of the afterlife of slavery,[32] Tran introduces the concept of the aftermarket of racial capitalism, arising as specific structures of economic opportunity within standing systems of racialized inequality. In common parlance, an aftermarket is a market for parts used in the maintenance of an earlier purchase, such as a car or computer. In the context of racial capitalism, "even as the political economies move on, the political arrangements leave in place inequality rife with opportunity for further exploitation."[33] Tran presents as a case study the Delta Chinese who settled in the South after Reconstruction, arguing that the racial capitalist political economy that was built up around chattel slavery and later exploited Chinese labor created "aftermarket opportunities for exploiting African American need." Here, the aftermarket is the food desert in Black Mississippi in the 1800s, which presented a business opportunity for Chinese Americans to open grocery stores, a model that grew to be so successful that it later drew Chinese from China and other parts of the United States there.

But the moral legacy of the Delta Chinese, as Tran's analysis shows, is complicated: here were African Americans in the segregated South desperate for goods and services no one else could or would provide, and Chinese Americans who were, despite not being White in the eyes of the law,[34] generating wealth by filling an aftermarket need created by the afterlife of slavery.[35] According to firsthand accounts, many Delta Chinese rationalized this as "strictly business," disavowing the consequences and exigencies of racial capitalism. Here the money form functions exactly as Marx critiqued it: the financial transaction alienates people not only from their labor but each other, severing social relations and obfuscating the racial dynamics and ethical questions at play.

The Delta Chinese grocery store was codependent upon the Black community, but it was still viewed with suspicion. The Delta Chinese eventually accrued enough material wealth and success that during the civil rights movement in the 1960s, the stores were the target of boycotts and Molotov cocktails.[36] Though the Chinese may have been viewed as "an extension of the whites," Tran shows that the Delta Chinese hardly saw themselves as becoming White but rather forged their own social class through the establishment of Chinese schools (with the help of White Southern Baptist missionaries), Chinese churches, and, of course, grocery stores. This complicated narrative also finds striking resonance in the 1992 LA riots.

In any case, this reading casts the afterlife of slavery in political-economic terms and situates the Delta Chinese as operating in the aftermarket of racial capitalism. But just as a Black/White racial binary is insufficient here, so is a Manichean ethic: we cannot simply adjudicate the Delta Chinese as either simply exploitative or survivalist. The moral tragedy, according to Tran, does not lie "in the extent of their racism or greed, but rather in the limits of their concern as a consequence of prior formations."[37] In other words, it is less important whether the Chinese were acting with racist or exploitative intent and more important that the political, economic, and legal structures in place were racist to begin with—that is, the game was rigged—which made it possible not only to defer moral culpability and ethical responsibility but, worse still, to be able to claim an equal victimhood such as through experiences of anti-Asian racism at the hands of both Whites *and* Blacks. It was just the way things were.

Tran further engages with Afro-pessimism, drawing on critiques by William Jones and Lewis Gordon of Afro-pessimism and Christian theodicy.[38] The optimism of bad-faith Christianity and the pessimism of Afro-pessimist thought, respectively, declare that either only God can liberate Black suffering or nothing can. Both equally foreclose the possibility of historical action. In this paradigm, the reality that social change is progressive, always contested and incomplete, lends itself *both* to arguments that the moral arc of the universe bends inevitably toward justice, as Martin Luther King Jr. famously said, and that efforts toward liberation—here the end of anti-Blackness—are ultimately doomed.[39] Tran's answer to this is Gordon's argument that "rejects transcendent intervention and focuses on commitment to political action, of taking responsibility for a future that offers no guarantees," so that "the movement from infinite resignation becomes existential political action."[40] This resonates with Marx's well-known critique of religion as the opiate of the masses. What Marx suggested was the abolition of religion *as* the illusory happiness of the people, a call to oppose the conditions that require illusions. I argue further that Asian American theology of liberation can hold *both* these truths: that transcendent intervention exists *and* can manifest in commitment to political action. With the weight of history behind us, we expect no guarantee from the immanent future. But still we bring the fight.

In any case, the finer points of academic debates around the primacy of race or capitalism need not ultimately concern us. Ours is a theology of the streets. Whether racism or capitalism came first has little material consequence: we already know that both must be dismantled simultaneously. The battle waged by the global Occupy movement against finance capitalism, however faltering, demands the attention of any radical Asian American theology. Indeed, such considerations as we have seen necessarily build upon all that we have discussed up to this point: the continuing settler occupation of the Americas, the anti-Black racism that structures the being of non-Black society in the afterlife of slavery, the migration and refugee flows from Asia to the United States through capitalism and imperialism in the form of alien capital, and, finally, the combined racialization and sexualization of proletarian Asian bodies.

In the wake of the pandemic, disaster capitalism has taken advantage of the preexisting inequalities not only within the structure of US society but also on a global scale.[41] Ranging from the unequal distribution of personal protective equipment to vaccine hoarding, the collapse of capitalism that both leftists and accelerationists had hoped for during the brief economic crash in March 2020 is nowhere in sight.[42] Instead, what followed was a strong recovery for the stock market, inflating the wealth of millionaires and billionaires, while for the working-class population the effects of the coronavirus not only lingered but continued to worsen as evictions increased, racial health disparities were exacerbated, and job losses among gig workers were not recuperated. While the pandemic represents a rupture whose significance and effects can only be accurately assessed decades later, it can be confidently said that racial capitalism has survived the pandemic and continues to barrel forward as strong as ever toward the climate apocalypse.

Just as liberation theology remains, as Wilmore described, a vision unfulfilled but not invalidated, so too does the popular critique of finance capitalism advanced by the Occupy movement and racial capitalism by the Black radical tradition. The theologies of the minjung and multitude resonate with any Asian American theology of liberation as theologies not only from below but also ones that reassert the preferential option for the poor. At the same time, it must be acknowledged that the multitude tautologically "contains multitudes" and is therefore, by necessity, complex and contradictory. There will be working-class Asian Americans interested in class mobility, belonging within the nation-state, and carceral systems that protect private property and small businesses. While the work of understanding these lived realities and empathizing with them is not beyond the ambit of theologies of liberation, there can be little compromise when it comes to dealing with the oppressive structures and relations of power that define the material and spiritual conditions of these multiple realities. It has not gotten easier for a rich man to enter into the kingdom of heaven than for a camel to pass through the eye of a needle. Our theology must be in the trenches of class struggle. There is no ethical alternative.

At the same time, post-colonial theorist Rey Chow warns of the potential for protest and resistance to be subverted and subsumed into the structure of capitalism itself.[43] Chow transposes Georg Lukács's model of class consciousness in Marxism onto a framework of ethnic consciousness, playing it against Weber's notion of the Protestant work ethic and the spirit of capitalism. In analyzing the relations between Chinese labor exploitation and US capitalist consumption, Chow describes them as the "commodified relations of ethnicity" wherein the "Protestant ethnic" is held captive within their own culture and whose salvation lies in resistance rather than work, as explained by Weber. But while such resistance might produce a race consciousness, and in fact forms the ontological basis of the ethnic person according to Chow, where "to be ethnic is to protest," its appearance of being grounded in moral universalisms such as democracy, human rights, freedom of speech—in a word, liberation—may be transfigured into a commodified spectacle.[44] Both Chineseness and Americanness here are produced through the configurations of global capitalism. As Chow warns, those eager to stage ethnic struggles are often not only the ethnics themselves: the most spectacular protestations of China as an abuser of human rights are often made by those in the United States with the most commercial interest in them, including politicians, missionaries, businesspeople, academics, and the media. In other words, protest generates profit. Pepsi made a commercial based on Black Lives Matter. Ethnic captivity, therefore, transubstantiates into global capital's flows. As can be seen from the increase in the wealth of the 1 percent in the wake of the pandemic and the cottage industry of anti-racism built on the George Floyd rebellion, anything short of a complete revolution that decisively ends racial capitalism will only produce greater profits while serving as what Fanon called, "hibernation therapy" or "hypnotherapy for the people."[45] Our commitment to class struggle must be ever vigilant against co-optation.

Similarly, Catherine Liu offered a self-critique of the professional-managerial class, or PMC for short. It was first articulated by John and Barbara Ehrenreich as "salaried mental workers who do not own the means of production and whose major function in the social division of labor may be described broadly as the reproduction of capitalist culture and capitalist class relations," thus a white-collar, middle-class parallel to the petite bourgeoisie.[46] In describing this class, the Ehrenreichs hoped that they would fulfill the "defining dream of the American left"—namely, that "discontented members of the middle class might join the working-class majority in a political effort to redistribute both power and wealth downward," their optimism buoyed by the New Left of the 1970s and the movements around ecology, women's liberation, and anti-war.[47] This hope was rekindled during the Occupy movement, as the Ehrenreichs concluded that "we expect to see the remnants of the PMC increasingly making common cause with the remnants of the traditional working class for, at a minimum, representation in the political process"—a hope that was not realized.[48]

In contrast, Liu cynically characterized the professional managerial class as shamelessly hoarding secularized virtue, in that "whenever it addresses a political and economic crisis produced by capitalism itself, the PMC reworks political struggles for policy change and redistribution into individual passion plays, focusing its efforts on individual acts of 'giving back' or reified forms of self-transformation."[49] Echoing Chow's analysis, the Protestant ethnic here is manifested through virtue signaling and the performance of transgression. Liu directs her polemic toward members of the professional-managerial class such as herself, with the stated purpose of identifying and liquidating the "PMC values" produced by this false consciousness. Actual transgressions in the form of class treason are called for: "We must be heretics. We should blaspheme."[50]

How should class struggle be waged from an Asian American position? Keeping in mind the gaping intraethnic inequality, we find ourselves again in the position of Choi's tragic hybridity, wherein Asians are widely perceived to occupy the middle rung of the US socioeconomic and racial order.[51] As it were, Asians continue to make gains in economic, political, and cultural arenas through growing representation in these areas, taking their place as civil society's junior partners or the petite bourgeoisie. Given this de facto position as the middle or model minority, it is useful to reflect on Amilcar Cabral's elaboration of the role of the "indigenous petite bourgeoisie" or "indigenous colonial elite" in the context of national liberation struggles in Africa. This elite, who emerged during the process of colonization, retain "some element of indigenous culture yet they live both materially and spiritually according to the foreign colonial culture."[52] While they may have strong links with the masses of the working class and local chiefs, they aspire to "a way of life which is similar if not identical with that of the foreign minority." They are "prisoners of the cultural and social contradictions of their lives" and cannot escape from their role as a marginalized class.

Cabral identifies the marginality of this class as being responsible for sociocultural conflicts of the colonial elite or the Indigenous petite bourgeoisie, played out "according to their material circumstances and level of acculturation but always at the individual level, never collectively." This daily drama produces a "frustration complex" and a compelling need to question their marginal status, and to re-discover an identity most acutely felt by African diasporas living in the colonial metropolis, represented by movements and theories such as Pan-Africanism and negritude. This diagnosis of African colonial elites and their diasporas maps onto the racial melancholy and anxieties of Asians Americans.

The solution, according to Cabral, is to "return to the source." It is not on its own an act of struggle against foreign domination; it must go beyond the individual, expressed through movements, transforming the contradiction into struggle. It is of no historical importance unless it brings "not only real involvement in the struggle for independence, but also complete and absolute identification with the hopes of the mass of the people, who contest not only the foreign culture but also the foreign domination as a whole."[53] Otherwise, it remains a form of political opportunism, a Protestant ethnic in the spirit of racial capitalism. This return is an uneven process that produces a minority that shares in the building and leadership of liberation movements and that does not truly identify with the masses except through struggle. This identification requires that in the face of destructive action by imperialist domination, the masses retain their identity, separate and distinct from that of the colonial power.[54] Yet, as Cabral writes, it is not the masses who need to assert or reassert their identity, as it is not they who have been confused but the "culturally uprooted, alienated or more or less assimilated" Indigenous petite bourgeoisie that engage in the "sociological battle in search of its identity." More pointedly, it is only a minority of the latter that does this, whereas another minority asserts the identity of the foreign dominant class, "often in a noisy manner," while the "silent majority is trapped in indecision."[55]

These historical lessons from the African liberation struggles, transposed onto the Asian American context, offer both hope and warning. It should not be expected then that a majority of Asians Americans, who do not identify as Asian American to begin with, will readily engage in revolutionary struggle and identify themselves with the racialized masses or the working-class "majority minority." At the same time, Cabral does not dismiss the contribution of the middle-class minority: even if it is expressed in forms legible to the minority colonial power rather than the masses, it still serves to activate its own class. More importantly, Cabral locates within colonial domination an apparent contradiction posed by the Indigenous petite bourgeoisie: they are simultaneously the victims of frequent humiliation by the foreigner and aware of the injustices to which the masses are subjected and of their resistance and spirit of rebellion, therefore it is from within this social class produced from colonialism itself that arise the first important steps toward mobilizing and organizing the masses for the struggle against the colonial power.[56] If Cabral is to be taken seriously, then this poses a monumental moral imperative for Asian Americans who view themselves as the "middle minority" within the imperial US racial capitalist order. Herein lies a path to Asian American liberation.

Elsewhere, writing in the context of the African diaspora in Jamaica, Guyanese revolutionary Walter Rodney suggests that the position of the Black educated person in the West Indies is "as much a part of the system of oppression as the bank managers and the plantation overseers."[57] The privileged position of the so-called intellectuals and academics is one of Babylonian captivity. In order to break free of this captivity, Rodney suggests first attacking the White hegemony within one's own discipline or line of work, then moving beyond to challenge the social myth of the multiracial society, and finally, attaching oneself to the activity of the Black masses.

One of the elements of Black power, according to Rodney, is sitting down together with any group of Black people that is prepared to sit down to talk and be listened to, to "ground": "We have to 'ground together.'" This inverts the power relation in a manner perfectly harmonious with the biblical narrative: out of the mouth of babes and sucklings God has ordained strength. In doing so "you get humility, because look who you are learning from. The system says they have nothing, they are the illiterates, they are the dark people of Jamaica."[58] The last shall be first. Cabral's return to the source and Rodney's groundings reinforce the earlier imperatives of Asian American theology of liberation: the preferential option for the poor, the invitation to social death, and landlessness as the capitulation of aspirations of belonging within the settler-colonial empire. But unlike the African or African diasporic context, the return to the source here calls for a further reconfiguration of identity that is not directly linked to any monolithic identity that the masses may possess, but rather a coalitional politics already inherent in Asian Americanness that chooses identification with the oppressed in every form.

SELL ALL THAT YOU HAVE:
A THEOLOGY OF STRUGGLE AND HAVELESSNESS

So where does this leave us? Despite the critiques of Chow and Liu of the protestant ethnic and the professional managerial class, the conclusion that each revolutionary thinker—Cabral, Rodney, and Fanon—all converge upon is that middle minorities can play a pivotal role in revolution. Whether it is phrased in terms of the colonized intellectual, Indigenous petite bourgeoisie, junior partners of civil society, or simply the Black educated person, they all identify a revolutionary possibility when this in-between person gains a radical political consciousness and casts their lot with the masses. They become race, caste, and class traitors, returning to the source, grounding with their brethren, and doing the dance of social death.

This grounding is a synergistic process: the middle minority does not lead the way; where this has happened in history, it has tended to form vanguard parties that end up betraying the masses, forming a neocolonial governing class where no fundamental transformation of social relations has taken place. We cannot be satisfied with such a jaundiced vision of liberation: we have to want it all and cannot rest until we all have it all. Across the liberative horizon, our jubilant vision is that of Isaiah: where all swords are beaten into plowshares, all spears into pruning hooks, the wolf and the lamb graze together, and the lions eat straw like the ox—demilitarization, decolonization, abolition, Indigenous sovereignty, ecological restoration, and the means of production.[59]

Having laid all the groundwork to arrive at this point, there is no need to mince words. For Asian Americans in a racial capitalist, anti-Black, settler-colonial society, what shall we do? One could start with the plain advice of John the Baptist: they that have two coats, let them give to those that have none; and those that have meat, likewise.[60] That is, freely give of our surplus. In the present capitalist mode of production, we are alienated not only from our labor and our neighbor but also our money: in Jesus's parable of the rich man with surplus grain, the latter ran out of storage for his surplus grain, and rather than give it away, he built a bigger barn. Today, the wealth of the wealthy is no longer constrained by physical storage space. What it means today, then, to limit our wealth—or, frankly, hoarding—and surplus requires much more deliberateness. The current financial system is theoretically limitless by design, and the endless accumulation of capital is antithetical to the idea of maximum wealth.

Even still, John was only preparing the way of Jesus, whose demands are even more radical, more than many of us can bear. Recall the rich, young ruler, who had kept the commandments from his youth up. Jesus, beholding him, loved him, and said to him, "Sell all that you have and distribute it to the poor; and you will have treasure in heaven; and come, follow me." [61] The idea that Jesus loved the man is striking, for in the Gospels the only individuals that Jesus was explicitly said to love were Mary, Martha, Lazarus, and perhaps also his disciple John. This makes the invitation to sell all and give to the poor and follow him so full of sincerity and meaning. Despite having faithfully kept the law of the Torah, there was still one thing lacking for wholeness.[62] The simplicity of the call is unsettling: there is nowhere to hide. What I mean by "havelessness," which can gesture to either John's "have less" or Jesus's "have not," captures not only the preferential option for the poor but also something akin to a vow of poverty, or Tran's notion of dispossession. Of course, the practice of the preferential option by Latin American Roman Catholics led to the development of liberation theology while Methodists became abolitionists active in the Underground Railroad of the 1800s. To many of us, the call to sell all that we have is either too radical or too impractical, depending on how one chooses to hear it. But even so, the past practices of others should guide us in our attempts to at least approximate this state of havelessness.

The unreasonable, unbelieveable call to havelessness, along with the many others from the Sermon on the Mount and other parables, are constant reminders of just how difficult it is to take Jesus at his word. More than faith or reason, it is an abiding love that obeys the call and not walk away grieved. What a theology of liberation asks of us is a serious political-economic commitment to continually experiment with literal interpretations of his demands. The extent to which Asian Americans have failed to see the blessedness of the poor, the mourner, the meek, the merciful, the peacemakers, the hungry, the thirsty, and the least of these is a measure of how far still the horizon of liberation is. It only makes sense to those who come to experience it and find their lot in it. Liberation theology is not a systematic theology but always an organic theology that one reaches for in the course of love and struggle with the multitude, the minjung, the 99 percent, such as when James Bui described the Vietnamese churches in the aftermath of Katrina. It may be that Bui knew about some forms of liberation theology, but there certainly was not an established Asian American or even Vietnamese one.[63]

If we are to go by national survey statistics, the median Asian American household is well above the median US household income, despite about one in every ten Asian Americans living below the poverty line.[64] This translates to saying that *most* Asians are not only better off than the average US person, but also quite likely to be upper-middle class or above. Calling Asian Americans to havelessness for the sake of wholeness, then, will quite certainly leave many sorrowful. Even John's simple redistributive vision goes against the immigrant mentality of upward mobility through hard work and individual merit, and it is important that this idea of giving should be according to the popular saying "Solidarity, not charity." Though we may give out of our abundance, we should not hold onto more than what is necessary. On the other extreme, others need to be cautioned to not too quickly martyr oneself or burn out in giving unsustainably, a passion that both religious organizations and Left movements have often exploited. Above all, we must ask, as Brazilian archbishop Dom Helder Camara did, *why* the poor are poor.

The various ideas marshalled in this chapter set a solid path toward collective liberation, particularly the practice of liberation theology in the Hong Kong movement and minjung theology against social and gender oppression, offering models of praxis in Asian American contexts. These all point to a call to be materially and spiritually engaged in mass struggle. Here, we may build on the Filipino theology of struggle, which Sano already drew upon earlier.[65] Developed by Filipino Christians involved in a broader struggle for national liberation, it was for a long time not formalized in writing because Filipino theologians were so active in struggle they had neither the time nor resources to do so.[66] Moreover, its early articulators were comfortable identifying their theological reflections with Latin American liberation theology, despite critically applying their own insights and contexts: it was less important to distinguish their theological method from others than it was that their work be useful in struggle.[67]

According to Eleazar Fernandez, the theology of struggle is a theology from below, coming from the perspective of poor and struggling people, enabling the common people to become theological subjects themselves. While it understands itself to be a contextual theology, it is not an adaptation of "some readymade theological goods from the European or North American supermarkets." Rather than asking: "How can we adapt theology to our needs?," it asks, "How can our needs create a theology which is our own?"[68] The needs of the people are what shape a theology of struggle—not a theology *about* struggle. It is an outcome of struggle, a theology *in* and *of* struggle. Being born from struggle instead of the academy, its orientation supports the praxis of struggle and does not satisfy some intellectual curiosity. Furthermore, as Fernandez writes, it is primarily a reflection of those who suffer and therefore struggle, together with those who struggle and therefore suffer. The latter are those who have chosen to struggle with the poor, resonating with every theme raised in this chapter. Rather than speaking for the people, we seek to *subjectivize*, enabling people to become theological subjects in their own right.[69] A theology of the people that denies the people their right to theologize, according to Fernandez, is an "antipeople" theology. Instead, a conversion to the people is required.

So havelessness is a material invitation to struggle along with those who suffer, to partake of their suffering in radical solidarity. Recalling a popular Tagalog saying that it is easy to be born but it is not easy to be human,[70] Fernandez writes that "it is only by way of struggle, through struggle, in being in and of the struggle, that this new humanity is to be born and find its present expressions"[71] And further, if the struggle of the poor is an expression and anticipation of a new humanity, it would also mean that one can only find one's humanity in solidarity with them.[72] This solidarity is characterized by its specificity and groundedness, not by universal assertions or denouncements about human rights. A process of disalienation takes place, as Isaiah also prophesied: "They shall not build and another inhabit, they shall not plant and another eat, for as the days of the tree, so the days of my people, and my chosen shall enjoy the work of their hands."[73] How radical this statement is should not be lost on those of us so conditioned by a capitalist system of production, which separates the worker from not only their labor but also their neighbor in capitalist competition.

It is thus as Charles Avilla describes the role of the theologian: like waves of the ocean; they happen to be more conspicuous parts of the ocean but themselves are part of the ocean, and of the same substance with it.[74] The ocean calls to us. Return to the source, ground with your brethren, sell all that you have, betray race and class, struggle with those who suffer. The economic redistribution that is a part of these calls is not so much about being someone's savior as it is about becoming dispossessed. In Tran's political-economic story of Asian Americans, vignettes are offered as models of refusal to participate in the aftermarket of racial capitalism. One example is Bobby Jue, whose family started a store in Hollandale, Mississippi, in 1948:

> He learned that while he worked a taxing eighty hours a week, his customers counted hours differently, from "can to can't." He visited homes and came to see that the cheap wallpaper he sold his customers did not cover so much as serve as walls. . . . As an adult, Bobby spent time picking cotton alongside some of his customers, simply to better understand their lives. He didn't last half the day, but he caught another glimpse of the gulf that separated their lives from his, which is to say he understood more fully their lives and his.[75]

But Bobby also knew that the grocery store he had operated was economically exploitative, a fact he still regrets.

THE YEARS THE LOCUST HATH EATEN: A NOTE ON REPARATIONS

In 1969, civil rights activist James Forman jumped onto the pulpit of Riverside Church in New York City, interrupting the service to demand $500 million in reparations from White churches and synagogues, corresponding to approximately fifteen dollars per Black person. It was the chief demand of a Black manifesto that began thus:

> We the black people assembled in Detroit, Michigan for the National Black Economic Development Conference are fully aware that we have been forced to come together because racist white

America has exploited our resources, our minds, our bodies, our labor. For centuries we have been forced to live as colonized people inside the United States, victimized by the most vicious, racist system in the world. We have helped to build the most industrial country in the world.

The manifesto goes on to outline how the reparations should be spent, including the establishment of a Southern land bank, four major publishing industries, four television networks, a research skills center, and a Black university in the South. It also outlined actions necessary to win their demands, such as sit-in demonstrations, "disruption of racist churches and synagogues," and "find within the white community those forces which will work under the leadership of blacks to implement these demands by whatever means necessary." Further, the manifesto asserts that "to win our demands we will have to declare war on the white Christian churches and synagogues and this means we may have to fight the total government structure of this country. Let no one here think that these demands will be met by our mere stating them."[76]

Unsurprisingly, the overall reaction to the manifesto was outright rejection, with *Christianity Today* reporting the headline "'Black Manifesto' Declares War on Churches"[77] and *Time* magazine exactly five months later wrote that "since Forman first issued his arrogantly worded 'Black Manifesto' in Detroit last April, only an estimated $22,000 has trickled into the coffers of his National Black Economic Development Conference. Forman's demands have been successful, however, as a catalyst in moving churches to examine their consciences."[78] The *Time* article continued in its patronizing tone, noting, for example, that the Central Committee of the World Council of Churches rejected the concept of reparations but voted to distribute $500,000 "not to Forman but to organizations of oppressed racial groups whose purposes are 'not inconsonant' with those of the World Council." Other Christian and Jewish organizations similarly rejected the idea of reparations but moved to support efforts to "fight poverty and racial discrimination" in ways that they retain ultimate control, keeping agency firmly in the hands of the White organizations. This is charity, not solidarity. Fifty years on, the response to the manifesto and reparations more generally continues to be framed more often as spiritual tests as much as financial ones, and almost always elides political-economic framing (despite mounting evidence that unconditional cash transfers are highly effective).[79]

Reparations, in part, is an attempt to financially quantify the downstream economic effects of certain historical injustices, such as the $20,000 and formal apology issued by Ronald Reagan to each Japanese American survivor of the Japanese incarceration during the Second World War. No reparation has been paid in any amount by the US government to African Americans, including the "Forty Acres and a Mule" promised to previously enslaved families by Union General William Sherman's 1865 wartime field order during the Civil War, which of course never materialized. An ongoing point of debate regarding reparations for slavery revolves around the question of whether reparations should be made to African descendants of slaves or Black people in general. Notably, Forman's Black manifesto did not demand payment to individuals but for the establishment of institutions that support Black flourishing, potentially sidestepping this bone of contention.[80]

Yet, as pastors Duke Kwon and Gregory Thompson point out, the economic aspect of reparations is a critical one but arguably not even the primary one—they frame White supremacy as a *cultural* theft, not merely of wealth but also of truth and power, so that the financial restitution of reparations is necessary but insufficient.[81] Still, what do these have anything to do with Asian Americans in particular? According to Kwon and Thompson, while Zacchaeus's position was one of culpability and restitution, the good Samaritan's is one of restoring the wronged to wholeness. Thus, they argue that reparations are the repair of White supremacy's cultural theft through both these points of view. All told, assembling together the ideas of this chapter and the last converges on the need for reparations—whether for slavery and its afterlives, or Land Back and Indigenous sovereignty—as a necessary aspect of Asian American liberation, no strings attached.

As case studies, Tran's historical analysis of the Delta Chinese and ethnographic account of Redeemer Community Church in Bayview/Hunter's Point, a historically under-resourced area of San Francisco, together show that the aftermarket effects of racial capitalism structure the political-economic reality in which we attempt to act justly, love mercy, and walk humbly. These ultimately lead to the most practical of questions regarding how we conduct our lives: where we live, where we shop, who we socialize with, how we make meaning. Most importantly, what the frame of racial capitalism shows is that individual choices alone are not sufficient to dismantle capitalism. Individualistic forms of pious or politically correct living may temporarily absolve guilt complexes while buying into capitalism's mechanism of penance.[82] Instead, the structure of liberation requires collective action, shared imagination, and a million experiments in living otherwise.

At the same time, while Tran comes close to rejecting the ontological reading of Afro-pessimism in favor of the political-economic frame of Black Marxism, I argue that *both* the material and metaphysical approaches can coexist and inform each other productively. Material relations, whether de jure or de facto, attempt to describe external processes such as racial capitalism while metaphysical relations focus on internal processes that become fashioned as ontology. The negotiation between the two forms the intersubjective experience that Eng and Han's work illuminates. It is a third space in which our identity is formed: ontology and materiality *together* structure how we live and move and have our being. That the drama of race plays out in both arenas should be clear, despite what sophisticated arguments or polemics may say. They are inextricably intertwined. Similarly, our desires—the libidinal economy of Afro-pessimism that attempts to supersede political economy—are shaped together by our internal longings, our social worlds, and capitalism, a point that will bring us to the final chapter. Fanon's lamentations in *Black Skins, White Masks* will be held together with those in *Wretched of the Earth*; one addresses the libidinal economy and the other the colonial, material world.

I moved to Dearborn, Michigan, for work in late 2021, after the coronavirus pandemic had run rampant across the country several times over, and by then the United States was largely ready to believe it was ready to move on and resume business as usual. Dearborn sits in the southwest corner of Detroit, having resisted annexation into the city of Detroit, arguably the largest Black city in the United States.[83] The birthplace of the automobile, a last stop on the Underground Railroad, the deathplace of Vincent Chin,[84] it is a historic city in decline. Here, you can find houses for sale ranging from millions of dollars to just a few thousand, the latter being either severely dilapidated or foreclosed and on auction. According to 2020 US Postal Service data, the vacancy rate in the city of Detroit is just about one in five, the lowest since 2015, and in some parts of the city it is one in three.[85] Dearborn, on the other hand, is the town of Henry Ford, where the company is headquartered along with its factories and developments. It is also the heart of Arab America, estimated to have anywhere from one- to two-thirds of its residents being of Arab heritage.[86] First arriving from Lebanon and Syria as a result of civil wars in the late 1800s, others began to migrate from Yemen, Palestine, Iraq, and elsewhere in the Middle East to service the auto industry until its collapse after the Second World War. But by then, a significant Arab American community had taken root, and they were fortunate enough to be counted White during the reign of its infamous segregationist mayor Orville Hubbard (1942–1978) that made Dearborn one of the Unites States' many sundown towns.[87] In this case, thousands upon thousands of Black laborers travelled to Dearborn to work in its auto industry but made sure to leave by the end of the day on the very real threat of death. Driving through the different parts of the larger Metro Detroit area, what seems to be a theoretical discussion on the aftermarket of racial capitalism or the afterlife of slavery turns into visceral experiences. The road signs change, the lawns and buildings change, the people change.

Then suddenly questions about how to live out one's politics and theology become uncomfortably tangible: What would it mean to buy a house, to own land, and if so, where? If you have children, where would you send them to school? Where do you go for food, or church, or work, or play? If someone asks for money, do you turn away? Where do you spend your money? Where do you form relationships? All these choices have ramifications in the social reality that will come to structure our lives and our health. Though the Flint water crisis that happened an hour's drive away is not related to Detroit's problems, Detroit remains a site of environmental racism, not least because it is still the heart of the US auto industry, with the Big Three: Chrysler, General Motors, and Ford.

At the end of the day, there is a cost. But at the same time, Detroit is a city that is full of life in the cracks. Even as abandoned lots and boarded-up houses pepper the urban landscape, so is there the most vibrant urban-farming communities I have seen in any large city, just as the Detroit Black Community Food Security Network recently replaced *Security* with *Sovereignty* in its name. Grace Lee Boggs has left a deep legacy of activism and activists (known affectionately as "Grace babies") who carry on her and James Boggs's work in Detroit, not least well-known activist adrienne marie brown. Long fights continue to be waged against eviction, high property tax, racist policing, surveillance technology, and food insecurity. But these signs of life, alternate ways of living and relating, are not narratives of a city that is "bouncing back," a poisonous narrative that whitewashes gentrification, capitalism, and co-optation. Instead, it is simply a continuation of a long legacy of survival, resistance, and fugitivity in a post-industrial city.

The call is not to fix or save or even heal but to be with, to struggle alongside, and to follow—to ground with one's brethren, to return to the source, to betray race and class. As Grace Lee Boggs writes, reading both Marx and Jesus as "the materialism of rooting ideas in real life and practice, going beyond talk and ideas alone," we come to see that real poverty is "the belief that the purpose of life is acquiring wealth and owning things" and real wealth is "not the possession of property but the recognition that our deepest need, as human beings, is to keep developing our natural and acquired powers and to relate to other human beings."[88] Further, "We must have the courage to walk the talk, but we must also engage in the continuing dialogues that enable us to break free of old categories and create the new ideas that are necessary to address our realities, because revolutions are made not to prove the correctness of ideas but to begin anew." [89]

Still, with reality pressing hard on all sides, what does it mean now to become Black and outcaste, to sell all that we have, to die and begin anew? Do we really want to know the answer?

POWER

7.

THROUGH THE GAS

Breaking the Immanent Frame

They are middle-class intellectuals. We are not intellectuals. We're working class, there's a gap there. They have this concept about fighting the police, that they wait for the police to strike first and then they respond. For us, we are being assaulted by the police our whole lives, they have always struck first, they treat us like shit, this is our justification. The whole structure of the police and the state is assaulting. How can you say we have to wait for them to hurt us first? They've been assaulting us our whole lives and nobody cares or listens. For us this is the only way to like, express ourselves, to have our voices heard. We've been completely excluded from society, but people need to know we exist, for us, this is class struggle, there's no other way.

—Thalugaz, "Thalugaz Interview"

I, John Brown, am quite certain that the crimes of this guilty land will never be purged away but with blood. I had, as I now think vainly, flattered myself that without very much bloodshed it might be done.

—John Brown, in W. E. B. Du Bois, *John Brown*

Was not Christ crucified. And by signs in the heavens that it would make known to me when I should commence the great work—and until the first sign appeared, I should conceal it from the knowledge of men—And on the appearance of the sign, (the eclipse of the sun last February) I should arise and prepare myself, and slay my enemies with their own weapons.

—Nat Turner, "The Confessions of Nat Turner (1831)"

In February 2020, student protests broke out in Thailand following the dissolution of the Future Forward Party, which appealed to a majority of young voters in the previous year's election. The party was replaced by the runner-up, the Phalang Pacharat Party, controlled by the military junta. Protests continued to escalate into the year, calling for the resignation of the prime minister Prayut Chan-o-cha, the drafting of a new constitution, and the reform of the Thai monarchy. The latter demand was unheard of, given Thailand's draconian lèse-majesté law, which forbids any insult of the monarchy. The movement declined later in the year following COVID-19 measures, prosecution of protest leaders, and violent crackdowns on protesters.

Still, protest activities resurged the following year. In August 2021, an independent group formed known as Thalugaz (through the gas), a play on the name of a larger, earlier group Thalufa (through the sky).[1] Centered around the economically depressed and over-policed Din Daeng area of Bangkok, the leaderless group largely consists of vocational students or youths of lower-class backgrounds.[2] According to one of its coordinators, Thalugaz was formed because some working-class protesters in Bangkok "felt excluded by the mainstream protest groups who always promote non-violent means of resistance." "For us that's not enough," they write: "We can't wait any longer for this confrontation with the state, we need to do something now, different from the mainstream."[3] They describe Din Daeng as a slum and the police like "a mafia that we have to live under. They take everything we have, they dominate us and we have to totally obey them. They're the main problem in the area, everyone hates them. It's like within the neighbourhood we're living in a totally corrupt mafia-run police state."

Many members attribute the reason for their participation in Thalugaz to the abuse of power by the government, the unjust use of violence against protesters, and the failed COVID-19 response. Annusorn Unno, a professor at Thammasat University who interviewed Thalugaz members, notes that the youths joined the protests for these reasons, but the ensuing violent clashes with the police stirred resentment, leading to an "anger that keeps the Thalu Gas protesters fighting."[4] In contrast to Thalufa as a whole, which also clashed with police forces through water cannons, tear gas, and rubber bullets (and later also live rounds), the faction of protesters who eventually became organized as Thalugaz resolved to fight back, including through the use of Molotov cocktails, slingshots, and firecrackers. One protester said, "I wanted to strike back at the police because they use violence first." A similar evolution from nonviolent to violent resistance can be seen in the escalation of Myanmar's nonviolent and creative Spring Revolution in 2021 into an armed People's Defensive War against the military junta, which had killed hundreds of unarmed protesters.[5]

The role of (non)violence in protest and resistance has long been a point of debate, both among observers and participants alike. It is a question with no universal answer, despite what popular discourse might lead us to believe, because agency ultimately lies in the hands of those who struggle against their oppressors. Still, general principles can be found, and in the spirit of asking as we walk, it is useful to reflect on praxis. In this chapter and the next, I discuss questions surrounding the role of (non)violence, first in the context of struggle for the freedom of oneself and others, and secondly when lethal violence is dealt toward our own. Discussions of violence in such contexts tend to focus on its *physical* manifestations, whether against humans or property, whereas the larger backdrop of structural violence and its material effects is left unexamined. To be certain, the themes discussed throughout this book—settler colonialism, racism, capitalism, sexism, and so on—can be understood as the structural aspects of various forms of violence that liberation theology struggles against. The following chapters shift the focus onto the physical aspects, even if theoretical ideas intervene, of everyday violence that we confront in struggle and otherwise.

Many of us may not be directly confronted with the question of whether or not to employ physical violence, or to "strike first," as Thalugaz insists (which may call for introspection with regards to our class position and interest in maintaining the status quo). Still, the considerations of this chapter regarding the role of violence will lead us to an open, indeterminate space of play beyond the limits of ethics and teach us something about the nature of law and grace. Further, various characteristics of an Asian American theology of liberation—subjectless, landlessness, beinglessness, and havelessness—all point to a broader analysis of power relations.

PACIFISM AS PATHOLOGY

If Asians are to be engaged in class struggle and downward mobility, and indeed as a form of incarnational politics, how is it to be carried out? Where is the place of Asians in Black riots, class warfare, and revolutionary struggle? While complexities exist in any mass uprising and rebellion, there also occur splittings forced by precipitating events that impose a binary logic, such as in partisan politics, revolutionary struggle, or conservative eschatologies. Will there be a clean separation of the chaff from the wheat and the goats from the sheep? Then there is the more immediate question of strategy, in particular the role of physical violence in the fight for liberation.

The obsession with absolute nonviolence as the singular means of achieving meaningful social change is deeply ingrained within the US moral character. Peaceful protests are often used to condemn violent ones; the destruction of private or even state property is deemed to never be an appropriate response to the destruction of Black life. Here the model-minority myth is often activated, legitimizing only certain kinds of protests, whereas riots, looting, and the burning of police cars and precincts are condemned. Following Chow, peaceful protests conveniently serve the purposes of the state and racial capitalism: they allow for the expression of dissent while leaving the broader structures—and indeed the sources of structural violence—intact. But both forms of protest express the voice of the minjung, the oppressed, the unheard, the blood of Abel crying to God from the ground. They are the key texts upon which theologians of the streets must perform exegesis.

The question of violence in the struggle for liberation has been much grappled with by revolutionaries and organic intellectuals engaged in actual struggle. It is those who have put their lives and safety at stake that we must listen to, not armchair theologians who pontificate from their positions of comfort. Guyanese revolutionary Walter Rodney asked, "By what standard of morality can the violence used by a slave to break his chains be considered the same as the violence of a slave master?" The violence of Blacks who have been "oppressed, suppressed, depressed and repressed for four centuries" cannot be equated with the violence of White fascists. According to Rodney, "Violence aimed at the recovery of human dignity and at equality cannot be judged by the same yardstick as violence aimed at maintenance of discrimination and oppression."[6] The point here is not to specifically advocate for armed struggle or even violence in general but rather to prevent the question from being foreclosed. The unquestionable moral high ground afforded to nonviolent resistance must indeed be questioned, and we must ask whom it truly serves and protects.

To broach the question of violence in the struggle for liberation, I first turn to Ward Churchill's study of the political and psychological—indeed, pathological—dimensions of pacifism. Pacifism is an ideology that precludes violence dealt toward others and, in practice, inanimate objects while not necessarily preventing violence inflicted on oneself. Whereas the emotional courage and at times costly sacrifice required by a true pacificist position is readily acknowledged, it is its effectiveness as a strategy in revolutionary struggle that is questioned.

Churchill first examines the extreme case of the Jewish Holocaust as an example of pacifism manifested in passivity in the face of genocide, grounded in a profound desire for "business as usual" and the belief that by continuing normal day-to-day activities and "not alienating anyone" a more or less humane Jewish policy might be morally imposed on the Nazi state.[7] This brings into question the moral superiority implied by pacifism's renunciation of physical violence, judging the legitimacy of any actor solely based on the presence of violence. As we know, the Holocaust ended not through pacifist or nonviolent methods but through the massive application of armed force, similar to the US war in Vietnam ending more as a result of Vietnamese communist resistance than anti-war protesters.[8]

Turning to less extreme examples, Martin Luther King Jr. and Mohandas Gandhi, his inspiration, won their political victories in no small part because of the violence enacted upon their opponents by others. Nonviolent appeals were rendered not only more reasonable but also as the only accepted form of protest. The essential contradiction of pacifist praxis, Churchill writes, is that survival in any confrontation with state power depends on the restraint of the state in its use of violence, whereas for victory it requires the active presence of a counterbalancing violence that renders the pacifist the more agreeable opponent. Indeed, King was aware of this contradiction and deliberately leveraged the threat of anti-state violence to advance his pacifist agenda.[9] The latter was a *strategic* choice that only worked within a larger system of violent *and* nonviolent actions. As the events following the George Floyd riots have similarly shown, the concessions of the state to pacifists—never mind armed shopkeepers defending against looters—act as counterrevolutionary forces that delegitimize the more violent factions, even if the violence is merely directed toward physical property.[10]

The general maintenance of nonviolence as the foundation of US activism, according to Churchill, constitutes a politics of the comfort zone rather than a truly pacifist formation. At its height are mass demonstrations that feature an impressive lineup of speakers critiquing the state, having secured permits for lawful assembly and the cooperation of the police, or performative, direct, nonviolent actions where specific plans are made for activists to be arrested, such as for the occupation of restricted areas and refusal to disperse, in the most cooperative manner with the police and released after a short time. In exchange for not disrupting business as usual and the functioning of the state, the general safety of the nonviolent dissenters is guaranteed. To the extent that such forms of counterrevolutionary resistance are tolerable to the state, they are in fact natural metabolic byproducts of capitalism produced through the commodification of ethnic relations, and in the end they produce a more functional and efficient form of capitalism. This form of ritualistic opposition, Churchill writes, can be readily sublimated within the comfort zone by the continuation of business as usual.

Within the parameters set by the state, nondisruptive dissenters are free to carry out activities that prefigure their revolutionary society yet which ironically cannot be brought into being by nonviolent tactics alone. This prefiguration allows inaction in the "mother country" to be linked rhetorically and symbolically to Third World liberation struggles and, from there, "solidarity" with non-White armed revolutionary struggles within the United States itself. And in the event that positive social transformation is achieved, the prefigurative nonviolent "experts" are well-positioned to be leaders in post-revolutionary society, whereas if the colonizing state prevails, the nonviolent movement has a natural fallback position, thus preserving "the comfort zone of "White skin privilege" regardless of the outcome.

Churchill identifies three characteristics of pacifism as pathology: delusion, regarding the efficacy of pacifism alone as a revolutionary agenda; racism, displacing state violence onto people of color and the Third World; and suicidal tendency, in attempting to impel a nonviolent state response.[11] That violence can be avoided in revolutionary movements in Western countries but not in the Third World amounts to American exceptionalism and, according to Canadian activist Mike Ryan, "has become a form of catharsis, a practice that allows us to cleanse our souls of the guilt of our white skin privilege for ourselves and for each other without posing a threat either to the state or ourselves."[12] All this applies quite readily to light-skinned professional-managerial class Asian Americans in their comfort zones.

But rather than replacing hegemonic pacifism with a "cult of terror," Churchill proposes:

> Any revolutionary movement within advanced capitalist nations must develop the broadest possible range of thinking/action by which to confront the state. This should be conceived not as an array of component forms of struggle but as a continuum of activity stretching from petitions/letter writing and so forth through mass mobilization/demonstrations, onward into the arena of armed self-defense, and still onward through the realm of "offensive" military operations (e.g., elimination of critical state facilities, targeting of key individuals within the governmental/corporate apparatus, etc.). All of this must be apprehended as a holism, as an internally consistent liberatory process applicable at this generally-formulated level to the late capitalist context no less than to the Third World. From the basis of this fundamental understanding—and, it may be asserted, only from this basis—can a viable liberatory praxis for North America emerge.[13]

In other words, to not forbid violence is not the same as requiring it. Instead, it becomes but one of the means by which liberation may be won, thus Malcolm X's call for freedom and justice "by any means necessary" and, further, that "tactics based solely on morality can only succeed when you are dealing with people who are moral or a system that is moral."[14] In any case, these reflections should begin to clarify the nature of violence in some of the recent mass protests in Asia, including the prodemocracy protests in Hong Kong and the anti-coup resistance in Myanmar.

Leaving the problem of nonviolence aside, I now turn to the question of violence itself. To reflect on violence at the intersection of liberation struggles, politics, and religion requires a particular degree of care. Religious fanaticism and nationalistic jingoism have easily recruited violence as a justified means to certain ends. Justifications of violence in service of liberation, in turn, even if in self-defense, must be made with extreme care, as often the same rationalizations are employed by those on the other side. With this caution in mind, the abolitionist John Brown provides an interpretive key to the role of violence in struggle, particularly within the context of what might be called militant allyship.

Inspired by the Haitian revolution, Brown led a band of twenty-one raiders—including escaped slaves and three of Brown's sons—in seizing the federal arsenal at Harpers Ferry in West Virginia in 1859, what was intended to have been the first step in a guerilla war in the Appalachian Mountains against slaveholders. The raid failed, as the local militia was reinforced by federal troops, and ended with ten of the raiders killed, five escaping, and the remaining seven tried and executed, including Brown. Through his writings, interviews, and courtroom speeches that were infused with appeals to ideals of the nation and the Bible, Brown divided the country in two, marking a prelude to the Civil War. Brown described both the violence he committed and the violence committed against him as part of a process by which the land was purged of its sins—the sins of slavery—with blood, lifting the interpretive frame into a realm that requires theological reasoning about politics, or political theology.

Brown's story reveals the limits of ethics in what Ted Smith calls the "frame of universalizable immanent ethical obligations," which roughly means moral duty based on ethical reasoning about cause and effect. Indeed, in Talal Asad's study of the phenomenon of suicide bombing, the suicide bomber is also cast as a figure through which liberal democracies work out the repressed knowledge of the lawless violence at work in their own founding and ongoing existence. As such, attempts to explain suicide bombing "tell us more about liberal assumptions of religious subjectivities and political violence than they do about what is being ostensibly explained."[15] Thus rather than seeking to explain John Brown, the prerogative here is to situate Brown's violence within his own political theology and to interpret it on his terms.

Brown was a polarizing figure, even in his time. The view of Brown as a fanatic turned into debates about the possibility of mental illness despite Brown's outright rejection of the insanity plea his lawyers attempted to introduce in his trial. Viewed as a freedom fighter on the other side, Brown's violence, placed alongside the violence of the soldiers in the American Revolution, could also be grafted onto legitimations of state violence. Placed in continuity with violent means used by the state to achieve the equality of all races, Brown could be refashioned as a national hero, as indeed present-day state-sponsored memorials at Harpers Ferry, North Elba, and Osawatomie show. Whether terrorist or heroic revolutionary, freedom fighter or fanatic, appeals to a "higher law" in either case end in religiously motivated violence, and in particular violence without state sanction.[16]

As Smith argues, both interpretations of Brown assume that violence can be justified in an "immanent frame of moral obligations," which can contain arguments in just war traditions and pacifism grounded in the belief that violence leads to more violence, but they cannot make sense of commitments to violence or nonviolence that "make no earthly sense." More importantly, both categories assume the monopoly of the state on legitimate violence.[17] Even as a freedom fighter, the figure of Brown can be assimilated into the state as the center of legitimate violence—it is Brown's violence that is the exception and requires justification. Smith therefore proposes political theology as the means to move beyond the frame of immanent ethics and to reason about divine violence. [18] Separating politics from theology does not solve the problem of extralegal violence, as critics of religious violence in a post-9/11 world might argue; instead it can underwrite new forms of violence, especially violence that serves to enforce the separation of religion and politics and also extralegal forms of state violence carried out domestically and abroad.[19]

In contrast, Walter Benjamin proposes an incomplete translation whereby the theological cannot be entirely secularized into the political. The gap between the two measures the distance between law and justice in Benjamin's *Critique of Violence*, which interrogates what distinctions among sanctioned and unsanctioned violence reveal about the nature of violence. The circle of justification created by legal means and ends gives rise to the state's monopoly on legitimate violence, so that violence, "when not in the hands of the law, threatens it not by its ends that it may pursue but by its mere existence outside the law."[20] Thus, for justified law to remain as such, it must either destroy or absorb any violence that exists outside of it. Benjamin calls this force exerted by the system "mythic violence," taking the form of lawmaking (*rechtsetzende*) and law-preserving (*rechtserhaltende*) violence, combining the binding obligation of justice with the arbitrariness of law. As the ends that mythic violence seeks exist outside of the circle of justification, its character is not instrumental but rather expressive, the same which resonates in the "shock and awe" strategy employed by the United States in Iraq and, before that, Hiroshima and Nagasaki. In its archetypal form, Benjamin writes, mythic violence is a "manifestation of the gods"—not a manifestation of their will but simply of their existence.

What breaks the cycle of mythic violence is divine (*göttliche*) violence. The manifestation of divine justice in this world, it destroys systems of obligation without creating new ones, as mythic violence does: "If mythic violence brings at once guilt and expiation, divine power only expiates."[21] Divine violence opens up an incommensurability between commandment and action, inviting free response and responsibility. Rather than translating this *Entsetzung* as the "suspension" of law, Smith proposes instead the "relief" or "deposition" of law, relieving the law of its binding power enforced by mythic violence. While Slavoj Žižek encourages us to "fearlessly identify divine violence with positively existing historical phenomena, thus avoiding any obscurantist mystification,"[22] Smith argues that the task rather is to see divine violence in the negation at work in every moment, a "critical discernment that can hear the groaning of all creation."[23] Within this framework, Brown should be properly understood as what Benjamin called a "great criminal," one who "in defying the law, lays bare the violence of the legal system, the judicial order itself."[24] Such a characterization does not legitimate nor condemn Brown's actions but instead, in the relief of the law, reveals the limits of ethical reasoning about certain forms of violence.

But what of this law? Language of a higher law defined a structured but relatively empty space that was charged with its own significance even as it was open to many different kinds of content and compatible with many different sorts of worldviews.[25] Most recently, resistance to discourse involving higher laws is bolstered by the predominance of both Islamic and Christian extremists who invoke such language.[26] To be sure, abolitionists also often invoke a higher law. The abolitionist imagination, according to Andrew Delbanco, occurs when one identifies "a heinous evil and want[s] to eradicate it—not tomorrow, not next year, but now," a sensibility that grates against a politics of the comfort zone.[27] Doing away wholesale appeals to a higher law does not remove the possibility of mythic violence and instead precludes any possibility of thinking critically about forms of higher law. Delbanco, along with others, including Brown, Smith argues, assume that this higher law takes the form of codes of obligation and prohibition—in other words, the same as earthly laws.[28]

Smith calls this "code fetishism," characterized not by a belief in a higher law or the content of any such law but rather the sense that the highest good could be expressed best in the form of a code, or "something like the perfection of public policy."[29] The fulfilment of the law in this sense, then, takes the form of perfect adherence to the code rather than transcending it. In contrast, the "messianic fulfilment of the law," as Giorgio Agamben interprets Benjamin's relief of law, is best understood as the turning of the imperative of law into an indicative of divine justice. This indicative, Smith writes, serves to negate absolute obligations in this age in ways that invite a free response in history that is permeated by the presence of God.[30] The divine violence of the higher law relativizes the whole imperative mood; the proclamation of the Kingdom of God does not issue a new set of commandments. The indicative of the Gospel relates to the world through *negation*, forming what Jacob Russelby calls an "iconoclastic utopia" rather than a "blueprint utopia."

These considerations, Smith argues, cannot legitimate Brown's violence through some divine code, but the notion of divine violence renders it legible: the raid was made possible by "a higher law that revealed the whole edifice of laws sustaining slavery for the organized violence that they were."[31] Divine violence can thus "break the hold of some particular ethical system and then invite but not determine responses that include ethical deliberation." It is outside the limit of ethics, "the end of visions of the normative that take it to be complete in itself,"[32] and therefore it is necessary to work in two registers: using the language of both divine and ethical violence.

FANON: DECOLONIZATION AS MYTHIC VIOLENCE

Smith's analysis of John Brown is productively complicated by Brown's identity as a White abolitionist. Once again, Asian American positionality, whether as middle minority or racially triangulated, say, in the sense of Claire Jean Kim,[33] precludes wholesale identification with neither John Brown nor Nat Turner. Moving laterally along Kim's foreigner/insider axis, I turn to Fanon's analysis of decolonial violence as a counterbalance. The first corrective that Fanon offers is a combined analysis of race and class: "In the colonies the economic infrastructure is also a superstructure. The cause is effect. You are rich because you are white, you are white because you are rich. This is why a Marxist analysis should always be slightly stretched when it comes to addressing the colonial issue."[34] Within the context of the settler-colonial state, a theology of landlessness offers Asian Americans the possibility of carefully identifying or being in solidarity with the colonized Indigenous people of the Americas.

The (settler)colonial context, according to Fanon, is characterized by the dichotomy it inflicts on the world, whereas decolonization unifies the world by a radical decision to remove its heterogeneity, by unifying it on the grounds of nation and sometimes race.[35] When an authentic liberation struggle has been fought, there is "an effective eradication of the superstructure borrowed by these [colonized] intellectuals from the colonialist bourgeois circles." In the meantime, the colonized world is stabilized by the release of constant "muscular tension" in the colonized, resulting from everyday life in the colonized world by means of fratricidal violence and internecine feuds, the fatalism of religion, and the emotional release of dance or possession.[36] In other words, violence is not absent when it is not employed in revolutionary struggle; it is merely sublimated in other potentially deadly means.

The challenge, Fanon declares, is to "seize this violence as it realigns itself. Whereas it once reveled in myths and contrived ways to commit collective suicide, a fresh set of circumstances will now enable it to change directions." For the colonized, this violence represents absolute praxis. The colonized person liberates themself in and through violence, and this praxis enlightens the militant because it shows them the means and the end. Here, the militant is one who works, where "to work means to works towards the death of the colonist."[37] In fact, Fanon points out, the colonist has always shown them the path they should follow to liberation: "The colonial regime owes its legitimacy to force and at no time does it ever endeavor to cover up this nature of things."[38]

Thus, while Smith's deliberations on Brown's crusade led to subtle meditations on the political theology of violence, Fanon offers an incisive and decisive assessment of what the colonized must do to be liberated from their colonizer. Indeed, "the work of the colonist is to make even dreams of liberty impossible for the colonized. The work of the colonized is to imagine every possible method for annihilating the colonist." The Manichaeanism of the colonist produces a Manichaeanism of the colonized: "The arrival of the colonist signified syncretically the death of indigenous society, cultural lethargy, and petrification of the individual. For the colonized, life can only materialize for from the rotting cadaver of the colonist."[39] But just as the colonial condition produces reductive binaries, so will the divine violence of decolonization break the mythic violence that sustains it. The liberation struggle, which "aims at a fundamental redistribution of relations between men, cannot leave intact either form or substance of the people's culture." More to the point, after the struggle is over, there is not only the demise of colonialism, but also the demise of the colonized, a meeting of divine violence and decolonial violence.[40] What arises in its stead is what Fanon calls a "new humanism."

The contradictions of Asian American identity can be read into Fanon's analysis of "colonized intellectuals" in the colonial setting, also Cabral's Indigenous petite bourgeoisie and Wilderson's junior partners in civil society. This "caste," according to Fanon, invests their repressed aggression in a "barely veiled wish to be assimilated to the colonizer's world" and "call for ways of freeing more and more slaves and ways of organizing a genuine class of the emancipated, whereas the masses have no intention of looking on as the chances of individual success improve."[41] The bourgeoisie in underdeveloped countries—relative to the metropolis of the colonizer—has "unreservedly and enthusiastically adopted the intellectual reflexes characteristic of the metropolis" and "alienated to perfection its own thoughts and grounded its consciousness in typically foreign notions." Indeed, Fanon says plainly, "theirs is a wish to identify permanently with the bourgeois representatives from the metropolis."[42]

In contrast, the masses want to take the place of the colonists, not simply to be equal to them and to sit with them in boardrooms and first-class lounges, as the project of neoliberal inclusion promises. "The colonized intellectual's insertion into this human tide will find itself on hold because of his curious obsession with detail," and so forgetting the very purpose of the struggle: the defeat of colonialism. The distractions and comforts afforded by White adjacency and promised by the model-minority myth go a long way toward disabling the return to source: "The people, on the other hand, take a global stance from the start. 'Bread and land: how do we go about getting bread and land?' And this stubborn, apparently limited, narrow-minded aspect of the people is finally the most rewarding and effective working model."[43]

Equally relevant is Fanon's diagnosis of the attempts of the Black diaspora to identify with an Africa that does not exist, resonating with the nostalgia of Asian diaspora. The Black diaspora in the United States, Central, and Latin America "needed a cultural matrix to cling to," and around the time of Fanon participated in a project of negritude, that unconditionally affirmed a universal African culture. But they soon realized that their "existential problems" differed from those faced by Africans, and that the only common denominator was that they all "defined themselves in relation to the whites. But once the initial comparisons had been made and subjective feelings had settled down, the black Americans realized that the objective problems were fundamentally different." Thus, negritude came up against the limitation posed by "phenomena that take into account the historicizing of men."[44] Similarly, Asian diasporic attempts to theorize or theologize through Asian cultural traditions run the risk of self-orientalization.

While this search may take one to "unusual heights in the sphere of poetry, at an existential level it has often proved a dead end." This "painful, forced search" is "but a banal quest for the exotic." Indeed, "the colonized intellectual who returns to his people through works of art behaves in fact like a foreigner" and "strangely reminiscent of exoticism."[45] It is worth quoting at length here:

> In order to secure his salvation, in order to escape the supremacy of white culture, the colonized intellectual feels the need to return to his unknown roots and lose himself, come what may, among his barbaric people. Because he feels he is becoming alienated, in other words the living focus of contradictions which risk becoming insurmountable, the colonized intellectual wrenches himself from the quagmire which threatens to suck him down, and determined the believe what he finds, he accepts and ratifies it with heart and soul.[46]

But this process is a necessity, Fanon argues, for "otherwise we will be faced with extremely serious psycho-affective mutilations: individuals without an anchorage." Unwilling or unable to choose between two nationalities or two determinations, such as Algerian and French or Nigerian and English—or Asian and American— these intellectuals "collect all the historical determinations which have conditioned them and place themselves in a thoroughly 'universal perspective.'"[47]

Yet eventually, this colonized intellectual "will realize that the cultural model he would like to integrate for authenticity's sake offers little in the way of figureheads capable of standing up to comparison with the many illustrious names in the civilization of the occupier" or any other form of representational politics. But then

> lucidly and "objectively" observing the reality of the continent he would like to claim as his own, the intellectual is terrified by the void, the mindlessness, and the savagery. Yet he feels he must

escape this white culture. He must look elsewhere, anywhere; for lack of a cultural stimulus comparable to the glorious panorama flaunted by the colonizer, the colonized intellectual frequently lapse into heated arguments and develops a psychology dominated by an exaggerated sensibility, sensitivity, and susceptibility.[48]

This movement of withdrawal resembles a muscular reflex, a contraction.[49] But sooner or later the colonized intellectual realizes that "the existence of a nation is not proved by culture, but in the people's struggle against the forces of occupation." In the context of North America, the settler-colonial state is this occupying force, and Fanon's diagnosis of the petite bourgeoisie's dilemma of straddling multiple identities describes what Asian American theologians have theorized as liminality or marginality—individuals without anchorage.

The solution lies in the destruction of colonialism itself, requiring a divine violence that destroys the colonial order and the Manicheanism that it produces. For such a revolution to occur, it is necessary for Asian Americans, particularly those of middle- or upper-middle-class status, to embrace a downward mobility, "groundings" that facilitate a return to the source. This naturally leads to new forms of coalitional politics, a commitment to desettlerizing, to social death, dispossession, and now, also, decolonization through the development of both race and class consciousness. In distinguishing decolonization from desettlerization, I mean to highlight the dual nature of US imperialism both as settler colony that continues its genocidal program of Indigenous nations and occupation of stolen land, and as colonial ruler of so-called US territories such as Puerto Rico, Guam, and the Virgin Islands, with military bases in places such as Hawaii, the Philippines, South Korea, and Japan.

Moreover, what undergirds the settler-colonial and military structure is racial capitalism, in which the Asian American imaginary is well-embedded as a junior partner despite the poverty faced by many Asians in the United States.[50] The structure of global capital determines much of the flow of migration, whether through economic dependency of post-colonial nations or exploitative labor practices. The massive violence required to undo capitalism itself and the complete disorder that decolonization is contingent upon must be recognized as entirely consonant with the divine violence necessary for breaking the spell of mythic violence maintained by the fusion of state, capital, and empire.

Fanon, again: "We should not therefore be content to delve into the people's past to find concrete examples to counter colonialism's endeavors to distort and depreciate. We must work and struggle in step with the people so as to shape the future and prepare the ground where vigorous shoots are already sprouting."[51] To identify these vigorous shoots requires the gift of sight, as Althaus-Reid recounted in her experience at a militant Protestant church in Buenos Aires: "After two years of popular bible readings and much discussion, and before reaching a conclusive decision on our praxis, we suddenly noticed that our church was full of beggars. The subjects of our praxis were already there, ignoring our meetings and discussions; it only required from us the gift to look around us."[52]

• • •

On the evening of June 12, 2020, Rayshard Brooks was sleeping in his car at a Wendy's restaurant in Atlanta, Georgia. Two police officers arrived, responding to a complaint that the car was blocking the drive-through lane. An altercation followed, in which Brooks was shot twice and later died in the hospital. The following evening, the Wendy's was set on fire. The majority Black Atlanta Police Department arrested Natalie White, a White woman believed to have been involved in the arson based on videos circulated on social media and in a romantic relationship with Brooks. Taking place only weeks after George Floyd's murder, the Wendy's became not only a memorial site for Brooks and a focal point of the Black Lives Matter protest in Atlanta, it was also occupied by protesters—some armed, some not—for a month after Brooks's killing.

In a reflection titled "At the Wendy's: Armed Struggle at the End of the World," the anonymous authors argue that while guns may have played a role in sustaining the occupation of the Wendy's by discouraging police from moving in during a moment of public outrage against the police, it also became an ersatz for thinking about how to keep the space safe, for a strategy of collective power.[53] The self-appointed leadership of the Wendy's occupation decided that the location should be made into a Peace Center. But

> the guns at the Wendy's were not going to magically make a Peace Center appear. Aside from replacing any real strategy, guns did not help the Wendy's leadership get any closer to their real goal, and in the end, they were still reliant on negotiations with the state to get what they wanted. At the same time, it is clear that there would have been no way to launch a critique of the guns from an unarmed position. Any plea for nonviolence would have been laughed at and brushed aside.[54]

Whereas questions abounded about whether a new civil war would erupt as a result of the George Floyd uprising—and as such the role of new John Browns in this civil war—the anonymous authors rightly point out that "the question of violence will be a decisive one for the future of revolutionary movements in America" and equally that "the strength of our movements will depend on broad social support more than on purely military victories." In other words, inasmuch as the Harper Ferry raid was indeed a decisive moment in the civil war and the abolitionist movement at large, it was far from the only one. Just as both pacifists and armed militants fetishize guns, to primarily dwell on questions of physical violence, however revolutionary, is short-sighted. Thus again the structure of liberation asks more of us: How do we keep ourselves safe, how to do we care for each other, how do we negotiate our conflicting desires well? What happens when we don't get along?

8.

BLACK PERIL, YELLOW POWER

Reckoning with the Violence of the Unthought

> *But I say unto you which hear, Love your enemies, do good to them*
> *which hate you, bless them that curse you, and pray for them which*
> *despitefully use you. And unto him that smites you on the one cheek*
> *offer also the other; and him that taketh away thy cloke forbid not to*
> *take thy coat also. Give to everyone that asks of thee; and of them that*
> *takes away your goods ask them not again.*
>
> —Luke 6:27–30

> *This is why I say it's the ballot or the bullet. It's liberty or it's death. It's*
> *freedom for everybody or freedom for nobody. America today finds her-*
> *self in a unique situation. Historically, revolutions are bloody, oh yes*
> *they are. They have never had a bloodless revolution. Or a non-violent*
> *revolution. That don't happen even in Hollywood. You don't have a*
> *revolution in which you love your enemy. And you don't have a revo-*
> *lution in which you are begging the system of exploitation to integrate*
> *you into it. Revolutions overturn systems. Revolutions destroy systems.*
>
> —Malcolm X, *The Ballot or the Bullet*

On January 15, 2022, a Saturday morning, forty-year-old Michelle Alyssa Go left her apartment in Manhattan's Upper West Side. As she waited for a subway train in Times Square, a man pushed her in front of an oncoming train, killing her immediately. When this made the news, my mother quickly texted my brother and me, telling us once again to be careful. Our parents live far away in Malaysia while my brother and I have lived mostly bicoastal lives in the last decade in the belly of the beast. Since the pandemic began, friends from home ask me tentatively about how it's been, looking Asian in the United States and all. Are you scared in the grocery store? Walking down the street? Wearing a facemask?

At first blush, it feels insensitive to write about *yet another* Asian person being attacked since the pandemic. It's been almost two years since the "China virus" had been so named; it was easy then to rag on a president who used unpresidential language and inspired bald-faced xenophobia. In the wake of the heightened attacks on East Asian people—often women or the elderly[1]—English-language commentaries appeared again about the history of anti-Asian racism in the United States; high-profile Asian Americans and organizations denounced these attacks, some even offering substantial financial reward for information leading to the arrest of the attacker.

Whereas opinions are divided over what the appropriate response might be, there is a general consensus on the reality of anti-Asian violence, regardless of its nature. The last decade of struggling over the worth of Black lives—and to a lesser extent Brown lives—has left us with the uncomfortable side effect of shifting the binary from White/non-White to Black/non-Black rather than exploding the binary itself. Now, to be certain, from music to politics, Blackness has a specificity, but when it comes to such tragedies, we are still looking for a language that doesn't quite exist, a language that adequately describes our realities, racial and otherwise, without doing injustice to others who have suffered differently.[2]

Michelle Go's assailant, Simon Martial, was a sixty-one-year-old Black man. The *New York Times* offered a sympathetic profile of Go's life and career, making it clear she was Asian, even as, according to police, there was no indication that the attack was racially motivated.³ Martial, on the other hand, was not racially identified and simply described as having a history of mental illness and a criminal record, possibly homeless. (A follow-up report on Martial by the *New York Times* appeared over two weeks later, detailing Martial's relationship to a failing mental health system.) Then again, less than a month later, in the early hours of Sunday, February 13, 2022, thirty-five-year-old Christina Yuna Lee was fatally stabbed in her Manhattan Chinatown apartment by Assamad Nash, a reportedly homeless Black man who had been arrested at least three times prior on misdemeanor charges.

Reading the news over the last two years, the same kind of story can be told again and again, many recorded on video even, of variations on the same theme. Of course, it should go without saying that Asians are also attacked by non-Black people—and at a higher rate at that—but the fact remains that these particular incidents did happen and more importantly that they have garnered the most attention, but only up to a point. Jay Caspian Kang alludes to this in *The Loneliest Americans*, where he articulates the uncomfortable question implied by the outcry of Asians in these times: "Why doesn't it count when people—especially Black people—commit hate crimes against us?" This question is rarely asked out loud, in English, but

> "on WeChat and KakaoTalk, platforms for the Chinese and Korean diaspora, a type of anti-Black nationalism emerged that asked why liberals seemed to care only when Black people got attacked by the police but not when helpless, elderly Asians were attacked by Black people. All of this was clumsy, of course, but these moments are always clumsy, because the point isn't quite political. It's cathartic: a way to hint at the contradictions we know exist but can never seem to articulate."⁴

This discontent is palpable but is also often beyond the range of hearing, at least in English. Asian anti-Blackness is real, and much ink has been spilled over it, but can the same be said for Black anti-Asianness? Is that even the point? (To be clear, eventually some things have been said about it, mostly falling along predictable partisan lines.)

Kang highlights the anachronism of the resurrected slogan "Yellow Peril supports Black Power" from the mid-twentieth century and points to the irony that Richard Aoki, who was famously photographed first holding the sign and later revealed to be an FBI informant on the Black Panther Party, as one of its few Asian members. This gestures to the transformation of historical figures and events into symbols and signifiers that are disconnected from their original referents: the shape of Asian America in 2020 is quite unrecognizable next to that of 1960. This subset of the immigrant population has become one of the fastest growing demographics, also the most ethnically diverse and economically unequal, in the country. The histories of the anti-Asian racism that are narrated largely deal with an earlier, more homogeneous and coherent past.

Let's first take a look at the data that we do have, for what it's worth. According to FBI hate crime statistics in 2020, reported anti-Black hate crimes were by far the most (34.7 percent), followed by anti-White hate crimes (10.5 percent), and anti-Asian hate crimes trailing far behind (3.4 percent). Compared to the previous year, this registers an increase for Black, (+45.6 percent), White (+35.1 percent), and Asian (+73.3 percent) populations, respectively, with the largest increase being for Asians. In comparison, the 2020 census data has White, Black, and Asian at 57.3 percent, 11.9 percent, and 5.9 percent, respectively.[5] Of course, as with all hate crime statistics, these crimes are under-reported and poorly classified, such as attacks not deemed racially motivated. It is difficult to empirically differentiate the increase in anti-Asian hate crimes as an uptick in actual events or in the willingness to report an incident, let alone as a hate crime. The latter can be argued based on the increasing awareness and reporting around anti-Asian violence.[6]

Still, it is quite unambiguous that there has been an increase in reports and videos of anti-Asian attacks, be they bodily harm, harassment, or property damage. One study on news coverage of anti-Asian racism in 2020 identified 1,023 reports of anti-Asian incidents (compared with, say, 279 reported hate crimes), 112 of which involved physical harassment and violence, about a third of which were incidents of being coughed at, spat at, or sneezed on.[7] But at this point, what the racial data of news reports can tell us is not always clear, as illustrated by the *New York Times* report on Simon Martial. Nonetheless, among the reports in which the race/ethnicity of the offender was explicitly identified, they were forty-four White, six Black, four Latine, and four Asian. While the FBI data reported 55 percent White, 21 percent Black, and 1 percent Asian offenders overall, it did not specify the breakdown in terms of specifically anti-Asian hate crime offenders.[8] In the least, we can infer from both these data sets that both anti-Asian hate crimes and Black hate crime offenders are far from the majority.

So why are reports of specifically Black anti-Asian violence sensationalized and most easily gone viral? Is there any reason to focus our attention on such events, which are in fact in the overwhelming minority of racist events? To answer the first question, perhaps implicit in such reports is the claim that *even Black people can be racist*, which, within the United States, is very much a case of whataboutism. If that were solely the case, there would be nothing more to say given the media's overall attraction to the spectacular, the newsworthy, the exception. The exception in this case, to be sure, is to the rule of dominant White racial violence. There is nothing here that needs to be said that has not been said before.

The answer to the second question, unfortunately, is yes, we still have to care, if nothing then for the simple fact that the outsize virulence of reports of Black anti-Asian violence feeds into an already existing anti-Blackness within the Asian American community, about which much has already been written. So, there is a need to address the issue whenever it arises, because on its own it easily reinforces a confirmation bias about the danger of Blackness. Combined with the first question, this perhaps resonates in an inverted sort of way with the LA riots in 1992. Certain accusations were made that the media helped to characterize the riots as a Black–Korean conflict, though the fact remains that a Korean shopkeeper really did shoot an unarmed Black girl. The resonances are not subtle, either: a well-known photo of "rooftop Koreans," picturing Koreans perched on a rooftop with rifles, ostensibly to ward off Black rioters, resurfaced in the wake of the riots following George Floyd's killing in 2020. The narrative that hardworking, immigrant, petit bourgeois Asian business owners ought to take up arms to defend their livelihoods at the expense of Black lives, as they had presumably done in the past, was convincing to many and a caricature of Asian anti-Blackness. But the answer to these sentiments cannot simply be open letters by younger Asians telling their elders to be less anti-Black. There is a Chinese proverb that roughly translates to: fear not ten thousand, but of the one in ten thousand.[9] A singular event of Black anti-Asian violence is enough to strike fear into a community already ambivalent about the fact of Blackness.

To get to the question of who or what we should really be talking about, let's first try to address the question that most, say, on the Left, would rather not: What do we do with Black anti-Asian violence? It's clear why it's hardly being talked about: it is uncomfortable and unpopular. It is tempting to quickly zoom out and point elsewhere—say, to capitalism or systemic racism, like a trick of misdirection. But how to not look away from neither the event nor the structure? What is the meaning of the violence in and beyond itself? Whatever the answers may be, grappling honestly and collectively with such difficult questions is necessary in order to move beyond the deadlock of identity politics that has failed to produce deep and enduring solidarities. The slogan "Stop Asian Hate" and the language of hate crimes in general obscure as much as they reveal, as it remains difficult as ever to conclusively prove that an attack was racially motivated. (Unless of course, a manifesto is posted online.) Often the assailants, when Black, are found to be mentally ill, criminals, or homeless, some form of undesirable attribute that somehow explains their action as an aberration. The assessment is made, then one quickly moves on from the uncomfortable scene until the next incident intrudes upon us. If this sounds like the characteristic pathologization of White lone-wolf shooters, that should be telling us something—namely, the reluctance to seek deeper structural and analytic explanations that reveal the individual behavior as symptomatic of something greater.

What if we viewed these manifestations of Black mental illness or criminality not as exceptional but instead as the actions of free agents, less inhibited than the average citizen, acting out a collective subconscious of anti-Asian violence? If this seems far-fetched at first, consider the banal human resource trainings to correct for unconscious bias and psychological studies that reveal associations of Blackness with danger, including dogs who learn their owner's racism through their owner's implicit behavioral response when confronted with otherness.[10] Though it may not have been articulated as such, the psychoanalytic dimension of race under capitalism has long been understood. Indeed, Blackness, as Frantz Fanon diagnosed, is a phobogenic object: it instills fear—the Black Peril, one might even say. The deadly consequences of this are career police officers reflexively shooting unarmed Black children because they instinctively fear for their lives. This claim may sound indefensible at first, but the fear—irrational or not—that subconsciously inflates Blackness into monstrosity is very much real and so are the deaths it produces. A pack of candy, a cellphone, a sandwich all metamorphose into guns.[11]

Taking the unconscious seriously, how should we think of anti-Asian racism? On its own, we might chalk it up to yet another aspect of the imperial, genocidal project of the United States. But when it manifests as specifically Black, what are we faced with? To ask which narrative, of Asian-Black racism or solidarity, is more true is misleading, because both are true as facts are facts. Both social relations exist. The question is: What do they *mean* when taken together, and what do they mean *for us*. One explanation is simple enough: Black life in the United States is one that is constantly in struggle for survival, for mattering, and its psychic stability is heavily eroded by the compounding of racial trauma, economic depression, and political subjugation. The wretched of the earth, in this case, are disproportionately Black and manifest the collective subconscious of a society unequally ravaged by the pandemic. Enough has been written about how the pandemic has disproportionately affected people of color, economically disadvantaged people, women, and LGBTQ people. But how the immediate and disproportionate effects of the pandemic continue to reverberate inward and outward, we have far from reckoned with.

The intersection of anti-Asian violence with gender violence in the 2021 Atlanta shootings has already been much highlighted and again manifests not only a racial but sexual unconscious. A nocturnal emission, if you will: the Asian female body is erotic as the Black male body is phobogenic. It matters less whether the attack was racially motivated, which the shooter later denied, or, as Chosun Ilbo reported, the shooter exclaimed, "I'm going to kill all Asians"; the fact of a gendered *and* racialized attack. But the high-profile murders of Alyssa Go and Christina Lee call for deeper reflection on the particular spectacle of a Black man "senselessly" murdering an Asian woman.

To diagnose this Black (male) anti-Asian (female) violence as a hysteric reflex of a societal unconscious may be unsatisfying to some. But notice that even the inability to properly name such violence builds a further cycle of repression that manifests itself in other ways, such as in racial animosity that verifies the claims of anti-Black violence dealt by non-Black people of color or the galvanization of new conservative voter constituencies. To simply understand it as a pathology of the Black community makes the same mistakes of identifying mass shooters as belonging to the domain of Whiteness alone. If the slave occupies the position of the unthought, as Saidiya Hartman put it, what should be implicated when the unthought commits physical violence, an act of much agency?[12] Whether or not there is a lack of an ontology, as Afro-pessimists argue, the surprise is that in the afterlife of slavery, the enslaved can not only act but also kill. Slave uprisings have taken place, and perhaps yet more are needed. But if we are to follow Fanon's diagnosis of the colonized Black person, would not such violence be simply a release of "muscular tension," of constantly living in a colonized society, and by which the colonized world is stabilized? Does this not make complete sense that Black anti-Asian violence, as a release of a pressure valve, stabilizes the United States both as a carceral state *and* dying empire?

The rallying of Asians against the specter of a deliberately unspecified anti-Asian violence risks further entrenching carceral logics, encouraging dutiful police reporting and pressing hate crime charges against Black people with histories of mental illness and incarceration. Police departments are only happy to be asked to police Black communities, just as the COVID-19 Hate Crimes Act was passed in 2021 more quickly and painlessly than any attempt to curtail anti-Black violence. On the other hand, it also moves toward liberal solutions of diversity and inclusion through media and political representation that have already proven ineffective many times over. More Yellow Power, say, as it was once called.

Clarion calls and op-eds about the need for Black and Asian solidarity (including my own, admittedly) have made little material difference in the lives of those most at risk of being attacked or becoming attackers. Instead, these proclamations often say more about an unresolved anxiety about the class mobility of Asians relative to Black populations, on the whole, in the span of one or two generations. If the violence were more clearly directed toward bourgeois Asians, we might be satisfied with an explanation there. But would any of this posturing solve the real problems in vulnerable Asian communities in the United States, who already struggle to be seen and heard? If the standard response to a mass shooting should be gun control, what solution do we have to fall back on in the case of a subway pushing, or knife attack, or drop kick? The general absence of firearms in these events leaves us more plainly to grapple with the difficult questions. Is the solution prosecution? Self-defense? Community patrols? How to address the chronic condition that produces the colonized Black (non)being? Free housing and mental health services, perhaps, would be part of a noncarceral remedy.

Not only is the Black body phobogenic, Fanon writes, it is also phobic. Accumulated within the Black body is the waste product of racial capitalism, settler colonialism, White supremacy, and a dying imperialism. And quite naturally so, as many of the sacrifice zones designated by the Environmental Protection Agency, which are geographic regions permanently impaired by environmental damage, are primarily located in or near low-income or majority-minority communities.[13] The circulation of commodities, as Marx theorized, produces money as a metabolic byproduct, but no metabolic process does not also produce waste. That these toxins act as triggers for mental illness, houselessness, and, yes, anti-Asian violence can be read as examples of such toxic byproducts, what is secreted from the unconscious. Anti-Asian violence, in particular, has been shown many times to be deeply woven into the fabric of the United States empire, along with anti-Blackness and settler violence.[14]

That Black life in the United States is assaulted at every level of being is unquestionable, but Asian suffering will not be similarly valorized by carefully constructing a parallel history of racial trauma that can match Black or Indigenous claims. Anti-Asian and anti-Black violence are qualitatively different, but they should not need to be the same in order to matter. And neither is mixing in a class or gender analysis adequate, as necessary as both may be, unfortunately. The language of difference, be it racial, class, or sexual, while important in identifying particularities of experiences, divides as much as it unites. Whereas the growing proliferation of gender identities points to more pluralistic and intersectional ways of being, much less can be said with regards to our fluency with race or even class. Disaggregating racial categories is an exercise in bean counting unless it is followed by an effective way of practicing coalitional politics. Asian American studies professors have made comfortable careers on the heterogeneity of Asian American identity, and still here we are.

The irony, of course, is that even as I attempt to trace Black anti-Asian violence to the institutional subconscious embedded within larger structures of oppression, the annoying question of what material difference this will make persists all the same. In the least, perhaps, we will have better reason to not be content with easy solutions or shiny diversions. Counter-narratives of Afro-Asian solidarity tend to preach to the choir. To risk a cliché, the point is to change the world, to make a material difference in the communities who are impacted by not simply anti-Asian violence but the larger, structural causes of which Black anti-Asian violence is but a secondary or even tertiary manifestation. That material conditions scaffold not only structures of feeling but also structures of the unfelt and unconscious should be at the forefront of our analysis and organizing.

None of this is fundamentally new. But as the violence continues to remind us, the inadequacy of language faces us yet again, to which I believe no satisfactory solution has yet been presented, but it remains a crucial question for revolutionary strategy: What tosses and turns in our collective unconscious, our fears, desires, and loves, remains partially submerged and is yet to be fully summoned, whether by language or praxis. What lies ahead is a path unknown, which almost certainly passes through the collapse of both the global climate and the US empire, but more pain will come if we look away or stay silent. For now, all that this reveals in the final accounting is our helplessness and limitations, despite all of our rhetoric and activism, our failure in uplifting *both* Asian and Black people together, not generically but specifically those who may well find themselves together in yet another horrific encounter going viral on the Internet.

ABSTRACT LABOR AND ORNAMENTALISM: ASIAN AMERICAN WOMEN

Up to this point, I have been discussing the nature of Black anti-Asian sentiment as a primarily racial phenomenon, a metabolic waste product of racial capitalism. But as indicated earlier, it should be understood as both a racialized *and* sexualized violence. Recalling Eng and Han's invocation of sexuality operating as the political unconscious of race, it is necessary to attend to the intersectional nature of the particular harms toward Asian American women. In the analysis that follows, I take as starting point the particularity of violence against what Anne Annlin Cheng calls the "Yellow woman," which we might functionally take to mean women of Northeast Asian descent in predominantly White societies, a transposition of Fanon's "racial epidermal schema."[15] This schema follows the collapse of a "body schema," the psychic integrity mediating between self and other, under the White gaze, wherein I am "very far, from my self, and gave myself up as an object." Whereas it would be a failure of a liberative approach to confine our analysis to that of so-called Yellow Asians, the particularity and spectacle of violence against Yellow women—as in the killings of Go, Lee, and the Atlanta massacres—are important points of departure.

In articulating a "feminist theory of and for the yellow woman," Cheng proposes *ornamentalism* as a conceptual lens for attending to "the afterlife of a racialized and aestheticized object that remains very much an object, even as the human stakes remain chillingly high."[16] Here Cheng plays on Said's orientalism and the use of ornamentalism in art history describing decorative art, a discourse noted to be both gendered and racialized. Decontextualized material objects, such as silk or satin imperial robes and cobalt-blue porcelain dragon jars, point to an Asia that is always ancient, excessive, feminine, available, and decadent. As an example, Cheng points to the "thingliness" of actress Anna May Wong on the Hollywood screen, whom Benjamin once referred to as a "moon" and a "bowl." Within this frame, Cheng's ornamentalism is an attempt to "take seriously what it means to live as an object, as aesthetic supplement" and to "attend to peripheral and alternative modes of ontology and survival." Put differently, while orientalism is about turning persons into things that can be possessed and dominated, ornamentalism is about a fantasy of turning things into persons. It is not simply the excess or the opposite of ontology but a precondition for embodiment, of how one is allowed to be embodied as a so-called Yellow woman. "Ornament is flesh for Asian American female personhood," according to Cheng. "Commodification and fetishization, the dominant critical paradigms we have for understanding representations of racialized femininity simply do not ask the harder question of what *being* is at the interface of ontology and objectness."[17] In comparison to the abjectness of the Black being of Afro-pessimism or the new humanism sought by Fanon, ornamentalism looks to the intersubjective racial-epidermal schema produced by cooperative forces of racialization and sexualization in the context of the Yellow woman.

In reflecting on the recent attacks against Asian women, Cheng herself pointed to an earlier work of hers, the *Melancholy of Race: Psychoanalysis, Assimilation, and Hidden Grief,* a predecessor of both *Ornamentalism* and Eng and Han's *Racial Melancholia,* asserting that her claim that "we are a nation at ease with grievance but not with grief" remains true. Cheng writes,

> In the desire to move past racial troubles—in our eagerness to progress—we as a nation have been more focused on quantifying injury and shoring up identity categories than doing the harder work of confronting the enduring, ineffable, at times contradictory and messier wounds of American racism: how being hated and hating can look the same; how the lesson of powerlessness can teach justice or, perversely, the ugly pleasures of power; how the legacy of anger, shame and guilt is complex.[18]

This unprocessed grief and unacknowledged racial dynamics continue to haunt our social relations, and in this context they point to the unresolved and unconscious processes of racialization at large that manifest in these discrete moments of spectacular violence. Such racial violence, of course, is not limited to anti-Asian violence.

To balance this ontological claim with a materialist analysis, I place Cheng's ornamentalism in dialogue with Iyko Day's interpretation of Asians in North America as the personification of abstract labor. Here, Day extends the idea of Asians as the "new Jews" through Moishe Postone's ideas on anti-Semitism under national socialism during the Third Reich. To properly describe Day's theory, it will be helpful to elaborate upon Postone first. Postone argues that the "apparent lack of functionality" of the Holocaust can be understood as a "foreshortened anti-capitalist movement," a convergence of anti-capitalism and anti-Semitism arising through the personification and identification of the Jew with the abstract domination of finance capital.[19] That is, not only were Jews stereotyped as owners and lenders of money, as in traditional European anti-Semitism, they were also "held responsible for economic crises and identified with the range of social restructuring and dislocation resulting from rapid industrialization."

Following Marx, abstract capital (money) is contrasted with concrete capital (commodity), an opposition or antinomy produced through capitalist social relations, in particular commodity fetishism. To explain the matter briefly, the commodity, according to Marx, possesses a double character: value and use-value. The use-value is the actual utility of the object, whereas its value is only realized in the act of exchange. In a barter system, the commodity immediately realizes both forms of value. In a money system, the commodity appears to only contain its use-value, its "thingliness," while money acts as the sole repository of value, the manifestation of this abstract, universal value—the root of all evil. On a larger scale, Postone argues, this dialectical tension is realized in the splitting of industrial capital as concrete and material versus finance capital that is abstract and parasitic.[20] This misunderstanding of the nature of capitalism leads to said foreshortened anti-capitalism, construed as a one-sided attack on abstract capital, rather than overcoming the antinomy itself by the abolition of capitalist social relations. At the same time, the manifest abstract dimension of capital is biologized—incarnated, if you will—as the Jews, whose extermination therefore realizes the destruction of the personification of the abstract, whence the anti-Semitism of the national socialist project of the Third Reich. In plain words, Jews represent money, so attacking Jews is like attacking capitalism, or so the logic goes.

Instead of capital, Day now looks at labor, the other aspect of Marx's theory. Day argues that the Asian in North America "personifies abstract processes of value formation anchored by labor."[21] The dual character of commodities is mirrored in a double character of labor: the concrete labor of physical activity and the abstract labor objectifies a commodity's value. Concrete labor determines how well-made a product is, capturing the qualitative dimension of use-value, whereas abstract labor is a quantitative expression of value, measured by the more intangible notion of "socially necessary labor time," which roughly means the average time needed for a society as a whole to produce the commodity. In particular, a slower worker might take more time to produce a product, but that does not make the given product more expensive on the market. It is in this sense that Day argues that Asians personify abstract labor, denigrated as "cheap" labor in the nineteenth century and valued as "efficient" in the twenty-first.

But how can the labor theory of value make sense of something so visceral as anti-Asian violence? Taken together with ornamentalism, we are led to ask how the Yellow woman (broadly interpreted) is embodied and, indeed, simultaneously racialized and sexualized under a White racial capitalist order. But rather than speaking of the Yellow or even Asian woman, I will here refer to the subject in question as the oriental woman, going back to Said's orientalism which was primarily concerned with representations of Middle Eastern and North African women. Under this schema, *both* forms of fetishization take place: the commodity fetish and the sexual fetish, if we view the alien capital represented by the oriental woman as not simply the personification of abstract labor but abstract *sexual* labor, which objectifies a sexual or sexualized value of the oriental woman as commodity. But this objectification is never complete, just as the beinglessness of the Afro-pessimist turn cannot completely negate the agency of the Black self. At the same time, reading this simultaneous fetish as a racial capitalist sexual fantasy, it becomes easy to place this within the larger order of repressed desires or sexual unconscious of a dominant White heteropatriarchal society. Such desires are most clearly borne out in interracial marriage trends, where Asian females and White males make up the majority of interracial marriages and, more generally, interracial marriages with one White partner predominating. Whereas such cross-racial romances often invoke strong reactions from many sides, all I wish to infer here is that the forces of race, class, sex, and gender that multivalently structure our sexual unconscious are deep, broad, and very much entangled.[22]

The question remains: Where do we go from here? The killing of Michelle Go on the subway tracks and Christina Lee in her own Chinatown apartment have left a heightened sense of terror and unsafety in Asian women, if the Atlanta spa shootings and general reports of anti-Asian violence were not enough. Theologian Grace Ji-Sun Kim, writing prior to these events, proposed a "theology of visibility" that works to "illuminate discriminatory acts of violence, xenophobia, sexism, and so on that target people of color, especially Asian American women."[23] This vacillation between the extremes of invisibility and hypervisibility similarly haunt Black women. But more than simple visibility is needed in order to demystify, or rather defetishize, the figure of the oriental woman. Our interrogations of the social construction of race and gender and the ways the multiple forms of oppression interlock must be sufficiently nuanced, able to move from the tropes and stereotypes that haunt our day-to-day lives, to the power structures that maintain these systems of domination, to what it will take to dismantle them and build the world anew. For many, our lived experiences are sufficient for grounding our critique, but they don't readily illuminate the path to liberation. That conscientization is a deliberate process, and one we cannot take for granted.

THE WILL TO POWERLESSNESS

The previous chapter asked what the means are by which we may get free, the role of violence in struggle against the powerful, in solidarity with the oppressed. This chapter instead forces a reckoning when those who harm us are not so clearly oppressors, when our so-called enemies, attackers, or hate crime perpetrators are other subjugated persons. Can we turn the other cheek? Can we offer our other coat? Here I am continuing to focus on the spectacular forms of violence: when a human strikes another human being or when a bank window is smashed, rather than the structural and systemic violence that forms the background of our everyday lives through settler colonialism, racial capitalism, heteropatriarchy, and citizenship.

In the previous chapter, I argued that it is a mistake to try to establish universal edicts by which we may adjudicate any acts of physical violence in the struggle for a more just world because it takes us beyond the limits of ethics. I believe that a principle may still be formulated based on the following hermeneutic reading: we are called to turn the other cheek when violence is dealt toward our individual being, but we do not get to demand the same of anyone else. No matter how many times victims of racial terror may forgive their assailants, such as in the Charleston massacre of nine Black people at the Emanuel African Methodist Episcopal Church in 2015, no obligation ever exists for the victims to extend forgiveness. The past makes no precedent. As Black feminist writer Roxane Gay wrote in response to the latter event,

The call for forgiveness is a painfully familiar refrain when black people suffer. White people embrace narratives about forgiveness so they can pretend the world is a fairer place than it actually is, and that racism is merely a vestige of a painful past instead of this indelible part of our present. Black people forgive because we need to survive. We have to forgive time and time again while racism or white silence in the face of racism continues to thrive. We have had to forgive slavery, segregation, Jim Crow laws, lynching, inequity in every realm, mass incarceration, voter disenfranchisement, inadequate representation in popular culture, microaggressions and more. We forgive and forgive and forgive and those who trespass against us continue to trespass against us.[24]

And even if forgiveness is not explicitly offered, the patient waiting for justice and reparations to be delivered is too often mistaken for forgiveness, to the point that it becomes expected. Even Martin Luther King Jr. wrote in his letter from a Birmingham jail, that the word "Wait!" rings "in the ear of every Negro with piercing familiarity," and this "Wait" has almost always meant "Never"; justice too long delayed is justice denied. Instead, I would argue that if someone else is being violated, it is my duty—as was the Samaritan's—to be my brother's keeper, to share their pain, to struggle alongside them. In other words, if you steal from me, I will offer you more; but if you steal from my neighbor, I will do everything in my power to care for them and bring you to account.

In a wide-ranging study on the biblical notion of power, J. P. Walsh argues that the Hebrew word *mishpat*, typically translated as "judgment," should be more broadly understood through the colloquial "having the say,"[25] whereas *tzedek* (or *tzdakah*) typically translated as "justice" or "righteousness," should be understood as "what is right," a consensus, a communal vision of common life.[26] Mishpat can be exercised according to tzedek, or it may not. Tzedek in the biblical tradition, according to Walsh, is more than obeying a set of rules such as those laid out in the Torah. It is "going beyond," to have concern for the other, and in failing to do so, in powerlessness, needfulness, and unrighteousness, we come to know and rely on God's mishpat, which is constant, self-emptying, gracious, and efficacious.[27] But this conception of power is still an individualistic one. Such power is not so much something to be attained—rather, it is our powerlessness in upholding what is right that should be acknowledged.

How are we to think of power when all I have argued up to this point is a relinquishing of desire for subjectivity, land, being, and possession? Recall that the subjectlessness of Asian American theology, in particular, points to the formations of Asian American identity itself: it is ultimately a power analysis. What Asian American theology affords us is the pulling back of the curtain on the interlocking power structures in which Asian American identity arises and is implicated. But rather than a will to power, be it, say, electoral, financial,[28] or even cultural power, which only serve to further assimilate Asian Americans into the standing structures of oppression, it is the will to powerlessness that undergirds all these moves away from these Faustian deals and toward collective liberation.

Powerlessness is what we feel when we read the news of yet another person of color—Black, Asian, or anyone else—being violently attacked or killed. Powerlessness is what many feel waiting for the subway, walking home, or going to the store. How can this kind of constant anxiety, insecurity be something to desire? Not on its own, it cannot. But an Asian American theology of liberation points us to the stubborn fact that we can only get free when all of us are free, and that so many of our neighbors, and sometimes we ourselves, experience powerlessness as a daily reality. But our power lies elsewhere: in-between the cracks, in spaces of fugitivity, not in the wind or quake or fire but in the stillness is God most keenly heard. In this sense I am not advocating for powerlessness entirely but instead self-determination for the disempowered and accountability for the powerful.

To finally close on the question of what might be done in the face of horrific violence, particularly against Asian women, the difficulties persist. Besides call for increased policing and prosecution of hate crimes, others have responded through offering self-defense classes, including physical maneuvers and pepper spray use. Interviews with participants show that they are under no illusion that it will end anti-Asian racism and misogyny, though for some it may offer psychological support and heightened vigilance.[29] These small efforts speak less to the limits of our imagination than to the amount of power that people feel they have in responding to such unpredictable dangers.

The mortal fear of being an Asian woman simply commuting to and from work is palpably real. There is no asking anyone to turn the other cheek, even if we may choose to when personally faced with the option. Instead, what the will to powerlessness draws us to is to simply and truthfully acknowledge that there might be little that we can do in the immediate future to protect all who are at risk, all who live under the shadow of death, who live in constant fear that their lives do not matter and may violently end while they are sleeping, driving, jogging, lying on the pavement, or waiting for the subway.[30] But it is also to be in struggle together, to work fiercely and tirelessly—but also full of care, rejuvenation, and healing—toward the end of all the powers that disempower the powerless, that enforce the false binaries that alienate us, that distort our desire.

9.

TOWARD USELESS JOY

The Erotics of Liberation and the End of Asian America

... and all these things shall be added unto you.
                                        —Matthew 6:33

Not one day passes without confirmation of the availability and the willingness to use force in the Third World. It is not the province of one people to be the solution or the problem. But a civilization maddened by its own perverse assumptions and contradictions is loose in the world. A Black radical tradition formed in opposition to that civilization and conscious of itself is one part of the solution. Whether the other oppositions generated from within Western society and without will mature remains problematical. But for now we must be as one.
                                        —Cedric Robinson, *Black Marxism*

May man never be instrumentalized. May the subjugation of man by man—that is to say, of me by another—cease. May I be allowed to discover and desire man wherever he may be. ... It is through self-consciousness and renunciation, through a permanent tension of his freedom, that man can create the ideal conditions of existence for a human world. Superiority? Inferiority? Why not simply try to touch the other, feel the other, discover each other? Was my freedom not given me to build the world of you, man?
                                        —Frantz Fanon, *Black Skin, White Masks*

The whole story of creation, incarnation and our incorporation into the fellowship of Christ's body tells us that God desires us, as if we were God, as if we were that unconditional response to God's giving that God's self makes in the life of the trinity. We are created so that we may be caught up in this; so that we may grow into the wholehearted love of God by learning that God loves us as God loves God.

—Rowan Williams, "The Body's Grace"

Throughout this book I have argued for Asian American liberation theology as a paradigm through which struggles of marginalized Asians in the United States—migrant, outcaste, poor, queer— become focal points of praxis and theological reflection through praxis. That is, Asian Americanness reveals more about the structures that produce it than the people it attempts to describe. The inherent dilemma of Asian Americanness can be glimpsed at first through an ahistorical sensibility produced by continuous waves of Asian arrivants or first-generation immigrants, complemented with attempts by activists and academics to construct coherent histories of Asian Americans. Further considerations of the racial formation of Asian Americans quickly reveal the instability of the imagined community, its construction through law, capital, and empire, producing a theoretical characteristic of subjectlessness and psychic conditions of racial melancholia and racial dissociation, structured by the landlessness of Asians who arrive as alien capital, international students or adoptees, and refugees of colonial wars. These definitions through absence are inherent and, in fact, become a feature to be embraced when faced with the calls to surrender belonging, being, possession, and power.

Asian American theology is pulled outward from itself by the calls of Black theology and Dalit theology while theological reflections on anti-Asian racism, divine and decolonial violence, and abolition propose a concerted movement inward to an ontological rupture that interrupts the mythic violence of the settler-colonial and racial-capitalist order, whose law enshrines itself as sovereign, and the many binaries enforced by colonial violence. On the other side of divine violence that breaks the immanent frame is a surrender of the will to power and possession. Rigidity softens. The will to material dispossession grounds the invitation to social death, both encapsulated in the blessedness of powerlessness.

The passing away of the dualism of settler and native, colonizer and colonized, citizen and alien, master and slave, worker and boss, simply extend Paul's proclamation of there being neither male nor female, Jew nor Gentile, slave nor free, but unity in the Messiah. This unity of many beings is established through the divine violence that transgresses boundaries while preserving individuality so that even past the horizon of revolution or revelation (apocalypse), nonviolent boundaries remain that distinguish between self and other, no longer structured by unequal power relations. In healthy, adaptive dissociation we can be many yet one. According to Althaus-Reid, "In theology it is not stability but a sense of discontinuity which is most valuable. The continuousness of the hermeneutical circle of suspicion and the permanent questioning of the explanatory narratives of reality implies, precisely, a process of theological discontinuity." As it were, liberation theology needs to be understood as a "continuing process of recontextualization, a permanent exercise of serious doubting in theology."[1] This serious doubting as a theological method clearly resonates with the undetermined nature of Asian American liberation theology.

Remember that liberation is a structure, not an event. Decolonization is an ongoing process, one that continues to take place following the event of national independence that produces postcolonial subjects. The abolitionist horizon demands, on the one hand, the dismantling of the prison industrial complex, all forms of policing, and the carceral system at large and, on the other hand, the building of dual power that produces alternate systems of care and protection, which allow the functioning of society without policing and prisons. This structure of liberation would include the redistribution of wealth and sustainable forms of adaptation in the wake of climate catastrophe, contingent upon a fundamental transformation of social relations. Relations such as the relations of production that constitute racial capitalism and the relations of social reproduction that determine the performance of race, gender, and sexuality.

To the extent that each axis of critique, whether abolition or decolonization or anti-capitalism, must work toward its irrelevance in liberation—the relief of law promised by divine violence—so must the racial formation of Asian American identity see its end at the horizon of liberation, in which every oppressive power structure is annihilated. The purpose of Asian American identity, then, is to bring forth a world in which Asian Americans *need not exist*. That is our liberation. Structures of oppression and racist violence both create and sustain what we have come to call Asian American identity, and without them it serves no purpose. In its place is the free response in history, the third space of play, permeated by the presence of God, where the instability of the Asian American subject is broken open and fit together with the broader dissolution of Manichean binaries. Neither Jew nor Greek, slave nor free, male nor female.

This degree of freedom can be frightening, destabilizing, and indeed, unsettling. Whereas critical theory provides orientations toward a liberative horizon, imagining *beyond* the horizon requires more expansive forms of thinking, such as Afrofuturism and queer theology. Political theology, as Smith has argued through the body of John Brown, offers ways of thinking of violence beyond the limits of ethics, where the relief of law gives way to the indicative of divine justice, an iconoclastic utopia that provides no fixed prescription of what might be prefigured. But utopia is a no-place, upon which desires and dreams are projected, a fantasy sustained by its unattainability, holding the same allure as a secret affair that lies just out of bounds.

Instead of this forbidden site of unreality, Foucault's notion of *heterotopia* is more useful for the project of liberation. Heterotopias are counter-sites, effectively enacted utopias in which the real sites are simultaneously represented, contested, and inverted. They are outside of all places, though it is possible to indicate their location in reality—like cemeteries or theaters or ships—which can contain several incompatible sites in a single real space.[2] Chuh argues for Asian America as a heterotopic project while Althaus-Reid also proposes a "Project of the Kingdom" built upon a heterotopic model that is multiple and changing: "It may present a kind of quicksand surface where theology may walk with uneasiness, but that is the crucial element of the Project of Liberation of the Kingdom: a certain uneasiness and a community made with the juxtaposition of elements which do not belong, who are outsiders to any hegemonic definitions."[3]

Whereas both Chuh and Althaus-Reid understand heterotopia in the abstract, Foucault's heterotopias are to be found in reality, even if they need not be "good places" (eutopias) such as colonies or brothels but can, as mirrors, both exist in reality but give sight to a no-place: "For now we see in a mirror, darkly; but then face to face: now I know in part; but then shall I know even as also I am known."[4] The projects of Asian America and of the Kin-dom,[5] as indicatives of beyond the horizon, must not be purely metaphysics: even if they may not be prefiguratively grounded in some spatial context, they can be embodied, inscribed in the flesh.

Queer theology is in part the revelation of queer theory that Christian theology is, at its core, a queering mission: the dissolution of boundaries between God and human, body and soul, spirituality and sexuality, life and death, and thus, again, Paul's indication of the centripetal oneness in the Messiah, the creation of a new humanism—and a new divinity, so to speak—whose primary orientation is toward God. Such radical love, theologian Patrick Cheng contends, is a love so extreme that it dissolves existing boundaries, revealing apparent binaries as ultimately fluid and malleable, making Christian theology a fundamentally queer enterprise.[6] This indeterminacy of the future, be it abolitionist or liberation or Christian, can thus be properly conceived of as a queer futurity, a queer pleasure that is collectively desired, which I refer to here as the *erotics of liberation*. As a counterweight to all the preceding historical, intellectual, ontological, and material analyses of Asian American liberation, I close this book with an embodied conclusion that carries us across the threshold.

To the extent that the free response of Smith's indicative of divine justice cannot prescribe discernible universal codes, all theology is indeed, as Althaus-Reid asserts, sexual theology. Salvation is the theological place of what Derrida called "the safe and sound" and, simultaneously, of what Anne Phillips describes as sensual excess, which carries with it "pleasures of insecurity, or the excitation of the unsafeness of the unknown."[7] Along these lines, Katherine Angel writes that in the current culture of affirmative consent, consent on its own cannot distinguish good sex from bad sex, and we should acknowledge that "we don't always know what we want" in order "to allow for obscurity, for opacity and for not-knowing." Moreover, Angel suggests an "ideal of joyful vulnerability," as sexual desire

> can take us by surprise; can creep up, unbidden, confounding our plans, and with it our beliefs about ourselves. But this giddiness is only possible if we are vulnerable to it. If asked, we might not say that what we want is sex in a hotel with a gruff stranger. It might be inaccurate to say either that we did, or that we didn't. Desire isn't always there to be known. Vulnerability is the state that makes its discovery possible.[8]

The nature of liberation is thus best described by a holy eroticism, which dialectically mediates both danger and safety, pleasure and pain, self and other. The indecenting of theology, including liberation theology, opens up a playful, creative, vulnerable space that liberation can properly inhabit.

This is the expanse that can hold all our dreams and futures.

According to Althaus-Reid, Latin American liberation theology is for the most part a decent theology, in the sense that it is concerned with authorship and the authorization or disauthorization of religiopolitical discourses of authority in Latin America:[9] "Decent theologies struggle for coherence, the coherence that sexual systems also struggle for," and "theology's permanent search for coherence is only an expression of its hegemonizing objectives."[10] Based on sexual categories and heterosexual binary systems, obsessed with sexual behavior and orders, Althaus-Reid asserts that every theological discourse is implicitly a sexual discourse, a decent one, an accepted one: "The liberationist hermeneutical circle has proved to be politically materialist and sexually idealist and is therefore a basic decent discourse."[11]

This sexual idealism, which Foucault showed to be a powerful form of social control, coordinates with decent theologies, including feminist or liberationist theologies, that simply attempt to invert rather than abolish unequal power structures.[12] In a theological materialist-feminist analysis, women need to be studied not only through a mere struggle of ideas about womanhood constructed in opposition to hegemonic definitions but by a process of deabstraction or materialist reversal.[13] This reversal is indispensable for a material and embodied liberation. Despite its commitment to the poor, liberation theology has not been immune to such pitfalls:

> The construction of knowledge, and theological knowledge in our present world, is technologically mediated. A truly liberationist, materialistic based movement ought to know that. Where are the popular publishing houses to give voice to the voiceless? Why did liberationists need to print their book in the USA? Why did they not change the production of theology in order to produce a Chiapas' style of "Intergalactic Flowers," that is, really a communitarian work of expression and reflection? Where were the

new institutions to train poor women and give them theological degrees? Evidently, the organisational standpoint of capitalism has not been challenged."[14]

Liberation theology, in this sense, was the surplus value of human suffering and commodified and sold according to the typical market forces. As decent theologies are built upon sexual idealism, so is capitalist economics, thus the perversion or indecenting of theology also produces a challenge to capitalism. Moreover, traditional liberation theology enshrines nationalism, which, Chuh has already pointed out, is a gendered affair. As Althaus-Reid writes, the *patriota* must "fully participate in the *machista* structure of the national myths of independence and the theological *imaginaire* of my people."[15]

When Gustavo Guttiérez was interviewed on Spanish television for his opinion on the vote on ordination of women in the Church of England, his answer suggested that women in Latin America only cared about feeding their children, not about ordination.[16] Here nationalism, capitalism, and sexual idealism intersect. "The homogenisation of sexuality and, specifically, the sexuality of the poor," according to Althaus-Reid, "serves as a basic pattern from which behaviour, aspirations and relationship to God and to economic systems are worked out and sacralised with an aura of immutability and eternity."[17]

In contrast, "our gods are Queer, because they are what we want them to be. There are no final definitions or models, just rubber-like, flexible identities ready to perform a divine act according to patterns of power."[18] The queerness of liberation thus presents itself as eminently natural, escaping definition and beyond imagination, just as the prophet Ezekiel and the apostle John struggled to convey their apocalyptic visions through crude metaphors. Yet, queerness is not to be misunderstood as confusion: the highest goal of charity work and activist organizing is to create the conditions that render oneself irrelevant; the radicalism of Asian American identity is to produce a future in which Asian Americans do not exist, or, rather, the oppressive structures that create the need for Asian American identity no longer exist. It is the relational third space of play, the free response in history. Open, boundless.

Concerning the disappearance of base ecclesial communities (BECs) in Latin America, Althaus-Reid writes: "I said that I was glad. BECs although very valuable at a certain time, are artificial structures. You cannot keep people in artificial structures for ever. You cannot expect people to live in restriction for the rest of their lives. Moreover, that would defeat the purpose of the very structure which is supposed to be a creative device to bring about something else that needs to happen in society."[19] As approximations to Asian American liberation, queerness presents itself as the space of free response, allowing for the multitudes that emerge in the passing of binary oppositions, whether it be settler/native, male/female, citizen/foreigner, or Black/White. This chaos is a generative chaos, the raw material of an earth "without form and void,"[20] as John Milton interpreted in *Paradise Lost*, whereas Althaus-Reid writes, "sexual chaos and the chaos of death are the two suppressed forces of Christianity, although paradoxically they constitute the Christian paradigm."[21]

That being said, Althaus-Reid's theological perversions and materialist reversals often hover at a theoretical level with clever wordplays and unorthodox theological readings, hence they remain to an extent disembodied, impersonal. To better locate a liberative heterotopia in physical reality, I turn to Rowan Williams's treatment of the body's grace.

While recent discourse in the wake of the Black Lives Matter movement have centered Black and Brown bodies as sites of reflection, and in Afro-pessimism bodies are meant to be accumulated and die,[22] the idea of the body's grace provides a soft landing beyond the liberative horizon. It is "a frontier that has been passed, and that has been and remains grace; a being present, even though this can mean knowing that the graced body is now more than ever a source of vulnerability." According to Williams, the life of the Christian community, its practical reality is the task of teaching us this:

> So ordering our relations that human beings may see themselves as desired, as the occasion of joy. It is not surprising that sexual imagery is freely used, in and out of the Bible, for this newness of perception. What is less clear is why the fact of sexual desire, the concrete stories of human sexuality rather than the generalising metaphors it produces, are so grudgingly seen as matters of grace, or only admitted as matters of grace when fenced with conditions.[23]

Indecent hermeneutics, according to Althaus-Reid, is not about tracing the path of methodological progress in our theological constructions. It is the art of pinpointing obscurities, twisted categories, and queer details that appear in disorder and with or without apparent continuation.[24]

Systematic theology, in contrast, attempts to present knowledge of the divine in a clean and orderly fashion and implicitly assumes that all that can be known is known and thus able to be catalogued. Such a taxonomy of divine revelation is most prominent in Protestant Christianity that assumes the existence of a closed canon, whereas even the Roman Catholic Church holds the doctrine of tradition as an extrabiblical source more akin to the oral traditions of the Hadith in Islam and the Mishnah and Talmud of Judaism. To the extent that liberation theology seeks to systematize itself through works like *Mysterium Liberationis* or incorporation into the academy, liberation theology betrays its own mission to avoid universal types or moral discourses instead of going to find "what was there."[25]

Similarly, when dealing with the body's grace we are confronted with unruly bodies: bodies that will not be policed, disabled and aging bodies, bodies that menstruate, ejaculate, and fart. Foucault's notion of biopower describes society's attempt to regulate the human body through forms of sexual control and discursive means, one crucial construction being the concept of purity. "Purity contradicts materiality," according to Althaus-Reid, and "like the Western whiteness which represents it, a single-frequency thought."[26] The concept of purity is a boundary construction: it sets up a binary of sexual dimorphism and sexual idealism, operating according to sexual economies built on Mosaic laws in which the sin of adultery is understood as a man infringing upon another man's property: his wife. This is anti-materialist to the extent that it is sustained by fantasies of purity, the disembodiment of sexuality through spiritualization and the disavowal of sexual deviance and abuse, not least in churches. Compulsory heterosexuality is so deeply embedded to the extent that even the terms *heterosexuality* and *homosexuality* assume the gender of the person as fixed assignments in a sexual dimorphism.[27] The current proliferation of new terminologies such as sapiosexuality, demisexuality, and asexuality reflect a growing search for a more expansive vocabulary that can describe a wider range of sexual experiences.

Instead, Williams suggests that it is sexual practices that rely on the agency of a single actor or asymmetrical power relation that should be called perverse, in that only one agent is in effective control of the situation, who "doesn't have to wait upon the desire of the other."[28] As such, the socially licensed norm of heterosexual intercourse should in many cases be called a perversion! More pointedly, this kind of sexual perversion is "sexual activity without risk, without the dangerous acknowledgement that my joy depends on someone else's as theirs does on mine," and distorted sexuality is "the effort to bring my happiness back under my control and to refuse to let my body be recreated by another person's perception."[29]

This maps perfectly onto my argument for collective liberation. Alienation of the body, whether by capitalism or Christianity, forms the grounds for sexual violence and dehumanization.

This suggests that sexual disorders are pervasively present in all sorts of disorders, constituting a paradigmatic case of wrongness, a distortion that shows us what it is like to refuse the otherness of the material world and to try to keep it other and distant and controlled. It is a paradigm of "how not to make sense, in its retreat from the uncomfortable knowledge that I cannot make sense of myself without others, cannot speak until I've listened, cannot love myself without being the object of love or enjoy myself without being the cause of joy."[30]

So we have arrived at the idea of joy at the end of liberation. Visions of abolition and revolution are longings of an eschatological nature, where various forms of salvation are attributed to the working-class and the colonized, as Revelation does to faithful Christians. Critiques of the former as an impure "social gospel" are again examples of an anti-materialist and disembodied cult of purity. In any case, while prophecies of blood and fire are common or even historically necessary in slave revolts and anti-colonial revolutions, the liberation dreams of the oppressed are much more: divine violence acts to negate and makes way for New Jerusalems that critical theory and liberation theology have not dared to theorize or fantasize about. Fanon's dreams are not of killing the White man but of running free. Considering the body's grace helps us to theorize liberation as an embodied future. Williams writes,

> All this means that in sexual relation I am no longer in charge of what I am. Any genuine experience of desire leaves me in something like this position: I cannot of myself satisfy my wants without distorting or trivialising them. But here we have a particularly intense case of the helplessness of the ego alone. For my body to be the cause of joy, the end of homecoming, for me, it must be there for someone else, be perceived, accepted, nurtured; and that means being given over to the creation of joy in that other, because only as directed to the enjoyment, the happiness, of the other does it become unreservedly lovable. To desire my joy is to desire the joy

of the one I desire: my search for enjoyment through the bodily presence of another is a longing to be enjoyed in my body.[31]

Here then is the apex of Asian American liberation, how we all get free. The surrender of our own joy, allowing it to be entirely dependent on the desire of another, perfectly describes the liberative horizon. True love, real love, according to Fanon, requires the mobilization of psychological agencies liberated from unconscious tension.[32] The muscular tension held in Fanon's colonized subject is also a sexual tension that finds release in liberation.

In this eroticism is an anti-capitalist inefficiency and a decolonial inversion, what Williams calls the "inefficiencies of exposed spontaneity." We take our time. While there is no guarantee that joy will arise in the encounter, there will at least be an indication of where joy does instead lie: "I can only fully discover the body's grace in taking time, the time needed for a mutual recognition that my partner and I are not simply passive instruments to each other." In this sense, sexual faithfulness is not an avoidance of risk but "the creation of a context in which grace can abound because there is a commitment not to run away from the perception of another."[33] Yet, when the container for this context is heterosexual marriage as the only absolute, exclusive ideal, it produces precisely the mythic violence that structures patriarchal society. We must transcend it.

The politics of desire, as with the erotics of liberation, is an ambivalent space that bursts with potential. In the essay *Does Anyone Have the Right to Sex?* philosopher Amia Srinivasan reflects on the 2014 massacre by Elliot Rodger and the nature of desire. Rodger stabbed three Chinese male students to death at his house, shot three White female students outside a sorority, killing two, and finally injured fourteen others near the University of California, Santa Barbara, campus before killing himself. It was revealed later from Rodger's manifesto that he belonged to online groups for "incels": involuntary celibates, self-described sexless men who blame women for their misfortune. Srinivasan compares incels, who believe they have the right to sex, with sex-positive, third-wave feminists, in particular lesbian, cisgendered women who exclude trans women as viable sexual partners.[34] This leads to the question of "how to dwell in the ambivalent place where we acknowledge that no one is obligated to desire anyone else, that no one has a right to be desired, but also that who is desired and who isn't."[35] Inherent in this is the recognition that sexual choices should be assumed to be free—until they are not—even while under patriarchy such choices are rarely free.

In other words, even if valuations such as the one Srinivasan lists as "the supreme fuckability of 'hot blonde sluts' and East Asian women, the comparative unfuckability of black women and Asian men, the fetishisation and fear of black male sexuality, the sexual disgust expressed towards disabled, trans and fat bodies" may be indeed desires of a free agent, they are also political facts. Sexual desires are subconsciously and dialectically formed by the political, economic, and racial structures that exert sexual control and discipline upon its subjects. That Rodger is not a specifically US phenomenon is underscored by his English and Malaysian parentage, furthermore by the recent 2021 knife attack by Yusuke Tsushima in Tokyo, injuring ten. When questioned by the police, he said, "When I was in college, I was looked down on by women in my club activities. I also didn't get along with the women I met on dating sites, so I started wanting to kill happy women."[36] Similarly in 2016, a twenty-three-year-old woman was stabbed to death in a karaoke bar restroom near Gangnam Station in Seoul by thirty-four-year-old Kim Seong-Min. The two were not acquainted; Kim confessed: "I did it because women have always ignored me."[37] The incident was widely viewed as a misogynistic act, sparking fear and public outcry.

Pushing back against the idea that one has a right to sex, the question becomes whether there is a duty to "transfigure, as best we can, our desires." In a nod toward the openness and promise of liberation, Srivinasa suggests that "desire can take us by surprise, leading us somewhere we hadn't imagined we would ever go, or towards someone we never thought we would lust after, or love. In the very best cases, the cases that perhaps ground our best hope, desire can cut against what politics has chosen for us, and choose for itself."[38]

Returning to Williams, thinking about sexuality in its fullest implications involves entering into a sense of oneself beyond the customary imagined barrier between the "inner" and the "outer," the private and the shared, precisely the queering of boundaries in liberation: "We are led into the knowledge that our identity is being made in the relations of bodies, not by the private exercise of will or fantasy: we belong with and to each other, not to our 'private' selves (as Paul said of mutual sexual commitment), and yet are not instruments for each other's gratification. And all this is not only potentially but actually a political knowledge, a knowledge of what ordered human community might be."[39] Sexual and political liberation are thus so intimately tied that in order to properly understand liberation as a form of politics—liberation as structure—it is necessary to listen to what Foucault called the "confessions of the flesh," how sexuality permeates socioeconomic and theological structures.

With this in mind, consider how Williams describes the challenge that same-sex love—indeed any queer love—poses to the meaning of desire itself:

> Same-sex love annoyingly poses the question of what the meaning of desire is in itself, not considered as instrumental to some other process (the peopling of the world); and this immediately brings us up against the possibility not only of pain and humiliation without any clear payoff, but—just as worryingly—of non-functional joy: or, to put it less starkly, joy whose material "production" is an embodied person aware of grace. It puts the question which is also raised for some kinds of moralist by the existence of the clitoris

in women; something whose function is joy. If the creator were quite so instrumentalist in "his" attitude to sexuality, these hints of prodigality and redundancy in the way the whole thing works might cause us to worry about whether he was, after all, in full rational control of it. But if God made us for joy?[40]

So queer love steers us toward useless joy. To rephrase this in Marx's materialist framework, joy has no use-value. One might argue its uses in the social if not biological reproduction of the worker and its potential for commodification, but such arguments falter. The body's grace, once again, is wonderfully inefficient. While Williams points out that "this sense of meaning for sexuality beyond biological reproduction is the one foremost in the biblical use of sexual metaphors for God's relation to humanity," and moreover, "When looking for a language that will be resourceful enough to speak of the complex and costly faithfulness between God and God's people, what several of the biblical writers turn to is sexuality understood very much in terms of the process of 'entering the body's grace,'" it is not a capitulation of the body in favor of the soul.[41] On the contrary, it is sexual joy—the erotic—that has no recourse to reproduction that offers itself as the paradigm of Asian American liberation, the political potential for human community.

Similarly, revolutionary Marxist Alexandra Kollontai describes "winged Eros" as that whose love is "woven of delicate strands of every kind of emotion." It attends a communist society built on the principle of comradeship and solidarity. Winged Eros triumphs over wingless Eros, the unadorned sexual drive that is easily aroused and soon spent, and among other things "rests on an inequality of rights in relationships between the sexes, on the dependence of the woman on the man and on male complacency and insensitivity, which undoubtedly hinder the development of comradely feelings"[42]—perverse heterosexuality, in other words.

A bourgeois system that divides the inner emotional world, complemented by the institution of private property such as in

Mosaic and Deuteronomic law, teaches that love is linked with property." "Bourgeois ideology has insisted that love, mutual love, gives the right to the absolute and indivisible possession of the beloved person. Such exclusiveness was the natural consequence of the established form of pair marriage and of the ideal of 'all-embracing love' between husband and wife."[43] This wingless Eros describes the efficient, functional, teleological sex that contradicts the useless joy of entering the body's grace.

In Kollontai's new and collective society, where interpersonal relations develop against a background of joyful unity and com-radeship, Eros will "occupy an honourable place as an emotional experience multiplying human happiness. What will be the nature of this transformed Eros? Not even the boldest fantasy is capable of providing the answer to this question. But one thing is clear: the stronger the intellectual and emotional bonds of the new human-ity, the less the room for love in the present sense of the word."[44]

The body's grace, borne on winged Eros, thus makes for the real heterotopic site of liberation, in which the dreams and dis-contents of Asian America may be inscribed: landless and racially dislocated aliens, called to surrender subjectivity, being, posses-sion, and power, to betray race and class for the erotic joy and risk of collective liberation. The queer futurity that Asian American theology points to is a boundless one, in the loosing of chains of all binaries that fix both oppressed and oppressor in dialectic oppo-sition, a multiverse of free responses and free associations, love without end.

Jose Comblin writes, "Bodies remind us that they exist when they suffer. This is when we are forced to remember them. No one who has never been truly hungry will fully understand that a human being is first and foremost a being who needs to eat. No one who has never been sick will know what health is. For the poor, the liberation of humanity is the liberation of suffering, crushed, humiliated bodies."[45] So we dream of what lies beyond the hori-zon, where Asian America ceases to exist because the oppressive politics and unequal power structures that sustained its existence have passed away. Imagination, according to Fernandez, is innate to a theology that is "expressive of the sighs, hopes, and longings of a subjugated people,"[46] and as Lester Ruiz writes, theology lies at the interface of the political and the sacred, both a bridge and a metaphor between that which is and that which is not.[47] Theological imagination carries us across the threshold into useless joy.

But until then, we fight for each other with every fiber of our being. In assessing the legacy of John Brown for the twentieth century, Du Bois pointed to the backward racial progress caused by the advent of social Darwinism, at odds with Martin Luther King Jr.'s famous remark about the moral arc of the universe that bends toward justice. The lesson of John Brown echoes in every revolutionary, that through the raising of consciousness they become people of history: "The cost of liberty is less than the price of repression, even though that cost be blood. Freedom of development and equality of opportunity is the demand of Darwinism, and this calls for the abolition of hard and fast lines between races, just as it called for the breaking down of barriers between classes." The cost of liberty is thus a "decreasing cost, while the cost of repression ever tends to increase to the danger point of war and revolution. Revolution is not a test of capacity; it is always a loss and a lowering of ideals. But if it is a true revolution it repays all losses and results in the uplift of the human race."[48] Once again: the world awaits.

EPILOGUE

HEALING AS WE FIGHT

In *The Trauma of Caste*, Dalit American Thenmozhi Soundararajan articulates the struggle of being a caste oppressed person through the lens of trauma. Trauma, from Soundararajan's initial discovery that she is Dalit, a painful truth drawn from her reluctant mother while in fifth grade, to experiencing discrimination firsthand when she naively began to reveal her caste status to other South Asians, to becoming a prominent leader in the anti-caste movement. Historical trauma, articulated by Maria Yellow Horse Brave Heart, is a trauma response that constitutes a constellation of features in reaction to the multigenerational, collective, historical, and cumulative psychic wounding over time, over one life span and across generations.[1] This kind of trauma leaves what Indigenous psychologist Eduardo Duran calls a soul wound.[2] We might think of historical trauma as intergenerational trauma that carries with it the weight of history.

For Asians who find themselves in the Americas, there is a genealogy that takes us back to Asia itself. By whatever means and whichever persons this occurs, we can almost invariably trace a complicated history involving colonialism, war, oppression, dreams, and desires. The ways in which we were or were not carried here—by parents who did not understand their own trauma, by older generations of whom we only know half-truths of, or by our lonesome selves in a strange land—leave their mark on our souls and in our bones.

Throughout this book I have leaned heavily on theories and theologies that attempt to parse out some of these complexities, trying to make them meaningful for anyone else troubled by the same contradictions that trouble me. But there is something missing, which I feel I had only begun to make up for in the last chapter: the embodied nature of our shared struggle, how this all sits with us as we eat, sleep, love, and work—the fundamental interconnectedness of the universe, a mycelial network, sometimes severed through intergenerational and interpersonal trauma. We might not yet know how to take care of each other in our dreams of liberation because we don't quite know how to take care of ourselves. This is also a part of entering the body's grace: to let ourselves be loved even while we still hurt.

Various theories have been proposed on how exactly our bodies remember the trauma of our biological forebears, whether it is how our parasympathetic nervous systems or genetic expressions are influenced by the stress responses induced in earlier generations. But the general consensus is that one way or another, our bodies remember what we don't or may have never known. As we involve ourselves in the work of liberation, we will as broken people encounter other broken people, and it is a sad truth that in the small world that constitutes radical organizing and activism, interpersonal conflicts are rife and often lead to the breakdown of such organizing activity. Of course, some efforts simply run their course and need no longer exist, but too often it is an acute blowup that leads to collapse. Then the people involved disperse and join groups elsewhere, bringing their pain with them, if unresolved. This fracture of the Left is sometimes about strategy and vision, which are important to debate, but it often also indicates a degree of not being able to come to terms with ourselves.

We might think that beyond the liberative horizon—heaven, swarga, or nirvana, some might say—we can freely love without pain, associate without hurt. There is no reality to this fantasy: as long as we live in relation to each other, there will always be variations in desires, preferences, and practice. I may like chocolate and you may like strawberry, and we will have to find ways to be happy. A perfect world that is free from all violence and hurt is one with no one in it. The psychoanalysis of Fanon and Nandy on the mind of the colonized and colonizer help us to understand our present situation, both structurally and personally; so do Eng and Han on the particular psychopathologies of Asian Americans. As useful as they are, these approaches don't quite tell us how to heal from our old wounds or how to manage new ones, how to listen to our bodies.

As Malaysian American journalist Stephanie Foo recounts in her memoir of complex trauma *What My Bones Know*, the stress response triggered by complex post-traumatic stress disorder (PTSD) can be debilitating and destructive when everything else around us is fine, but during times of crisis—in a pandemic, for example—it is in fact a proportionate and appropriate response.[3] It prevents the self from collapsing, stabilizing it enough to manage the crisis at hand. In other words, complex PTSD is a defensive mechanism that the body learns from a lifetime of constant traumatic injury, such as by child abuse or perpetual racism, that seems inappropriate to those who have not experienced the same. This does not necessarily justify one's actions or responses, but it at least explains them and places them in the wider view of history. The title of Foo's book refers to the intergenerational trauma that she uncovered in discovering fragments of her family's past suffering, such as during Malaysia's anti-communist era, and that her body inherited without her knowing.

In the context of getting free, this reminds us that a fundamental part of being free is finding healing. Not so much to be completely healed, for as anyone who grieves knows, the sorrow never quite leaves, at least in this life, but becomes integrated into our selves. We carry the pain of our parents, our ancestors, and, of course, our own selves in our bodies; intergenerational trauma sometimes spills over into interpersonal conflict, but this is also our inheritance. We can learn to regulate our emotional responses, to better attune to others, to empathize when they lash out, hold space for all of our feelings, and manage conflicts as they arise.

To heal as we fight is to deeply value the internal healing that needs to be done alongside the external struggle for a new world. It recognizes that the two are intimately linked and cannot be achieved without the other. If we only tend our wounds while the world burns and injustice remains, we will surely be torn open again by structures designed to do violence; if we try to fight for a world where all are free without transforming the old social relations, our unresolved hurts and blurred vision will shackle us and any win will be short-lived. Even contemporary anarchists have begun to absorb these lessons, moving away from rigid radicalism toward joyful militancy and rebellious mourning.[4] Whereas in this book I have argued for a position of something akin to detachment—to subjecthood, land, being, possessions, and power—we might also think of it as a secure attachment, as opposed to anxious or avoidant attachment, to each of these things that we need not be afraid nor possessive of but set in right relation to. As in the body's grace, my joy waits upon yours.

• • •

It is Lunar New Year's Eve, January 21, 2023. In the majority Asian city of Monterey Park in Los Angeles County, festivities were being held. That evening, seventy-two-year-old Tran Huu Can walked into Star Ballroom Dance Studio and shot and killed eleven people. The victims were elderly Chinese, Taiwanese, and Vietnamese, all but one in their sixties and seventies. Shortly after, Tran appeared at the Lai Lai Ballroom three miles away, where a young Brandon Tsay wrestled Tran's gun away, causing Tran to flee. Stopped by police the next day, Tran shot himself before any confrontation could take place.

Two days after the incident, at Mountain Mushroom Farm in Half Moon Bay, California, about thirty miles south of San Francisco, sixty-six-year-old worker Zhao Chunli shot and killed four people then drove three miles to Concord Farm where he killed another three. The victims were middle-aged to elderly Chinese and Mexican workers. Two hours later, he surrendered himself at a police station.

I thought I had done the best I could to write a book about Asian Americans, God, and liberation, but to have this pair of tragedies happen at the close leaves me at a loss. So many questions, so little answers: What pushed these Asian elders to do this? What had they gone through that led them down this path? Does the rhetoric of "anti-Asian hate" and the political work motivated by it have anything to offer here? What about the Asian American community, or leadership, or intelligentsia? What have they—we—done for the Trans and Zhaos who live in trailers and earn a pittance for wages in their old age? What does it mean when this "hate" is a rage turned inward? If nothing else, these events make the stakes so painfully clear: all our agitating, writing, organizing, and fighting must make real material change for the Trans and Zhaos, also the Martials and Nashes; to fail them is to fail ourselves.

It is also certain, sadly, that the healing as we fight will include a lot of grieving. There is much more harm and pain and loss in store—sometimes because we did not fight hard enough; other times because we did. The liberation that we struggle for must also be an expansiveness that can contain our grief and joy and hurt and healing, both as collective and private processes.

By the time you read this, it will likely be true that the climate has collapsed. Not in any catastrophic sense but in the slow violence of environmental change. It is widely expected that the anticipated 2–3°C increase in global temperatures within the next decade or two will trigger climate tipping points leading to negative feedback loops of cascading effects.[5] Standing at the precipice of catastrophe, feelings of anxiety and helplessness are natural and appropriate, but at the same time, the words of abolitionist Mariame Kaba in the wake of the acquittal of White supremacist killer Kyle Rittenhouse should ground us: "Let this radicalize you rather than lead you to despair."[6] For all the reckoning that the turmoil of the recent years may or may not have brought, the worst—and best—is yet to come, and we had better be prepared—brass knuckles, boba tea, and all.

Notes

ACKNOWLEDGMENTS

1. Callaci, "On Acknowledgments."
2. Geertz, "Deep Hanging Out."

INTRODUCTION

1. I use the word *American* here very reluctantly throughout the book. It conflates the US settler-colonial state with the geological formation that Whites call the Americas and which some of its Indigenous people call Turtle Island. A preferable alternative might be the once popular and provocative "Amerikkka." Noam Chomsky had once suggested that "American" is used because "United States of America" is not easily made into an adjective; this may be a linguistic accident, but its implications are broad and serious.
2. The capitalization of *White* in this text may appear disconcerting to some. It is certainly controversial. While this might signal notions related to White power, and some employ the lowercase "white" as a way of taking this power away, I choose to use the capitalized form in this book to denaturalize Whiteness and remind the reader of the social construction of Whiteness. See, for example, Theodore W. Allen, *The Invention of the White Race: Racial Oppression and Social Control.* Though in this book I focus on the constructedness of Asian Americans, similar care is also required with regards to broad categories such as White, Black, Asian, East, and West.
3. Tachiki and Ono, *Roots*, vii.
4. Seung, "Asian Americans," 181.
5. I carefully unbound the reader, scanned the pages, and have made it available online; more was generously provided from the archive by the Graduate Theological Union.

6. While liberation theology and theology of liberation are often used inter-changeably, as I shall also do, it is at times useful to refer to liberation the-ology as the historical form that theologizing about liberation has taken, whereas the latter might be better understood as something that is always in process, ongoing.

7. Althaus-Reid, *Indecent Theology*, 25.

8. Althaus-Reid, 26.

9. Althaus-Reid, *Indecent Theology*, 27.

10. Althaus-Reid, *Indecent Theology*, 33.

11. I use the term *refugee* in a sense broader than, say, that of the United Nations Human Rights Commission (UNHCR), and instead as a particular kind of exile, so as to include asylum seekers, undocumented persons, and migrants who have unwillingly left their home countries. In particular, they may be on either side of the state border of the country in which they seek refuge. For a more nuanced theorization, see, for example, Gandhi, *Archipelago of Resettlement*.

12. The use of the term *the poor* here is a crude analytic, unless qualified. In this book, I use the word in the thick, substantive sense of the Tanakh—namely, the Hebraic root *ani* (עָנִי), variously referring to the afflicted, lowly, humble, and poor, also *ebyon* (אֶבְיוֹן), referring to the poor or needy. It corresponds to the Greek *ptochos* (πτωχός), describing a beggarly posture. Taken together, *the poor* refers to both a material and metaphysical position, not reducible to a class analysis: "The *anawim*—the scum and refuse of society—have, like all dung, a contradictory status: the more they reveal dissolution and decay, the more fertile they become. . . . In embracing its *anawim*, a society is embrac-ing its own death; in the act of opening itself to its absurdities it is bound to disintegrate, since it survives only by excluding these from its precariously maintained world of meaning." Eagleton, *The Body as Language*, 70–71.

13. Corcoran et al., "An Anthropogenic Marker Horizon in the Future Rock Record."

14. Bergmann et al., "White and Wonderful?"; Ragusa et al., "Plasticenta."

15. Sometimes referred to as ELAB (Extradition Law Amendment Bill).

16. In England, for comparison, Asians are to this day generally assumed to be of South Asian origin and in the 1970s identified with political Blackness until the rise of Islamophobia in the late 1980s fractured this alliance. See Rama-murthy, *Black Star*, and Modood, "Political Blackness and British Asians." This separation can be seen in the now-outdated acronym BAME (Black, Asian, and Minority Ethnic), reminiscent of the term BIPOC (Black, Indige-nous, and Persons of Color).

17. Those in the nonprofit world will note the ironic use of "riches." The competition for grants has been darkly referred to as the "nonprofit Hunger Games," in reference to the popular young-adult dystopian novel *Hunger Games*. Even so, and despite devastating critiques of the nonprofit industrial complex, it continues to be the main channel of Asian American organizing.

18. Another possible formation is Third World liberation theology, following historian Gary Okihiro's *Third World Studies: Theorising Liberation*, but to the uninitiated the term *Third World* seems an anachronism, obscuring more than it enlightens. Admittedly, *Asian American* is also subject to this charge, though arguably to a lesser degree.

19. The terms *Global South* and *Global North* perhaps obscure more than they illuminate, if viewed primarily as geographical designations, especially as I will consider the flows of migration and transnationality whereby South and North are mutually constituted.

20. Wilmore, "A Revolution Unfulfilled"; Fernandez and Segovia, *A Dream Unfinished*.

21. It should be clear by now that I am writing from a particular Judeo-Christian theological perspective. I use it as my own point of entry, but there is much to be said from the perspectives of other spiritual and religious traditions. On the streets there is little we can assume about each other, and the conviviality arises precisely in discovering the commonalities and differences that define us.

22. Kim et al., "Asian American Religious History," 362: "Indeed, in charting the intellectual roots of the subfield of Asian American religions, at least one significant stream can be traced to the development of Asian American theologies of liberation, which spawned a series of networks developed for Asian American ministers and scholars." The authors point to PACTS, founded in 1972 by Lloyd Wake and Roy Sano; the Pacific Asian North American Asian Women in Theology and Ministry (PANAAWTM), founded in 1984 by Kwok Pui-Lan and Letty Russell; and the Institute for Leadership Development and Study of Pacific and Asian North American Religion (PANA Institute), which began in 2000 by Fumitaka Matsuoka.

23. The suffix *e* here reflects the current trend within Spanish-speaking LGBTQIA+ communities, such as in *Latine* as a gender-neutral alternative to *Latinx* commonly used in English-speaking communities. While the use of Latinx has entered mainstream English in the last decade, it has gained little traction within Spanish-speaking populations itself, in part due to its difficulty in pronunciation and lack of generalizability to other gendered words such as *amigxs*, whereas the suffix *e* has allowed for smoother linguis-

tic transitions such as *amiges* and the gender-neutral, third-person pronoun *elle* interpolating the masculine *el* and feminine *ella*.

24. Park, "Minjung Theology."

25. Boggs and Kurashige, *The Next American Revolution*, 64–72.

26. Herzog, *God-Walk*.

27. Torre, *Liberation Theology for Armchair Theologians*.

28. Fanon, *The Wretched of the Earth*, 145.

29. Day, *Alien Capital*.

30. The choice of language surrounding riots, uprisings, and rebellions is a subject of debate. For the use of riot in particular, see, for example, Clover, *Riot. Strike. Riot.*

31. Eng and Han, *Racial Melancholia, Racial Dissociation*.

32. Graeber, *The Utopia of Rules*.

33. Trask, "Settlers of Color and 'Immigrant' Hegemony."

34. Coulthard, *Red Skin, White Masks*.

35. Robinson, *Black Marxism*.

36. Hebrews 13:12–13.

37. Kenosis is the theological term derived from Philippians 2:7, describing Jesus's renunciation or emptying of his godly attributes when he became human.

38. Tuck and Yang, "Decolonization Is Not a Metaphor," 11.

39. Anzaldúa et al., *Borderlands / La Frontera*.

40. Fanon, *Black Skin, White Masks*, 204.

41. Wolfe, *Settler Colonialism and the Transformation of Anthropology*, 2.

42. Okihiro, *American History Unbound*, 20. A similar theme can be found in Evyn Lê Espiritu Gandhi's theorization of the Vietnamese nước (water, country, homeland) to connect the archipelago of Vietnamese refugee resettlement. Gandhi, *Archipelago of Resettlement*.

43. Fanon, *Black Skin, White Masks*, 194.

44. McAlister, "A Kind of Homelessness."

45. Tang, "A Gulf Unites Us," 125.

46. Fanon, *The Wretched of the Earth*, 131.

47. Fanon, *Black Skin, White Masks*, 199.

48. Fanon, 205. Whereas Cone's Black theology of liberation comes as a natural inspiration, my heavy reliance on the work of the Martinican psychiatrist and revolutionary Fanon may be surprising to some. Fanon's *Wretched of the Earth* was a crucial text for anti-colonial revolutionaries across the Third World while his *Black Skin, White Masks* is a key reference for the newer Afro-pessimist school of thought. The first primarily concerns revolutionary struggle; the second concerns psychoanalytic dimensions of anti-Black racism. In

articulating an Asian American theology of liberation, both of these powerful works will help ground our thinking and acting.

49. Cone, *A Black Theology of Liberation*, 40.
50. Szasz, *The Second Sin*, 20.
51. Lorde, "The Master's Tools," 27.

CHAPTER 1

1. A notable exception is the work of Wonhee Ann Joh and Nami Kim, who have argued for a critical theology that "considers the tasks of Christian theology in relation to critical studies of US imperialist militarism in Asia," providing a theological interrogation of United States militarist expansionism rationalized through specifically Christian language that further buttresses notions like the White man's burden, manifest destiny, the civilizing mission by the West, and the broader role of Christianity in empire-building. See Kim and Joh, eds., *Critical Theology against US Militarism*, xv. See also Chen, *Asia as Method*.
2. Coe, "Contextualizing Theology," 19–24.
3. Ruiz, "Revisiting the Question Concerning (Theological) Contextualization," 85
4. Pieris, *Asian Theology of Liberation*, 124–26.
5. In arguing against a pluralistic theology of difference (a potential pitfall of inculturation projects such as Pieris's), Kwok Pui-lan has proposed instead a "postcolonial theology of religious difference" that attends to the transformation of religious symbols and institutions in migration, exile, diaspora, and transnationalism, drawing attention to hybridized religious identities in the new contexts, which cannot be pinned down by fixed and reified notions of religion and how patriarchal relations in the religious arena intersect with and are transformed by colonial and other unequal relations. See Kwok, *Postcolonial Imagination and Feminist Theology*, 206–7.
6. Sharon Tan, quoted in De La Torre, *Ethics*; and De La Torre, *Handbook of US Theologies of Liberation*, 136–39.
7. Min, *The Solidarity of Others in a Divided World*, 3.
8. Phan, *Christianity with an Asian Face*, xx.
9. See, for example, Martey, *African Theology*, for a related perspective.
10. Fabella and Park, eds., *We Dare to Dream*.
11. Kyung, *Struggle to Be the Sun Again*, 110.
12. Kwok, *Postcolonial Imagination and Feminist Theology*, 20, 146.
13. Wong, "The Poor Woman," 61.

14. Blankenship, *Christianity, Social Justice, and the Japanese American Incarceration*, 215.
15. Tan, *Introducing Asian American Theologies*, 94–95.
16. Asian Center for Theology & Strategies, Pacific School of Religion, "Inventory of the Pacific and Asian American Center for Theology and Strategies Collection," Online Archive of California, accessed February 28, 2023, https://oac.cdlib.org/findaid/ark:/13030/kt75804087/entire_text/.
17. Loo, "Why an Asian American Theology of Liberation?," 209–213.
18. Sano, "Ministry for a Liberating Ethnicity," 290.
19. Sunoo, "Roots of Social Resistance in Asia and its Impact on Asian Americans," 9-10. "Serve the People" is a political slogan of the Chinese Communist Party, originating from a speech of Mao Zedong in 1944. Maoism more generally resonated with United States social movements in the 1960s. See Ishizuka, *Serve the People*.
20. Sunoo, 1–4.
21. Woo, "Theologizing: An Asian American Perspective," 355–56.
22. As captured by the Yellow Power movement then, "Asian" and "Yellow" were oftentimes equated, rendering invisible other Asians who might not identify as Yellow and revealing the limits of organizing based on skin color and of Asian American panethnicity; Sano, "Toward a Liberating Ethnicity," 21–24.
23. Kimoto, "From Silence to Sounds," 369–70.
24. Loo, "You Decide!," 374–75.
25. Tseng, "Asian American Religions," 83. See also Tseng, "Trans-Pacific Transpositions," 241–72.
26. Barger, *The World Come of Age*.
27. Bhabha and Spivak are dominant-caste Indians.
28. Sano, "Toward a Liberating Ethnicity," 14.
29. Choi, "Racial Identity and Solidarity," 144–45.
30. Choi, 132.
31. Matsuoka, *Out of Silence*, 96–97.
32. Choi, 148–50.
33. Zhou and Gatewood, *Contemporary Asian America*, 129.
34. Choi, *Disciplined by Race*, 69.
35. Matsuoka, *Out of Silence*, 90.
36. Fernandez, *Toward a Theology of Struggle*, 26.

CHAPTER 2

1. By the time the ban ended in January 2021 after Joe Biden's inauguration, it had mostly faded from public consciousness. The Biden administration

also largely ended the detention of migrant families in favor of surveillance technologies such as ankle bracelets and traceable cellphones, but in March 2023 announced that it was considering reinstating family detention again as a public health measure known as Title 42 that has allowed authorities to swiftly expel migrants expires in May.

2. Blankenship, *Christianity, Social Justice, and the Japanese American Incarceration*, 4.

3. Filipino, because they were essentially all men.

4. According to 2019 data, those of Chinese (24 percent), Indian (21 percent), Filipine (19 percent), Vietnamese (10 percent), Korean (9 percent), and Japanese (7 percent) make up the majority (85 percent) of Asian Americans, the remaining national origins each making up 2 percent or less. See Budiman and Ruiz, *Key Facts about Asian Origin Groups in the US.*

5. Here I am referring to Asia as the geographical landmass designated by early colonial powers. While this definition is open to being challenged, it remains one the operational definitions in popular discourse despite its fraught meaning.

6. The "brown paper bag test" refers to colorism within the Black American community, particularly in the twentieth century, where allegedly only those whose skin was lighter or the same as a brown paper bag were granted admission or other privileges.

7. Ignatiev, *How the Irish Became White*; Brodkin, *How Jews Became White Folks and What that Says about Race in America.*

8. This statistic can be calculated directly from the preceding data. See also Ramakrishnan and Shah, "One Out of Every 7 Asian Immigrants Is Undocumented."

9. Budiman and Ruiz, "Key Facts about Asian Americans, a Diverse and Growing Population." At the same time it is interesting to compare the increases relative to 2013–2015 survey data.

10. A 2018 census bureau study noted that Asians, relative to Black, White, and Hispanic populations, were the least familiar with and likely to fill out the census. It is certainly natural to expect that such Asians would lean lower on the socioeconomic ladder, resulting in data being skewed upward. McGeeney et al., *2020 Census Barriers, Attitudes, and Motivators Study Survey Report.*

11. This recounting of exclusionary laws hardly captures the harshness of life under this racial regime and should be supplemented by the broader anti-Chinese sentiment during this period. Most notable is the 1871 massacre in Los Angeles, involving the lynching of seventeen Chinese men by a mob of over five hundred people, the largest mass lynching in US history. (See, for example, Zesch, *The Chinatown War.*) Also in 1885, at least twenty-eight Chi-

nese miners were massacred in Rock Springs, Wyoming, setting off a wave
of further anti-Chinese violence in the Pacific Northwest. But even these
killings are eclipsed both in terms of number and historical memory by the
massacre of over three hundred Asian Mexicans, largely Cantonese and Japanese, in Torreón over the course of three days in March 1911. See, for example,
Herbert, *The House of the Pain of Others*.

12. Indeed, the Amerasian is derivative of the earlier Eurasian, produced in turn
by European colonialism in Asia.

13. Day, *Alien Capital*, 24.

14. Crenshaw, "Intersectionality, Identity Politics, and Violence against Women
of Color."

15. Similarly, some Iranians share a nationalist narrative of Aryan descent, giving
a pseudoscientific basis to the insistence of certain Iranian Americans on
their own inclusion into Whiteness. See Maghbouleh, *The Limits of Whiteness*.

16. Espiritu and Espiritu, *Asian American Panethnicity*.

17. Chuh, *Imagine Otherwise*.

18. Budiman and Ruiz, "Key Facts about Asian Americans, a Diverse and Growing
Population."

19. Rah, *The Next Evangelicalism*.

20. Lee, *The Making of Asian America*, 21.

21. Free native Filipinos were classified as *indios* rather than *chinos* or *negros*.
They were the first to be prohibited from enslavement under the Spanish
Crown in the 1540s. The Catholic Church came to associate chino slaves with
indios, embracing them as missionary targets and eventually ceasing to view
chinos as slaves. Free Filipinos were sometimes called Indian chinos, lending
to the blurring of boundaries between indios and chinos. For an account of
this complex history, see Seijas, *Asian Slaves in Colonial Mexico*.

22. Lee, *The Making of Asian America*, 24.

23. One striking outlier is the story of an enslaved South Asian turned popular
saint Catarina de San Juan in Puebla, Mexico. Much has been written about
her, including the early hagiographies of Alonso Ramos and José del Castillo
Grajeda. Catarina is said to have been abducted at about nine years old by
Portuguese enslavers from the western coast of India around 1610, sold at a
market in Manila, and brought to the port of Acapulco in 1619. From there
she was made to walk a difficult road, the *vía de china* to Mexico City, then to
Puebla. She was first purchased by a Portuguese merchant and his wife. After
they died, she was left free but moneyless and became the domestic servant of
a neighborhood priest. From early on she had adopted Christianity, the religion of her masters, and become the model of piety and an exemplary captive,

dutifully bearing the physical burdens of bondage to free her soul. By the time of her death in 1688, Catarina was considered a beloved popular saint by the residents of Puebla, who sought to have her beatified. Notably, the contemporary Juana Esperanza de San Alberto was similarly famous for her piety, but her African ancestry was likely seen by the poblanos as an insurmountable barrier to sainthood and they never advocated for her canonization.

24. Lee, *The Making of Asian America*, 35.
25. Lee, 43.
26. Lee, 44.
27. Ramnath, *Haj to Utopia*.
28. Lee, *The Making of Asian America*, 54
29. Ferriss and Sandoval, *The Fight in the Fields*.
30. Barajas, *Curious Unions*.
31. Dong, "*Jung Sai Garment Workers Strike of 1974.*"
32. Chang, Introduction to *Serve the People*.
33. Chan, "End Your Racist War," 5.
34. Not that a middle-class education serves as much of a shield from extrajudicial violence. In 1975, a White driver hit a parked car in Manhattan Chinatown and drove off, while a crowd of witnesses followed the driver past a nearby police station. When the police tried to control the crowd and knocked over a teenager, Chinese American architectural engineer Peter Yew tried to intervene, an act for which he was arrested, stripped, beaten, and charged with a felony. The incident ignited demonstrations numbering in the thousands— twenty thousand, by one account—and further clashes with the police.
35. Kim, "A Conversation with Chol Soo Lee and K. W. Lee," 81.
36. Lee, *Freedom without Justice*, 6.
37. Kim, "A Conversation with Chol Soo Lee and K. W. Lee," 103.
38. Kim, 105.
39. Mrie, "Photos."
40. Fanon, *Black Skin, White Masks*, 201–2.
41. Mignolo, *The Idea of Latin America*, 38–39.

CHAPTER 3

1. Kang, "What a Fraternity Hazing Death Revealed about the Painful Search for an Asian-American Identity."
2. Chen, "Corky Lee and the Work of Seeing."
3. Althaus-Reid, *Indecent Theology*, 34.
4. Althaus-Reid, 36.

5. Kim, "The 'Indigestible'Asian." Going beyond a reductive East/West binary, Kim notes that this rhetoric was also used by Japan as an ideological justification for imperialism and colonization of its neighboring countries under the banner of "Pan-Asianism," even as anti-Asian sentiment in the United States intensified following the Japanese attack on Pearl Harbor.

6. Wong, *The Poor Woman.*

7. Kim, "The 'Indigestible'Asian," 30.

8. Kim, 37.

9. Kim, 39.

10. A similar question was posed by the artist Fred Ho in the context of jazz: What makes Chinese American music Chinese American? An Asian American playing jazz does not make it Asian American jazz. Ho, "Beyond Asian American Jazz," 45-51.

11. Kim, "Critical Thoughts on Asian American Assimilation in the Whitening Literature"; Zhou, "Are Asian Americans Becoming 'White?'"

12. Such a story is told in celebrity chef Eddie Huang's memoir and subsequent sitcom adaptation *Fresh off the Boat*, wherein a young Eddie is embarrassed by his Chinese lunchbox meal compared to the other kids' Lunchables.

13. Nguyen, "Asian-Americans Need More Movies, Even Mediocre Ones." Five years on, Asian and Asian American shows have captured the attention of the US mainstream, most notably *Parasite* (2019), *Squid Game* (2021), and *Everything, Everywhere, All at Once* (2022), among many others. Even Nguyen's Pulitzer Prize–winning novel *The Sympathizer* is being adapted into a television series.

14. Matsuoka, *Out of Silence*, 56.

15. Kao and Ahn, *Asian American Christian Ethics*, 3–8.

16. Eng and Han, *Racial Melancholia, Racial Dissociation*, 115–16.

17. Eng and Han, 63.

18. Harris, "Whiteness as Property."

19. Du Bois, *The Souls of Black Folk.*

20. Eng and Han, *Racial Melancholia, Racial Dissociation*, 87–90.

21. Eng and Han, 122.

22. Eng and Han, 126.

23. Eng and Han, 109.

24. Eng and Han, 170.

25. Eng and Han, 19.

26. Eng and Han, 140.

27. Fanon, *Black Skin, White Masks*, 14.

28. Fanon, 27–29.

29. Fanon, 165.
30. Fanon, 170.
31. Fanon, 168.
32. Fanon, 33.
33. Fanon, 54–58.
34. Fanon, 45. It is perhaps worth noting that Fanon's wife, Josie Fanon, was a White Frenchwoman.
35. Fanon, 37.
36. Fanon, 36.
37. Fanon, 133.
38. Fanon, 154–57.
39. Day, *Alien Capital*, 5–7.
40. There is also a complex convergence of anti-Semitism (specifically, anti-Jewish sentiment) and anti-Sinicism in Southeast Asia. See, for example, Vajiravudh, "Jews of the Orient," and Ainslie, *Anti-Semitism in Contemporary Malaysia*.
41. Day, *Alien Capital*, 15–16.
42. Said, *Orientalism*, 167.
43. Said, 219.
44. Fanon, *Black Skin, White Masks*, 80.
45. Fanon, 83.
46. Fanon, 63.
47. Lee, *Journeys at the Margin*; Song, *Tell Us Our Names*.
48. Kuan and Foskett, *Ways of Being, Ways of Reading*, xiii
49. Fernandez and Matsuoka, *Realizing the America of Our Hearts*, 1.
50. Chuh, *Imagine Otherwise*, 4.
51. Chuh, 7.
52. Chuh, 10.
53. Chuh, 127.
54. Chuh, 32.
55. Chuh, 47.
56. Chuh, 55.
57. Chuh, 63.
58. Chuh, 87.
59. Chuh, 110.
60. Chuh, 82–83.
61. Lowe, *Immigrant Acts*, 83
62. Freire, *Pedagogy of the Oppressed*.
63. Okihiro, *Third World Studies*, 19.

CHAPTER 4

1. The 2021 song by singer Dhee and anti-caste rapper Arivu, originally in Tamil, describes the problematic repatriation of Tamil Dalits from Sri Lanka to South India, after ancestors including those of Arivu were taken there by British colonizers to work tea plantations over two centuries ago. See, for example, Bentz Goreau-Ponceaud, "To Be or Not to Be a Refugee?," 176–92, and Deeksha, "India's Failure to Protect Tamils Sent Back from Sri Lanka."

2. "Population Estimates, July 1, 2022," US Census Bureau. This data does not include those with two or more races, which constitute 2.9 percent.

3. For example, the 2022 admission statistics indicate that 25.9 percent of the 84.4 percent of domestic students are Asian Americans, which comes out to 21.9 percent of admitted students. This is in comparison to 15.9 percent African American, 1.1 percent Native American, 0.5 percent Native Hawaiian, 12.5 percent Hispanic or Latino, and 44.1 percent non-Hispanic or Latino Whites. See "Admission Statistics," Harvard College.

4. Hartocollis, "Asian-Americans Suing Harvard Say Admissions Files Show Discrimination."

5. Qin, "Applying to College, and Trying to Appear 'Less Asian.'"

6. The diffuse nature of the current climate crisis, what Rob Nixon calls "slow violence," makes it difficult at times to pinpoint exactly when a migration is due to climate change.

7. I use the terms *Native* and *Indigenous* interchangeably, within the US context.

8. For a treatment of the Jewish context, see Ellis, *Toward a Jewish Theology of Liberation*.

9. Wolfe, *Settler Colonialism and the Transformation of Anthropology*, 163.

10. Young and Veracini, "'If I Am Native to Anything.'"

11. Wolfe, *Settler Colonialism and the Elimination of the Native*, 387. The opposite is also true: genocide often takes place absent of settler colonialism, such as the Jewish Holocaust and the ongoing Rohingya, Darfuri, and Syrian genocides.

12. Veracini, *Settler Colonialism*.

13. Kosasa, "Sites of Erasure," 197.

14. Hauerwas and Willimon, *Resident Aliens*, 12

15. Hixson, *American Settler Colonialism*, 198.

16. Gutiérrez, "Internal Colonialism."

17. Deloria, "A Native American Perspective on Liberation."

18. Kim, "At Least You're Not Black."

19. Deloria, *God Is Red*. The other possibly more famous work being *Custer Died for Your Sins*.

20. Deloria, 304. This view is supported by a deficiency in biblical hermeneutics whereby man is interpreted to have been given dominion over the planet, supplemented by a naive and feeble understanding of stewardship.

21. Deloria, 79–82.

22. Deloria, 304.

23. Deloria, 296.

24. Tinker, "American Indian Theology," 2

25. Tinker, 2–3.

26. Tinker, 11–12.

27. Las Casas's mission compound is still in use by fundamentalist Christian groups such as the Summer Institute of Linguistics—formerly the Wycliff Bible Translators—in the Southern Hemisphere as a way of separating converts from their families and home communities, a strategy that holds continuity with the Indian boarding schools of the past. Thus, the cultural genocide of Native American culture persists and is an important reminder of the structural nature of settler-colonial invasion.

28. Tinker, "American Indian Theology," 7.

29. Coulthard, *Red Skin, White Masks*.

30. Tinker, "American Indian Theology," 129.

31. Trask, "Settlers of Color and 'Immigrant' Hegemony."

32. Young and Veracini, "If I Am Native to Anything."

33. Day, *Alien Capital*, 22.

34. Day, 10.

35. Day, 31.

36. Wolfe, "Recuperating Binarism."

37. Day, *Alien Capital*, 21.

38. Smith, "Heteropatriarchy and the Three Pillars of White Supremacy." In citing Andrea Smith, it is important to acknowledge that Smith's claimed Cherokee heritage has long been a subject of dispute. Smith is particularly important to consider because she continues to be productive in evangelical circles. See Viren, "The Native Scholar Who Wasn't." The article also describes the case of Ward Churchill, whom I cite in chapter 7. For the general problem of ethnic fraud and playing Native, see TallBear, *Native American DNA*, and Leroux, *Distorted Descent*.

39. Gjelten, "Killing of American Missionary Ignites Debate over How to Evangelize."

40. The critique in this book of the Israeli settler state that I make is an anti-settler position, not an anti-Semitic one. A critique of an ethnostate should not be conflated with a critique of a people group. Moreover, though the Semitic race was first coined by the Göttingen School of History in the early

1770s to describe the descendants of Shem, its modern usage within linguistic and archaeological anthropology refers to a broader geographic and cultural designation, such that the Israel–Palestine conflict might be better understood as an *intra*-Semitic issue. At the same time, it is important to acknowledge that even as anti-Asian sentiment has been on the rise, so has anti-Jewish violence (a more accurate term than anti-Semitism). As with anti-Asian racism, it is also possible and needful to historicize anti-Jewish racism; I do not undertake this but do explore their overlap in chapter 8.

41. Such conflicts have much to do with Asian Americans, as seen in the politics behind the May 2022 mass shooting at Irvine Taiwanese Presbyterian Church by David Chou, killing one and wounding five others. It reveals the deep geopolitical tensions that carry over to the United States. Born and raised in Taiwan, Chou opposed Taiwanese independence from China and viewed himself as an angel of death, destroying Taiwanese independence. See, for example, Hioe, "Confusion About 'Chinese' or 'Taiwanese' Identity of Gunman after Shooting at Taiwanese Church in California"; and Yang, "The Laguna Woods Shooting Wasn't Driven by Anti-Asian Hate."

42. Not to mention forcibly taken from Japanese Americans during their mass incarceration, not unlike the seizure of Jewish capital during the Holocaust.

43. Cone, *The Cross and the Lynching Tree*.

44. James 2:15–18.

45. Coates, "The Case for Reparations."

46. On the Left, proposals to invoke eminent domain for the use of public, affordable housing, while noble in intention and realpolitik, reinforce the settler state. See, for example, Gustavussen, "We Can Decommodify Housing through Eminent Domain."

47. Sakai, *Settlers*, 9.

48. Sakai, 6

49. Sakai, 431.

50. Luke 19:8.

51. Tuck and Yang, "Decolonization Is Not a Metaphor."

52. Trask, "Settlers of Color and 'Immigrant' Hegemony," 2.

53. See, for example, *Introducing Asian American*; Lee, *From a Liminal Place*; Kato, *Religious Language and Asian American Hybridity*.

54. The brutal British partition of India, Pakistan, and Bangladesh, to give but one example.

55. Hall, *The Bowl with One Spoon*, 238.

56. Tuck and Yang, "Decolonization Is Not a Metaphor," 31.

57. Ateek and ʿAtīq, *Justice, and Only Justice*.

58. Ateek, "A Palestinian Perspective."
59. Tuck and Yang, "Decolonization Is Not a Metaphor," 27.
60. Aldred, "First Nations and Newcomers," 193–206.
61. "Un programme de désordre absolu."
62. Fanon, *The Wretched of the Earth*, 2.
63. Fanon, 3.
64. Trask, "Settlers of Color and 'Immigrant' Hegemony," 21.
65. Fanon's *The Wretched of the Earth* translates from *Les Damnés de la Terre*. Fanon never explicitly says who he means by the wretched, but a likely answer would be the colonized.

CHAPTER 5

1. Twenty years earlier, sixteen-year-old Yong Xin Huang was killed in Brooklyn by an NYPD officer who shot him in the back of the head. Huang was shooting a pellet gun at a friend's house when the neighbor called the police. The officer was not indicted. Huang's older sister, Qianglan Haung, spoke in support of Akai Gurley and said in an interview that she feels her family never received the same support from Asian Americans as Liang had. See Fuchs, "Decades after a Cop Shot Her Brother, Qinglan Huang Speaks Up for Akai Gurley."
2. Kang, "How Should Asian-Americans Feel about the Peter Liang Protests?"
3. See "Home," Letters for Black Lives.
4. Less well known is that Alex Keung, one of the other two officers indirectly involved in George Floyd's murder, was African American. See Barker, "The Black Officer Who Detained George Floyd Had Pledged to Fix the Police."
5. Lee, *The Cold War Origins of the Model Minority Myth*.
6. The Hmong American community, though similarly divided, was much less outspoken. If anything, Hmong support for Black lives was more prominent in media coverage and protests.
7. Moreover, as Jonathan Tran argues, the model-minority myth refutation cottage industry has tended to *remythologize* the myth itself by effectively bracketing political-economic considerations. For example, counterarguments that rely on disaggregating Asian American demographics follow a deficit model while ignoring the opportunity hoarding that also takes place. Tran, *Asian Americans and the Spirit of Racial Capitalism*, chapters 1 and 6.
8. Lee, "When Is Asian American Life Grievable?"
9. Ho and Mullen, *Afro Asia*, 3.
10. Shilliam, *The Black Pacific*; Sharma, *Hawai'i Is My Haven*.

11. Cohen, *Chinese in the Post-Civil War South.*
12. Rickford, "Malcolm X and Anti-Imperialist Thought."
13. Prashad, *Everybody Was Kung Fu Fighting*, 145.
14. Aoki, importantly, was alleged much later in 2012 to have been an FBI informant. See Dong, "Richard Aoki's Legacy and Dilemma?," 102–15.
15. Prashad, *Everybody Was Kung Fu Fighting*, 141.
16. Uyematsu, "The Emergence of Yellow Power in America." Today the notion of Yellow Power, even as it has been invoked again in solidarity with Black uprisings in 2020, is inadequate at best to describe the complexity of what constitutes Asian Americans and how their solidarities are to be represented. The 1969 slogan "Yellow Peril supports Black Power" was revived in an attempt to offer a form of solidarity connecting the racist attacks against East Asians during the coronavirus pandemic in the United States with the George Floyd rebellion against police killings of Black people but ends up flattening the incommensurable forms of violence. For example, a picture of Aoki holding this slogan circulated widely during this resurgence of interest.
17. Okihiro, *Third World Studies*, 15.
18. Lee, *The Making of Asian America*, 375.
19. Much has been written about the various dynamics of the so-called Black–Korean conflict. See, for example, Park, "Black-Korean Tension in America," 60; and Kang, "The Managed Hand," 820–39.
20. Kang, *The Loneliest Americans*, 161–64.
21. In attempting to draw directly from Cone's Black theology of liberation, it is necessary to qualify the use of it in light of Asian American subjectlessness. I argue that it is possible to historicize and even deconstruct Blackness without losing the ontological argument—the fact of being and nonbeing, human and nonhuman. Here Fanon's interpretation is most expedient: Blackness is as an intersubjective reality, a racial epidermal schema that objectively exists as melanin but functions variously according to social construction. Similar remarks can be made of Asianness, which I revisit in Chapter 8.
22. Cone, *For My People*, 155.
23. Cone, 167.
24. The name itself originates from an 1863 raid on the Combahee River by Harriet Tubman, in which she led 150 Black Union soldiers in a campaign that freed more than 750 enslaved people in South Carolina. It was the only United States military campaign planned and led by a woman.
25. Wynter, "Unsettling the Coloniality of Being/Power/Truth/Freedom," 264.
26. Fanon, *The Wretched of the Earth*, 42
27. Martinot and Sexton, "The Avant-Garde of White Supremacy."
28. Haynes, *Noah's Curse.*

29. Wynter, "Unsettling the Coloniality of Being/Power/Truth/Freedom," 302.
30. Said, *Orientalism*, 39.
31. Fanon, *Black Skin, White Masks*.
32. Hartman et al., *Afro-Pessimism*, 8.
33. Hartman et al., 24.
34. Murakawa, *Ida B. Wells on Racial Criminalization*, 218.
35. Fanon, *Black Skin, White Masks*, 108.
36. Fanon, 95.
37. Hartman et al., *Afro-Pessimism*, 20–24.
38. Being should not be confused with humanness, especially at the brink of ecological collapse. Connecting the themes in this book to ecology and environment is an important undertaking to be made, but that I do not take up.
39. Hartman et al., *Afro-Pessimism*, 8.
40. Hartman et al.
41. Fanon, *The Wretched of the Earth*, 182.
42. Gutiérrez, *A Theology of Liberation*, 56.
43. Gutiérrez, 69.
44. Sattayanurak, "The Construction of Mainstream thought on 'Thainess' and the 'Truth' Constructed by 'Thainess.'"
45. Fanon, *Black Skin, White Masks*, 90.
46. Slabodsky, "It's the Theology, Stupid!"; Carter, *Race*.
47. Lloyd and Prevot, *Anti-Blackness and Christian Ethics*.
48. Wilderson, "The Prison Slave as Hegemony's (Silent) Scandal."
49. Hartman et al., *Afro-Pessimism*, 30.
50. Cone, *A Black Theology of Liberation*, 12–14.
51. Cone, 20.
52. Cone, 13.
53. Cone, 26–27.
54. Cone, 48.
55. Cone, 54.
56. Desai, "What B. R. Ambedkar Wrote to W. E. B. Du Bois."
57. Wilkerson, "America's 'Untouchables.'"
58. Wilkerson, *Caste*; Burden-Stelly, "Caste Does Not Explain Race."
59. Ambedkar and Roy, *Annihilation of Caste*, 238.
60. The English word *caste* derives from the Portuguese *casta*, carrying the connotations of race, clan, lineage, tribe, or breed. It was first used in the modern sense of caste when the Portuguese first arrived in India in 1498. It was also used by the Spanish to describe hierarchies of mixed-raced people in colonial Latin America.

61. This identification of work and caste inverts Marx's theory of alienation wherein the worker is separated from their labor and its product.

62. Roy, "The Doctor and the Saint."

63. Nelavala, "Caste Branding, Bleeding Body, Building Dalit Womanhood," 271.

64. Nelavala.

65. Roy, "The Doctor and the Saint."

66. Gandhi established a volunteer ambulance corps of Indian stretcher-bearers to support the British during the Battle of Spioen Kop in the Second Boer War in 1900, against native South African anti-colonial fighters. See Desai and Vahed, *The South African Gandhi*.

67. Ambedkar and Roy, *Annihilation of Caste*, 66–78.

68. Zwick-Maitreyi et al., "Caste in the United States," 1–51.

69. Ambedkar and Roy, *Annihilation of Caste*, 222. As with Wilkinson, this identification should not be taken literally.

70. Ambedkar and Roy, 233.

71. Sitha's real name was later found to be Chanti Jyotsna Devi Prattipati. The suffix *Reddy* indicates a dominant caste origin while *Prattipati* indicates a Dalit one. By one account, an autopsy found her to be pregnant when she died.

72. Shah, "South Asian Border Crossings and Sex Work."

73. Ambedkar and Roy, *Annihilation of Caste*, 311.

74. Ambedkar and Roy, 306.

75. Chitrajaya, "Jesus and Ambedkar," 123.

76. Clarke, "Dalit Theology," 19.

77. "The Bangkok Declaration and Call" Global Ecumenical Conference on Justice for Dalits.

78. Clarke et al., eds., *Dalit Theology in the Twenty First Century*, 13.

79. Dayanandan, "Who Needs a Liberation Theology?," 9.

80. The name change was in part a recognition of Indigenous sovereignty and of Seattle as being occupied by settlers, an increased consciousness since the days of Occupy Wall Street.

81. Hakim, Saul, and Oppel Jr, "'Top Cop' Kamala Harris's Record of Policing the Police."

82. Soundararajan, *The Trauma of Caste*.

83. Molchanova, "Modern Slavery in India."

84. Shubadra, "Arundhati Roy Does Not Know What Caste Pain Is About."

85. Robinson, *Black Marxism*, 167.

86. Robinson, 168.

87. Particularly inspiring is the story of Chinese indentured laborer Bu Tak, or

José Bu, who became a celebrated Cuban freedom fighter in the 1860s, known for charging into battle, ferociously waving a machete, and shouting in Spanish, "For Cuba! Spanish go to hell!"

88. Douglass, "No Progress without Struggle."
89. Cone, *The Cross and the Lynching Tree*, 30.
90. United Nations, "Statement to the Media by the United Nations' Working Group of Experts on People of African Descent, on the Conclusion of Its Official Visit to USA, 19–29 January 2016."
91. Matthew 16:24.
92. Bonhoeffer, *The Cost of Discipleship*, 89.
93. Hartman, Martinot, Sexton, Hortense, and Wilderson. *Afro-Pessimism*, 78.
94. Philippians 2:7 and John 3:30.
95. Munoz and Solis, "As Free as Blackness Will Make Them."
96. Munoz and Solis.
97. Fernandez, *Toward a Theology of Struggle*, 67.
98. *Compañero*, or *compa* for short, carries different connotations to *camarada* in Spanish depending on national history. Both translate to "comrade." The former tends to have more socialist leanings, while the latter more militant communist, sometimes fascist, leanings. But compa also connotes companionship, a softer togetherness than comradeship.

CHAPTER 6

1. Rogers, Jakes, and Swanson, "Trump Defends Using 'Chinese Virus' Label, Ignoring Growing Criticism."
2. Kim, Keenan, and Fausset, "Protesters Gather in Atlanta to #StopAsianHate."
3. A month later, on April 17, 2021, nineteen-year-old Brandon Hole shot and killed eight people at his former workplace, a FedEx ground facility near Indianapolis' main airport. Four of the victims belong to the local Sikh community, as did nearly all the workers at the facility. The Sikh community called for unity and support from other Asian American communities, but little support was given from East Asian American communities.
4. Swanson, "Atlanta Killings Underscore Troubling Rise in Anti-Asian Violence."
5. Ho, "Migrant Massage Workers Don't Need to Be Rescued."
6. Uprety, "Sociologist Tamara Nopper Discusses Anti-Asian Violence."
7. Historically, around 10 percent of hate crime reports have been of anti-White bias. See Federal Bureau of Investigation, "Hate Crime in the United States Incident Analysis."

8. The question of criminalization, or what *is* a crime, is also incredibly important and reveals the how little the criminal justice system really is about justice.

9. Red Canary Song, "Red Canary Song Response to 8 Lives Lost in Atlanta."

10. The phrase "We are the 99%" originates in the 2011 Occupy Movement, generally referring to the enormous wealth inequality between the richest 1 percent of the US population and the rest. While this is a catchy slogan, and despite the incontrovertible fact that the wealth of the ultrarich does indeed eclipse the rest, it still elides the gradation of inequality pointed out by Matthew Stewart's book *The 9.9%* and many others. In particular, many Asian Americans find themselves in the upper-middle class—according to one definition, the fourth-highest income quintile, above the middle and below the wealthiest, between roughly $85,000 and $140,000 in annual household income; other possible measures might involve wealth, including homeownership. By the former measure, we might call the "economic masses" those around or below median household income or personal income, around $67,000 and $35,800, respectively, according to 2020 statistics. At the same time, what economic statistics do not see are (1) those whose wealth is not primarily gained through income and (2) what Marxists refer to as the lumpenproletariat—the underclass of undocumented, unemployed, incarcerated, and the like.

11. Another possible answer lies in broad arguments around shared anti-imperialisms and the struggle against US militarism in general and in relation to China in particular, but such an approach is often liable to a sort of leftist form of a Monroe Doctrine. The Monroe Doctrine was a US policy in the 1800s that opposed European colonialism in the Americas in favor of US interests. In this context, the danger lies in committing ideological protectionism of a geographic region that one's connection to is only imagined.

12. Cone, *A Black Theology of Liberation*, 25.

13. Harris, "Whiteness as Property."

14. Admittedly, this song was much less popular than others such as the "Glory to Hong Kong," the de facto national anthem of the Hong Kong protests.

15. Lai, "Understanding the Use of Violence in the Hong Kong Protests."

16. This perhaps forms a shared locus with Asians born in the United States who feel most strongly the pain of rejection when they are told to go back to their own country. In contrast, first-generation Asian immigrants in the United States often *expect* to be victims of racism and to not feel welcome, thus slightly complicating the question of perpetual foreignness as it relates to the Asian search for belonging and what a theology of landlessness has to offer.

17. Tse and Tan, *Theological Reflections on the Hong Kong Umbrella Movement*, 5.
18. Rieger and Pui-Lan, *Occupy Religion*.
19. Tse and Tan, *Theological Reflections on the Hong Kong Umbrella Movement*, 96–100.
20. Kung, *Liberation Theology and Hong Kong's Predicament*.
21. Tse and Tan, *Theological Reflections on the Hong Kong Umbrella Movement*, 136–42.
22. Tse and Tan, 151–56.
23. Park, "Minjung Theology," 2.
24. It is perhaps needful to comment on the use of han here, where earlier I had critiqued the overreliance on or caricatures of certain East Asian philosophies or cultural concepts. Here, I refer to han in the larger context of minjung theology, which has its own well-developed Korean theological tradition, and it is that broader, established school of thought that I build upon.
25. Park, "Minjung Theology," 3.
26. In fact, there is also the specific Korean medical diagnosis of *hwabyung*, literally "fire illness," known as a Korean culture-bound syndrome that can be understood as the somatization of the repression of one's han. While it is interesting also to note that hwabyung is most often studied in Korean women, perhaps not unlike outdated notions of hysteria, it has also been used as a framework to understand the school shootings at Oikos University in 2013 by One Goh and at Virginia Tech in 2007 by Seung-Hui Cho, both Koreans. Cho's in particular is the deadliest school shooting in US history and was at the time the deadliest one-man shooting. See Kang, "That Other School Shooting."
27. Hong, Southall, and Watkins, "He Was Charged in an Anti-Asian Attack."
28. Kyung and Chung, *Struggle to Be the Sun Again*, 76–77.
29. Rieger and Pui-Lan, *Occupy Religion*, 102.
30. Rieger and Pui-Lan, 133.
31. Robinson, *Black Marxism, Revised and Updated Third Edition*.
32. Hartman, *Scenes of Subjection*; Sexton, "People-of-Color-Blindness."
33. Tran, *Asian Americans and the Spirit of Racial Capitalism*, 80–97.
34. The case *Gong Lum v. Rice* (1927) affirmed the separate-but-equal doctrine articulated in *Plessy v. Ferguson* (1896) and denied Gong Lum's nine-year-old Chinese American daughter Martha Lum entry to a "White" school because she was a member of the "Yellow" race.
35. Tran, *Asian Americans and the Spirit of Racial Capitalism*, 146.
36. Tran, 88–108.
37. Tran, 148.

38. Jones, *Is God a White Racist?*; Gordon, *Bad Faith and Antiblack Racism*; Gordon, *Freedom, Justice, and Decolonization*.

39. Tran, *Asian Americans and the Spirit of Racial Capitalism*, 277–87.

40. Gordon, *Freedom, Justice, and Decolonization*, 110.

41. Klein, *The Shock Doctrine*.

42. I refer to the right-wing appropriation of the heterodox Marxist notion of accelerationism, the hope to precipitate violent racial conflict in order to establish a White ethnostate.

43. Chow, *The Protestant Ethnic and the Spirit of Capitalism*, 47.

44. Chow, 48.

45. Fanon, *The Wretched of the Earth*, 28.

46. Ehrenreich and Ehrenreich, "The Professional-Managerial Class."

47. Ehrenreich, *Fear of Falling*, 256.

48. Ehrenreich and Ehrenreich, "Death of a Yuppie-Dream."

49. Liu, *Virtue Hoarders*, 71.

50. Liu, 78.

51. Though, it is important to note, a significant number of Asians in the United States see themselves as being at the bottom, perceiving Asians to be the most invisible and neglected by US policy, media, and general discourse, contributing to the acute sense of indignity and discrimination relative to other racialized groups.

52. Cabral, *Return to the Source*, 61.

53. Cabral, 63.

54. Cabral, 64.

55. Cabral, 67.

56. Cabral, 69.

57. Rodney, *The Groundings with My Brothers*, 62.

58. Rodney, 67.

59. See Isaiah 2:4, 11:6–9, 65:25.

60. Luke 3:11–14. The other advice to tax collectors and soldiers is also worth meditating on, especially to the latter: Μηδένα διασείσητε, variously meaning do not blackmail, extort, shake thoroughly, or intimidate anyone; or, as in the King James Version, "do violence to no man."

61. Mark 10:21. ἠγάπησεν, the root word *agape*, the exact same famously used in John 3:16. A variant of the Greek text further adds at the end: "Take up the cross, and follow me," thus combining the call to social death, or dying to oneself, with a rejection of capitalism and private property.

62. Matthew 19:21. τέλειος, whose root word is *telos*, meaning complete, also translated to *shalem* in Hebrew.

63. Phan, *Christianity with an Asian Face*, makes some indications toward this.

64. In 2019, it was $85,800 compared to $61,800, which translates to about 39 percent more. Poverty rates are 10 percent compared to the national average of 13 percent, though the disparity ranges from 6 percent (Indian) to 25 percent (Mongolian). See Budiman and Ruiz, "Key Facts about Asian Americans."

65. Sano, "A Theology of Struggle from an Asian American Perspective," 8–11.

66. Fernandez, *Toward a Theology of Struggle*, 22–24.

67. By some interpretations, the Philippines *is* a part of Latin America. Some call it the Mexico of Asia.

68. Fernandez, 25–27.

69. Even Spivak's famous work *Can the Subaltern Speak?* ironically repeats this transgression. While itself a groundbreaking work, there are important related questions here for practical consideration: To whom should the subaltern be speaking? Are they not already speaking? Perhaps they are simply not being listened to, or may not even want to be heard. If the subaltern manages to speak in the "right" circles (such as Columbia University, Spivak's institution), are they still subaltern anymore? The challenge of subjectivization is a much more difficult representation. See Spivak, "Can the Subaltern Speak?," 66–111.

70. Madaling maging tao, mahirap magpakatao.

71. Fernandez, *Toward a Theology of Struggle*, 96.

72. Fernandez, 88.

73. Isaiah 65:22.

74. Avila, "Peasant Theology."

75. Tran, *Asian Americans and the Spirit of Racial Capitalism*, 149–50.

76. "Black Manifesto," *New York Review of Books*.

77. "'Black Manifesto' Declares War on Churches," *Christianity Today*.

78. "Churches," *Time*.

79. Cressler and Banks, "Reparations and Religion"; Pega et al., "Unconditional Cash Transfers for Reducing Poverty and Vulnerabilities." Indeed, a 2020 investigation by the *Detroit News* revealed that the city had overtaxed homeowners by at least $600 million when it failed to reduce assessed values when property values fell after the 2008 recession. While the city council approved a number of measures in 2023 to benefit overtaxed residents, none of them included direct repayments, arguing that it was unconstitutional to issue direct payments to individuals.

80. A parallel debate concerns who owes these reparations: the descendants of enslavers or non-Black people in general? A possible model that might be held in consideration are the reparations paid to Holocaust survivors and the

solidarity tax paid by former Western Germany for the rebuilding of Eastern Germany after 1991.

81. Kwon and Thompson, *Reparations.*

82. Related critiques have arisen under the notions of greenwashing and pink-washing, in which corporations market their products as supportive of environmentally conscious and progressive gender rights, respectively, while exploiting and committing violence against other communities.

83. By the US 2020 census, Detroit was 80 percent Black out of a population of 639,111, trailing after Jackson, Mississippi (80 percent; 153,701), and South Fulton, Georgia (93 percent; 107,436). The next largest Black cities were Memphis, Tennessee (63 percent; 633,104), Baltimore, Maryland (60 percent; 585,708), and Atlanta, Georgia (50 percent; 498,715).

84. Technically, Chin was killed in Highland Park, a separate city entirely within the city of Detroit, which, like Dearborn, refused incorporation into Detroit. In the mid-1900s, Highland Park had a significant Japanese American community that relocated there after their incarceration during the Second World War. Many Japanese companies had branches in Detroit, facilitated in part by the booming auto industry there. Despite the racism that followed the war and the decline of the US auto industry, the Japanese American community found economic success and moved out to form enclaves in majority-White, wealthy suburbs: Novi, West Bloomfield, and Farmington Hills.

85. To the USPS, the address is either occupied and requires mail service or is vacant and does not. An address is deemed vacant if it did not collect mail for ninety days or longer. In addition to occupied and vacant addresses, there are also "no stat" addresses. A "no stat" address is deemed that if it is under construction and not yet occupied or is in an urban area and identified by a carrier as not likely to be active for some time. See, for example, "USPS Reports Decreased Vacancy Rates in Detroit."

86. As alluded to in Chapter 2, demographic data about Arab Americans is difficult to assess accurately because it is not an official census category, counted officially instead as White, and thus has to be approximated through various proxies.

87. Good, *Orvie.* Sundown towns are all-White towns—or counties or, in the case of Oregon, the entire state up to 1926—in which "colored people" are to leave by sundown or else. This practice was so widespread that the annual publication *The Negro Motorist Green Book,* indicating which places were safe to travel to, was widely used as a survival tool.

88. Boggs and Kurashige, *The Next American Revolution,* 60.

89. Boggs and Kurashige, 51.

CHAPTER 7

1. *Thalu* is a romanization of the Thai ทะลุ, meaning "to penetrate" or "to go through." The *gas*, of course, refers to tear gas.
2. Unno, "'Thalu Gas.'"
3. DinDeng, "Thalugaz Interview."
4. The romanized spelling "Thalugaz" is used by their Facebook and Twitter accounts of the same name. There also exists another student group under the name Thalugas, which one of the coordinators of Thalugaz informs me are organized hierarchically and oppose the monarchy but not the state in general. The two are often conflated or confused by outside observers.
5. The historical and political context of Myanmar differs greatly from Thailand, except for the overlapping feature of military coups. Interestingly, but also tangentially, inciting others to commit crimes or conspiracy in order to make an arrest is also a common FBI tactic.
6. Rodney, *The Groundings with My Brothers*, 22.
7. Churchill, Ryan, and Jensen, *Pacifism as Pathology*, 49–51.
8. Deserting soldiers and draft dodgers, on the other hand, are a different story.
9. Churchill, Ryan, and Jensen, *Pacifism as Pathology*, 55–57.
10. Not to mention that the riots were not entirely without communal logic: within many lootings were moments of collective economic redistribution and sharing, not a chaotic free-for-all.
11. Churchill, Ryan, and Jensen, 84–86. At the same time, it might well be argued that armed struggle within the United States, especially for non-White people, is at least as much a suicidal prospect.
12. Churchill, Ryan, and Jensen, 141.
13. Churchill, Ryan, and Jensen, 94.
14. The language of necessity, though, must be exercised with much caution, as it has also been used to enshrine state violence, such as the Gulf of Tonkin Resolution of 1964 that allowed authorizing the president to take all necessary steps, including the use of armed force to assist any member of the Southeast Asia Collective Defense Treaty, and the Authorization for Use of Military Force (AUMF) following the 9/11 attacks in 2001 granting the president authority to use all "necessary and appropriate force" against those determined to be involved.
15. Asad, *On Suicide Bombing*.
16. Whereas Brown's own appeal to a higher law challenged the state's monopoly on violence, it was imperative for then governor of Virginia Henry Wise, at a time when the sovereignty of the states was a central issue, to execute John

Brown in a manner that enshrined the sovereignty of the commonwealth of Virginia. He did so by ensuring that Brown was protected both from vigilantes who wanted to lynch him and from sympathizers who might attempt to rescue him, and that Brown's execution would impress upon its witnesses what one commentator called the "awful majesty of the law." The law of the state was sovereign. Smith, *Weird John Brown*, 27.

17. Smith, 35–36.

18. Smith, 60.

19. But even attempts to employ political theology can run afoul, such as Carl Schmitt's insistence on the need for both some sovereign power beyond the system of law and some clear earthly identity for that legal power—a legal system that depends on a sovereignty that exceeds the system itself—all of which led Schmitt to support Hitler's regime.

20. Benjamin, *Critique of Violence*, 281.

21. Benjamin, 297.

22. Žižek, *Violence*, 167.

23. Smith, *Weird John Brown*, 81.

24. Smith, 83.

25. Smith, 98.

26. A relevant example is the anti-abortion activist Paul Hill, who murdered Dr. John Britton and his bodyguard James Barrett at the Pensacola Ladies Center in 1994, with the intention that the event would be to anti-abortionists what Harpers Ferry was to abolitionists.

27. Delbanco et al., *The Abolitionist Imagination*, 23.

28. Smith, *Weird John Brown*, 109.

29. Smith, 111.

30. Smith, 117.

31. Smith, 123.

32. Smith, 176.

33. Kim, "The Racial Triangulation of Asian Americans."

34. Fanon, *The Wretched of the Earth*, 5.

35. Fanon, 10.

36. Fanon, 19–21.

37. Fanon, 44.

38. Fanon, 42.

39. Fanon, 50.

40. Fanon, 178.

41. Fanon, 22–23.

42. Fanon, 122.

43. Fanon, 13.
44. Fanon, 153.
45. Fanon, 160.
46. Fanon, 155.
47. Fanon, 155–56.
48. Fanon, 157.
49. Fanon, 156–57.
50. Or, as is often the case, *because* of poverty, debt, and citizenship status many people of color enlist in the army or take up jobs in the carceral system. Another reminder that the best way to see that all these things are interconnected is to just *look* around us.
51. Fanon, *The Wretched of the Earth*, 168.
52. Althaus-Reid, *Indecent Theology*, 6.
53. "At the Wendy's."
54. "At the Wendy's."

CHAPTER 8

1. On the other end of the age spectrum is the 1989 Cleveland Elementary School shooting in Stockton, California, where a White man shot and killed five children and wounded thirty others, many of whom were Cambodian and Vietnamese refugees. Though little remembered, it was one of the largest shootings at an elementary school before the 2012 Sandy Hook Elementary School shooting.
2. The same day of the incident in New York City, Rabbi Charlie Cytron-Walker and three congregants were held hostage by British national Malik Faisal Akram at a Texas synagogue, demanding the release of Pakistani neuroscientist Aafia Siddiqui, allegedly connected to the Islamic State group. FBI officials called it an act of terrorism and a federal hate crime.
3. Closson and Newman, "Woman Dies after Being Pushed Onto Subway Tracks in Times Square."
4. Kang, *The Loneliest Americans*, 160.
5. US Department of Justice, "2020 Hate Crimes Statistics."
6. Moreover, what currently figures as the *Asian* imaginary in the United States has been overdetermined by *yellowness*, so to speak—meaning the primarily Northeast Asian.
7. Borja and Gibson, "Virulent Hate + Reports."
8. US Department of Justice. "2020 Hate Crimes Statistics."
9. 不怕一万, 只怕万一.

10. Hawkins and Vandiver, "Human Caregivers Perceive Racial Bias in their Pet Dogs," 901–17.
11. Trayvon Martin, Andrew Hill, Casey Goodson Jr.
12. Hartman and Wilderson, "The Position of the Unthought."
13. Hedges and Sacco, *Days of Destruction, Days of Revolt*. The concept of sacrifice zones and their impact on low-income communities of color have been well-documented by environmentalists and journalists, among others.
14. That Europeans arrived in the Americas by Chinese and Filipino sailors, bringing enslaved Africans and Asians as they killed the Natives, should remind us that none of these forms of violence should be thought about separately for very long.
15. Fanon, *Black Skin, White Masks*, 92.
16. Cheng, "Ornamentalism," 429–30.
17. Cheng, 432.
18. Cheng, "What This Wave of Anti-Asian Violence Reveals about America."
19. Postone, "Anti-Semitism and National Socialism."
20. Postone, 109–10.
21. Day, *Alien Capital*, 8.
22. To be doubly clear, I make no judgment about anyone's individual decisions. This is about the statistical reality.
23. Kim, *Invisible*, 145.
24. Gay, "Why I Can't Forgive Dylann Roof."
25. The root *safah* (שָׂפָה) refers anatomically to the lip, also language.
26. Walsh, *The Mighty from Their Thrones*, 3–7.
27. Walsh, 179.
28. The opening scene of Kevin Young's book and movie adaptation *Crazy Rich Asians* comes to mind: A Singaporean Chinese family is turned away at the posh Calthorpe Hotel in London, 1986, with no uncertainty that it is because of their race, only to have Lord Calthorpe arrive and reveal that Eleanor Young of the family is its new owner, who proceeds to fire the bewildered hotel clerk. Here, money does not buy happiness: it trumps racism. Kwan, *Crazy Rich Asians*, 1–8.
29. Geng, "On Pepper Spray and Preventing Anti-Asian Violence"; Wong, "Asian Women Don't Feel Safe in Public." Yu and Me Books, a Manhattan Chinatown bookstore dedicated to Asian American literature that opened in 2021, gave out free pepper spray to hundreds of people, most of whom were young Asian women.
30. Breonna Taylor, Daunte Wright, Ahmaud Arbery, Charles Kinsey, Michelle Go, to name but a few. Black liberation is a precondition for Asian liberation.

CHAPTER 9

1. Althaus-Reid, *Indecent Theology*, 4.
2. Foucault, "Of Other Spaces."
3. Althaus-Reid, *Indecent Theology*, 147.
4. 1 Corinthians 13:12.
5. The eschatological notion of "Kin-dom," as a play on *Kingdom*, popularized by mujerista theologian Ada María Isasi-Díaz, gestures to the idea of liberation being grounded in relations of kinship and care. See Isasi-Díaz, "Kin-dom of God."
6. Cheng, *Radical Love*, 10.
7. Althaus-Reid, *Indecent Theology*, 152.
8. Angel, *Tomorrow Sex Will Be Good Again*.
9. Althaus-Reid, *Indecent Theology*, 20.
10. Althaus-Reid, 24.
11. Althaus-Reid, 21.
12. Foucault, *The History of Sexuality*.
13. Althaus-Reid, *Indecent Theology*, 36.
14. Althaus-Reid, 35. Althaus-Reid's publisher, Taylor & Francis, is also based in England.
15. Althaus-Reid, 133.
16. A more generous reading of Guttiérez's response might be: the Church of England does not care about the material lives of Latin American women, so why should they care about who it ordains?
17. Althaus-Reid, *Indecent Theology*, 45.
18. Althaus-Reid, 67.
19. Althaus-Reid, 35.
20. Genesis 1:2.
21. Althaus-Reid, 68.
22. Wilderson, "Gramsci's Black Marx," 238.
23. Williams, "The Body's Grace," 44
24. Althaus-Reid, *Indecent Theology*, 110.
25. Althaus-Reid, 117.
26. Althaus-Reid, 102–3.
27. Even rabbinic interpretations have much more expansive gender and sexual categories.
28. Williams, "The Body's Grace," 46.
29. Williams, 47–48.
30. Williams, 51.

31. Williams, 6.
32. Fanon, *Black Skin, White Masks*, 24.
33. Williams, "The Body's Grace," 9.
34. Related to what are colloquially known as *terfs*, transexclusionary radical feminists. Also, there is a newer, smaller group of female incels, or femcels, who also believe in the right to have sex. Both male and female incels are structured by heteronormativity: "They feel the same sense of "humiliation and exclusion" that incels do, but they react to those feelings differently. . . . Though society is discussed as inherently 'lookist' and unfair, femcels are not out to change it, because they don't see it as changeable." Tiffany, "What Do Female Incels Really Want?"
35. Srinivasan, "Does Anyone Have the Right to Sex?"
36. Montgomery, "Knife Attacker on Tokyo Train Says He Wanted to 'Kill Happy Women.'"
37. Park and Park, "Gangnam Murderer Says He Killed 'Because Women Have Always Ignored Me.'"
38. Srinivasan, "Does Anyone Have the Right to Sex?"
39. Williams, "The Body's Grace," 12.
40. Williams, 14–15.
41. Williams, 15–16.
42. Kollontai, *Make Way for Winged Eros*, 291.
43. Kollontai, 288.
44. Kollontai, 290.
45. Comblin, *Retrieving the Human*, 4.
46. Fernandez, *Toward a Theology of Struggle*, 186.
47. Ruiz, "Towards a Theology of Politics," 32.
48. Du Bois, *John Brown*, 170–71.

EPILOGUE

1. Duran et al., "Healing the American Indian Soul Wound."
2. Duran, *Healing the Soul Wound*.
3. Foo, *What My Bones Know*.
4. Montgomery and Bergman, *Joyful Militancy*.
5. Armstrong McKay et al., "Exceeding 1.5°C Global Warming Could Trigger Multiple Climate Tipping Points."
6. Hayes and Kaba, "Let This Radicalize You."

Bibliography

Achebe, Chinua. *Home and Exile*. New York: Canongate Books, 2003.

"Admission Statistics." Harvard College, accessed March 5, 2023. https://college .harvard.edu/admissions/admissions-statistics

Ainslie, Mary J. *Anti-Semitism in Contemporary Malaysia: Malay Nationalism, Philosemitism and Pro-Israel Expressions*. New York: Springer, 2019.

Aldred, Ray. "First Nations and Newcomers: Treaty." In *Strangers in This World: Multireligious Reflections on Immigration*, edited by Hussam S. Timani, Allen G. Jorgenson, and Alexander Y. Hwang, 193–206. Minneapolis: Fortress Publishers, 2015.

Althaus-Reid, Marcella. *Indecent Theology*. London: Routledge, 2001.

Ambedkar, B. R., and Arundhati Roy. *Annihilation of Caste: The Annotated Critical Edition*. Edited by S. Anand. New York: Verso, 2016.

Anderson, Benedict. *Imagined Communities: Reflections on the Origin and Spread of Nationalism*. Rev. ed. New York: Verso, 2016.

Angel, Katherine. *Tomorrow Sex Will Be Good Again: Women and Desire in the Age of Consent*. New York: Verso, 2021.

Anzaldúa, Gloria, Norma Cantú, and Aída Hurtado. *Borderlands / La Frontera: The New Mestiza*. 4th ed. San Francisco: Aunt Lute Books, 2012.

Armstrong McKay, David I., Arie Staal, Jesse F. Abrams, Ricarda Winkelmann, Boris Sakschewski, Sina Loriani, Ingo Fetzer, Sarah E. Cornell, Johan Rockström, and Timothy M. Lenton. "Exceeding 1.5°C Global Warming Could Trigger Multiple Climate Tipping Points." *Science* 377, no. 6611 (September 9, 2022): eabn7950. https://doi.org/10.1126/science.abn7950.

Asad, Talal. *On Suicide Bombing*. New York: Columbia University Press, 2007.

"At the Wendy's: Armed Struggle at the End of the World." Ill Will, November 9, 2020. https://illwill.com/at-the-wendys.

Ateek, Naim Stifan. "A Palestinian Perspective: Biblical Perspectives on the Land." In *Voices from the Margin: Interpreting the Bible in the World*, edited by R. S. Sugirtharajah, 280–86. Maryknoll: Orbis Books, 2015.

Ateek, Naim Stifan, and Naʿīm S. ʿAtīq. *Justice, and Only Justice: A Palestinian Theology of Liberation*. Maryknoll, NY: Orbis Books, 1989.

Avila, Charles R. *Peasant Theology: Reflections by the Filipino Peasants on Their Process of Social Revolution*. Bangkok: World Student Christian Federation, Asia-Pacific Region, 1976.

"The Bangkok Declaration and Call" Global Ecumenical Conference on Justice for Dalits, March 21–24, 2009, Bangkok, Thailand.

Barajas, Frank P. *Curious Unions: Mexican American Workers and Resistance in Oxnard, California, 1898–1961*. Omaha: University of Nebraska Press, 2021.

Barger, Lilian Calles. *The World Come of Age: An Intellectual History of Liberation Theology*. New York: Oxford University Press, 2018.

Barker, Kim. "The Black Officer Who Detained George Floyd Had Pledged to Fix the Police." *New York Times*, June 27, 2020. https://www.nytimes.com/2020/06/27/us/minneapolis-police-officer-kueng.html.

Benjamin, Walter. "Critique of Violence." In *On Violence: A Reader*, edited by Bruce B. Lawrence and Aisha Karim, 268–85. Durham, NC: Duke University Press, 2007.

Bentz, Anne-Sophie, and Anthony Goreau-Ponceaud. "To Be or Not to Be a Refugee? Reflections on Refugeehood and Citizenship among Sri Lankan Tamils in India." *Citizenship Studies* 24, no. 2 (2020): 176–92.

Bergmann, Melanie, Sophia Mützel, Sebastian Primpke, Mine B. Tekman, Jürg Trachsel, and Gunnar Gerdts. "White and Wonderful? Microplastics Prevail in Snow from the Alps to the Arctic." *Science Advances* 5, no. 8 (August 1, 2019): eaax1157. https://doi.org/10.1126/sciadv.aax1157.

"Black Manifesto." *New York Review of Books*, July 10. 1969. https://www.nybooks.com/articles/1969/07/10/black-manifesto/.

"'Black Manifesto' Declares War on Churches." *Christianity Today*, May 23, 1969. https://www.christianitytoday.com/ct/1969/may-23/black-manifesto-declares-war-on-churches.html.

Blankenship, Anne M. *Christianity, Social Justice, and the Japanese American Incarceration during World War II*. Chapel Hill: University of North Carolina Press, 2016.

Boggs, Grace Lee, and Scott Kurashige. *The Next American Revolution: Sustainable Activism for the Twenty-First Century*. Berkeley: University of California Press, 2012.

Bonhoeffer, Dietrich. *The Cost of Discipleship*. New York: Touchstone, 2012.

Borja, Melissa, and Jacob Gibson. "Virulent Hate + Reports: Anti-Asian Racism in 2020." Virulent Hate Project, accessed March 12, 2023. https://virulentha te.org/wp-content/uploads/2021/05/Virulent-Hate-Anti-Asian-Racism-In-20 20-5.17.21.pdf.

Brock, Rita Nakashima. *Off the Menu: Asian and Asian North American Women's Religion and Theology.* Louisville: Presbyterian Publishing, 2007.

Brodkin, Karen. *How Jews Became White Folks and What that Says about Race in America.* New Brunswick, NJ: Rutgers University Press, 1998.

Budiman, Abby, and Neil G. Ruiz. "Key Facts about Asian Americans, a Diverse and Growing Population." Pew Research Center, April 29, 2021. https://www .pewresearch.org/fact-tank/2021/04/29/key-facts-about-asian-americans/.

Budiman, Abby, and Neil G. Ruiz. *Key Facts about Asian Origin Groups in the US.* Washington, DC: Pew Research Center, 2019.

Burden-Stelly, Charisse. "Caste Does Not Explain Race." *Boston Review,* December 14, 2020. http://bostonreview.net/race/charisse-burden-stelly-caste-does-not -explain-race.

Cabral, Amílcar. *Return to the Source.* New York: New York University Press, 1974.

Callaci, Emily. "On Acknowledgments." *American Historical Review* 125, no. 1 (February 1, 2020): 126–31. https://doi.org/10.1093/ahr/rhz938.

Carter, J. Kameron. *Race: A Theological Account.* New York: Oxford University Press, 2008.

Chakrabarty, Dipesh. "Provincializing Europe: Postcoloniality and the Critique of History." *Cultural Studies* 6, no. 3 (1992): 337–57.

Chan, Patsy. "End Your Racist War." *Gidra,* June 1971, 5.

Chang, Jeff. Introduction to *Serve the People: Making Asian America in the Long Sixties,* by Karen L. Ishizuka, xi–xiii. New York: Verso Books, 2016.

Chang, Jeff. *We Gon' Be Alright: Notes on Race and Resegregation.* New York: Picador, 2016.

Chen, Ken. "Corky Lee and the Work of Seeing." n+1, accessed April 18, 2023. https://www.nplusonemag.com/online-only/online-only/corky-lee-and-the -work-of-seeing/.

Chen, Kuan-Hsing. *Asia as Method: Toward Deimperialization.* Durham, NC: Duke University Press, 2010.

Cheng, Anne Anlin. "What This Wave of Anti-Asian Violence Reveals about America." *New York Times,* February 21, 2021. https://www.nytimes.com/2021/02/21 /opinion/anti-asian-violence.html.

Cheng, Anne Anlin. "Ornamentalism: A Feminist Theory for the Yellow Woman." *Critical Inquiry* 44, no. 3 (March 2018): 415–46. https://doi.org/10.1086/696921.

Cheng, Patrick S. *Radical Love: Introduction to Queer Theology.* 1st ed. New York: Seabury Books, 2011.

Choi, Ki Joo. *Disciplined by Race: Theological Ethics and the Problem of Asian American Identity*. Eugene, OR: Wipf and Stock, 2019.

Choi, Ki Joo. "Racial Identity and Solidarity." In *Asian American Christian Ethics: Voices, Methods, Issues*, edited by Grace Y. Kao and Ilsup Ahn, 144–45. Waco, TX: Baylor University Press, 2015.

Chow, Kat. "If We Called Ourselves Yellow." NPR, September 27, 2018. https://www.npr.org/sections/codeswitch/2018/09/27/647989652/if-we-called-ourselves-yellow.

Chow, Rey. *The Protestant Ethnic and the Spirit of Capitalism*. New York: Columbia University Press, 2002.

Chuh, Kandice. *Imagine Otherwise: On Asian Americanist Critique*. Durham, NC: Duke University Press, 2003.

"Churches: Catalyst of Conscience." *Time*, August 29, 1969. https://content.time.com/time/subscriber/article/0,33009,901311,00.html.

Churchill, Ward, Mike Ryan, and Derrick Jensen. *Pacifism as Pathology: Reflections on the Role of Armed Struggle in North America*. Chico, CA: AK Press, 2007.

Clarke, Sathianathan. "Dalit Theology: An Introductory and Interpretive Theological Exposition." In *Dalit Theology in the Twenty-First Century: Discordant Voices, Discerning Pathways*, edited by Clarke, Deenabandhu Manchala, and Philip Vinod Peacock. New Delhi: Oxford University Press, 2011.

Clarke, Sathianathan, Deenabandhu Manchala, and Philip Vinod Peacock, eds. *Dalit Theology in the Twenty-First Century: Discordant Voices, Discerning Pathways*. New Delhi: Oxford University Press, 2010.

Closson, Troy, and Andy Newman. "Woman Dies after Being Pushed onto Subway Tracks in Times Square." *New York Times*, January 15, 2022. https://www.nytimes.com/2022/01/15/nyregion/woman-pushed-on-train-death.html.

Clover, Joshua. *Riot. Strike. Riot: The New Era of Uprisings*. New York: Verso Books, 2019.

Coates, Ta-Nehisi. "The Case for Reparations." *Atlantic*, May 22, 2014. https://www.theatlantic.com/magazine/archive/2014/06/the-case-for-reparations/361631/.

Cohen, Lucy M. *Chinese in the Post-Civil War South: A People without a History*. Baton Rouge: Louisiana State University Press, 1999.

Coe, Shoki. "Contextualizing Theology." *Mission Trends* 3 (1976): 19–24.

Comblin, Jose. *Retrieving the Human: A Christian Anthropology*. Eugene: Wipf and Stock, 2003.

Cone, James H. *A Black Theology of Liberation: 50th Anniversary Edition*. Maryknoll, NY: Orbis Books, 2020.

Cone, James H. *For My People: Black Theology and the Black Church*. Maryknoll, NY: Orbis Books, 1984.

Cone, James H. *The Cross and the Lynching Tree*. Maryknoll, NY: Orbis Books, 2011.

Corcoran, Patricia L., Charles J. Moore, Kelly Jazvac. "An Anthropogenic Marker Horizon in the Future Rock Record." *GSA Today* (2013): 4–8. https://doi.org .10.1130/GSAT-G198A.1.

Coulthard, Glen Sean. *Red Skin, White Masks: Rejecting the Colonial Politics of Recognition*. Minneapolis: University of Minnesota Press, 2014.

Crenshaw, Kimberlé W. "Mapping the Margins: Intersectionality, Identity Politics, and Violence against Women of Color." In *Foundations of Critical Race Theory in Education*, 3rd ed., edited by Edward Taylor, David Gillborn, and Gloria Ladson-Billings, 223–50. New York: Routledge, 2023.

Cressler, Matthew, and Adelle Banks. "Reparations and Religion: 50 Years after 'Black Manifesto.'" ABC News, December 30, 2019. https://abcnews.go.com /US/wireStory/reparations-religion-50-years-black-manifesto-67989717.

Day, Iyko. *Alien Capital: Asian Racialization and the Logic of Settler Colonial Capitalism*. Durham, NC: Duke University Press Books, 2016.

Dayanandan, P. "Who Needs a Liberation Theology?" *Dalit International News Letter*, February 2005, 9.

Deeksha, Johanna. "India's Failure to Protect Tamils Sent Back from Sri Lanka." Scroll.in, accessed November 12, 2022/ https://scroll.in/article/1036907/indi as-failure-to-protect-tamils-sent-back-from-sri-lanka.

De La Torre, Miguel, ed. *Ethics: A Liberative Approach*. Minneapolis, MN: Fortress Press, 2013.

De La Torre, Miguel, ed. *Handbook of US Theologies of Liberation*. St. Louis, MO: Chalice Press, 2004.

Delbanco, Andrew, John Stauffer, Manisha Sinha, Darryl Pinckney, and Wilfred M. McClay. *The Abolitionist Imagination*. Cambridge, MA: Harvard University Press, 2012.

Deloria, Vine. "A Native American Perspective on Liberation." *Occasional Bulletin of Missionary Research* 1, no. 3 (July 1977): 15–17. https://doi.org/10.1177/2396 93937700100303.

Deloria, Vine. *God Is Red: A Native View of Religion*. Wheat Ridge, CO: Fulcrum, 2003.

Derrida, Jacques. *Specters of Marx: The State of the Debt, the Work of Mourning and the New International*. London: Routledge, 2006.

Desai, Manan. "What B. R. Ambedkar Wrote to W. E. B. Du Bois." South Asian American Digital Archive, April 22, 2014. https://www.saada.org/tides/article /ambedkar-du-bois.

Desai, Ashwin, and Goolem Vahed. *The South African Gandhi: Stretcher-Bearer of Empire*. Stanford, CA: Stanford University Press, 2015.

DinDeng. "Thalugaz Interview." *DinDeng (ดินแดง)* (blog), August 31, 2021. https://www.dindeng.com/thalugaz-interview/.

Donnella, Leah. "Can East Asians Call Themselves 'Brown'?" NPR, November 16, 2017. https://www.npr.org/sections/codeswitch/2017/11/16/563798938/the-gray-area-between-yellow-and-brown-skin.

Dong, Harvey. *"Jung Sai Garment Workers Strike of 1974: 'An Earth-Shattering and Heaven-Startling Event.'"* In *Ten Years that Shook the City: San Francisco 1968–1978*, edited by Chris Carlsson and Lisa Ruth Elliott, 303–16. San Francisco: City Lights Books, 2011.

Dong, Harvey. "Richard Aoki's Legacy and Dilemma: Who Do You Serve?" *Amerasia Journal* 39, no. 2 (2013): 102–15.

Douglass, Frederick. "No Progress without Struggle." W. E. B. DuBois Learning Center, n.d. http://www.duboislc.org/html/BlackStruggle.html.

Du Bois, W. E. B. *John Brown*. New York: Oxford University Press, 2014.

Du Bois, W. E. B. *The Souls of Black Folk*. South Carolina: CreateSpace, 2014.

Duran, Eduardo. *Healing the Soul Wound: Trauma-Informed Counseling for Indigenous Communities*. New York: Teachers College Press, 2019.

Duran, Eduardo, Bonnie Duran, Maria Yellow Horse Brave Heart, and Susan Yellow Horse-Davis. "Healing the American Indian Soul Wound." In *International Handbook of Multigenerational Legacies of Trauma*, edited by Yael Danieli, 341–54. Boston: Springer US, 1998.

Eagleton, Terry. *The Body as Language: Outline of a "New Left" Theology*. New York: Sheed and Ward, 1970.

Ehrenreich, Barbara. *Fear of Falling: The Inner Life of the Middle Class*. New York: Grand Central Publishing, 2020.

Ehrenreich, Barbara, and John Ehrenreich. "Death of a Yuppie-Dream." Rosa-Luxemburg Stiftung, February 2013. https://www.rosalux.de/publikation/id/6796/death-of-a-yuppie-dream/.

Ehrenreich, Barbara, and John Ehrenreich. "The Professional-Managerial Class." *Between Labor and Capital* 5 (1979): 45.

Ellis, Marc H. *Toward a Jewish Theology of Liberation: The Challenge of the 21st Century*. Waco, TX: Baylor University Press, 2004

Eng, David L., and Shinhee Han. *Racial Melancholia, Racial Dissociation: On the Social and Psychic Lives of Asian Americans*. Durham, NC: Duke University Press Books, 2019.

Espiritu, Yen, and Yến Lê Espiritu. *Asian American Panethnicity: Bridging Institutions and Identities*. Philadelphia: Temple University Press, 1992.

Fabella, Virginia, and Sun Ai Lee Park, eds. *We Dare to Dream: Doing Theology as Asian Women*. Eugene, OR: Wipf and Stock, 2015.

Fanon, Frantz. *Black Skin, White Masks*. Rev. ed. Translated by Richard Philcox. New York: Grove Press, 2008.

Fanon, Frantz. *The Wretched of the Earth*. New York: Grove, 2002.

Federal Bureau of Investigation, "Hate Crime in the United States Incident Analysis." Crime Data Explorer, accessed March 11, 2023. https://cde.ucr.cjis.gov /LATEST/webapp/#/pages/explorer/crime/hate-crime.

Fernandez, Eleazar S. *Toward a Theology of Struggle*. Maryknoll, NY: Orbis Books, 1994.

Fernandez, Eleazar, and Fernando F. Segovia. *A Dream Unfinished: Theological Reflections on America from the Margins*. Eugene: Wipf and Stock, 2007.

Fernandez, Eleazar, and Fumitaka Matsuoka. *Realizing the America of Our Hearts: Theological Voices of Asian Americans*. Des Peres, MO: Chalice Press, 2003.

Ferriss, Susan, and Ricardo Sandoval. *The Fight in the Fields: Cesar Chavez and the Farmworkers Movement*. New York: Houghton Mifflin Harcourt, 1997.

Foo, Stephanie. *What My Bones Know: A Memoir of Healing from Complex Trauma*. New York: Random House, 2022.

Foucault, Michel. "Of Other Spaces." In *Heterotopia and the City*. New York: Routledge, 2008.

Foucault, Michel. *The History of Sexuality*, volume 1: *An Introduction*. New York: Vintage Books, 1980.

Freire, Paulo. *Pedagogy of the Oppressed*. New York: Penguin Books, 1972.

Fuchs, Chris. "Decades after a Cop Shot Her Brother, Qinglan Huang Speaks Up for Akai Gurley." NBC News, April 11, 2016. https://www.nbcnews.com/news /asian-america/two-decades-after-cop-shot-her-brother-qing-lan-huang-n5 54146.

Fujino, Diane Carol. *Heartbeat of Struggle: The Revolutionary Life of Yuri Kochiyama*. Minneapolis: University of Minnesota Press, 2005.

Gandhi, Evyn Lê Espiritu. *Archipelago of Resettlement: Vietnamese Refugee Settlers and Decolonization across Guam and Israel-Palestine*. Berkeley: University of California Press, 2022.

Gay, Roxane. "Why I Can't Forgive Dylann Roof." *New York Times*, June 23, 2015. https://www.nytimes.com/2015/06/24/opinion/why-i-cant-forgive-dylann-ro of.html.

Geertz, Clifford. "Deep Hanging Out." *New York Review of Books*, October 22, 1998. https://www.nybooks.com/articles/1998/10/22/deep-hanging-out/.

Geng, Lucia. "On Pepper Spray and Preventing Anti-Asian Violence." Pulitzer Center, August 23, 2021. https://pulitzercenter.org/stories/pepper-spray-and -preventing-anti-asian-violence.

Gjelten, Tom. "Killing of American Missionary Ignites Debate over How to Evangelize." NPR, November 27, 2018. https://www.npr.org/2018/11/27/671285330/killing-of-american-missionary-ignites-debate-over-how-to-evangelize.

Good, David L. *Orvie: The Dictator of Dearborn: The Rise and Reign of Orville L. Hubbard.* Detroit: Wayne State University Press, 1989.

Gordon, Lewis R. *Bad Faith and Antiblack Racism.* n.p.: Humanity Books, 1999.

Gordon, Lewis R. *Freedom, Justice, and Decolonization.* New York: Routledge, 2020.

Graeber, David. *The Utopia of Rules: On Technology, Stupidity, and the Secret Joys of Bureaucracy.* New York: Melville House, 2016.

Gray, Thomas, Nat Turner, and Paul Royster. "The Confessions of Nat Turner (1831)." *Electronic Texts in American Studies*, University of Nebraska, January 1, 1831. https://digitalcommons.unl.edu/etas/15.

Gustavussen, Mathilde Lind. "We Can Decommodify Housing through Eminent Domain." Jacobin, February 2022. https://jacobin.com/2022/02/decommodify-housing-los-angeles-eminent-domain-affordable-housing.

Gutiérrez, Gustavo. *A Theology of Liberation: History, Politics, and Salvation.* Maryknoll, NY: Orbis Books, 1988.

Gutiérrez, Ramón A. "Internal Colonialism: An American Theory of Race." *Du Bois Review: Social Science Research on Race* 1, no. 2 (September 2004): 281–95. https://doi.org/10.1017/S1742058X04042043.

Hakim, Danny, Stephanie Saul, and Richard A. Oppel Jr. "'Top Cop' Kamala Harris's Record of Policing the Police." *New York Times*, August 9, 2020. https://www.nytimes.com/2020/08/09/us/politics/kamala-harris-policing.html.

Hall, Tony. *The Bowl with One Spoon: The American Empire and the Fourth World.* Montreal: McGill-Queen's University Press, 2003.

Harris, Cheryl I. "Whiteness as Property." *Harvard Law Review* 106, no. 8 (1993): 1707.

Hartman, Saidiya. *Scenes of Subjection: Terror, Slavery, and Self-Making in Nineteenth-Century America.* New York: W. W. Norton, 2022.

Hartman, Saidiya, Steve Martinot, Jared Sexton, Spillers Hortense, and Frank Wilderson. *Afro-Pessimism: An Introduction.* Minneapolis: racked & dispatched, 2017.

Hartman, Saidiya V., and Frank B. Wilderson. "The Position of the Unthought." *Qui Parle* 13, no. 2 (2003): 183–201.

Hartocollis, Anemona. "Asian-Americans Suing Harvard Say Admissions Files Show Discrimination." *New York Times*, April 4, 2018. https://www.nytimes.com/2018/04/04/us/harvard-asian-admission.html.

Hauerwas, Stanley, and Bishop William H. Willimon. *Resident Aliens: Life in the Christian Colony.* Nashville, TN: Abingdon Press, 2014.

Hawkins, Carlee Beth, and Alexia Jo Vandiver. "Human Caregivers Perceive Racial Bias in their Pet Dogs." *Group Processes & Intergroup Relations* 22, no. 6 (2019): 901–17.

Hayes, Kelly, and Mariame Kaba. *Let This Radicalize You Organizing and the Revolution of Reciprocal Care*. Chicago: Haymarket Books, 2023.

Haynes, Stephen R., and Stephen Ronald Haynes. *Noah's Curse: The Biblical Justification of American Slavery*. Oxford: Oxford University Press, 2002.

Hedges, Chris, and Joe Sacco. *Days of Destruction, Days of Revolt*. London: Hachette UK, 2014.

Herbert, Julián. *The House of the Pain of Others: Chronicle of a Small Genocide*. Minneapolis, MN: Graywolf Press, 2019.

Herzog, Frederick. *God-Walk: Liberation Shaping Dogmatics*. Eugene, OR: Wipf and Stock, 2008.

Hioe, Brian. "Confusion About 'Chinese' or 'Taiwanese' Identity of Gunman after Shooting at Taiwanese Church in California." *New Bloom Magazine*, May 17, 2022. https://newbloommag.net/2022/05/17/tw-church-shooting/.

Hixson, Walter. *American Settler Colonialism: A History*. New York: Springer, 2013.

Ho, Fred. "Beyond Asian American Jazz: My Musical and Political Changes in the Asian American Movement." *Leonardo Music Journal* 9 (1999): 45–51.

Ho, Fred, and Bill V. Mullen. *Afro Asia: Revolutionary Political and Cultural Connections between African Americans and Asian Americans*. Durham, NC: Duke University Press, 2008.

Ho, Rosemarie. "Migrant Massage Workers Don't Need to Be Rescued." The Nation, April 2, 2021. https://www.thenation.com/article/activism/red-canary-song-wu-interview/.

"Home." Letters for Black Lives, accessed March 7, 2023. https://lettersforblacklives.com/.

Hong, Nicole, Ashley Southall, and Ali Watkins. "He Was Charged in an Anti-Asian Attack. It Was His 33rd Arrest." *New York Times*, April 6, 2021. https://www.nytimes.com/2021/04/06/nyregion/nyc-asian-hate-crime-mental-illness.html.

Ignatiev, Noel. *How the Irish Became White*. New York: Routledge, 2012.

Isasi-Díaz, Ada María. "Kin-dom of God: A Mujerista Proposal." *Our Own Voices: Latino/a Renditions of Theology* (2010): 171–89.

Jayachitra, L. "Jesus and Ambedkar: Finding Common Loci for Dalit Theology and Dalit Movements." In *Dalit Theology in the Twenty-First Century: Discordant Voices, Discerning Pathways*, edited by Sathianathan Clarke, Deenabandhu Manchala, and Philip Vinod Peacock, 121–36. New Dehli: Oxford University Press, 2011.

Jones, William Ronald. *Is God a White Racist? A Preamble to Black Theology*. New York: Anchor Press, 1973.

Kalahele, 'Imaikalani. *Kalahele: Poetry and Art*. Honolulu: Kalamaku Press, 2002.

Kang, Jay Caspian. "How Should Asian-Americans Feel about the Peter Liang Protests?" *New York Times*, February 23, 2016. https://www.nytimes.com/20 16/02/23/magazine/how-should-asian-americans-feel-about-the-peter-liang -protests.html.

Kang, Jay Caspian. "That Other School Shooting." *New York Times*, March 28, 2013. https://www.nytimes.com/2013/03/31/magazine/should-it-matter-that -the-shooter-at-oikos-university-was-korean.html.

Kang, Jay Caspian. *The Loneliest Americans*. New York: Crown, 2021.

Kang, Jay Caspian. "What a Fraternity Hazing Death Revealed about the Painful Search for an Asian-American Identity." *New York Times*, August 9, 2017. https://www.nytimes.com/2017/08/09/magazine/what-a-fraternity-hazing -death-revealed-about-the-painful-search-for-an-asian-american-identity .html.

Kang, Miliann. "The Managed Hand: The Commercialization of Bodies and Emotions in Korean Immigrant-Owned Nail Salons." *Gender & Society* 17, no. 6 (2003): 820–39.

Kao, Grace Y., and Ilsup Ahn, eds. *Asian American Christian Ethics: Voices, Methods, Issues*. Waco, TX: Baylor University Press, 2015.

Kato, Julius-Kei. *Religious Language and Asian American Hybridity*. New York: Springer, 2016.

Kim, Claire Jean. "The Racial Triangulation of Asian Americans." *Politics & Society* 27, no. 1 (March 1, 1999): 105–38. https://doi.org/10.1177/00323292990270 01005.

Kim, Elaine H. "'At Least You're Not Black': Asian Americans in U.S. Race Relations." *Social Justice* 25, no. 3 (73) (1998): 3–12.

Kim, Grace Ji-Sun. *Invisible: Theology and the Experience of Asian American Women*. Minneapolis, MN: Augsburg Fortress, 2021.

Kim, Helen Jin, Timothy Tseng, and David K. Yoo. "Asian American Religious History." In *The Oxford Handbook of Asian American History*, edited by David K. Yoo and Eiichiro Azuma, 360. Oxford: Oxford University Press, 2016.

Kim, Juliana, Sean Keenan, and Richard Fausset. "Protesters Gather in Atlanta to #StopAsianHate." *New York Times*, March 20, 2021. https://www.nytimes.com /2021/03/20/us/stopasianhate-protest-atlanta.html.

Kim, Nadia Y. "Critical Thoughts on Asian American Assimilation in the Whitening Literature." *Social Forces* 86, no. 2 (2007): 561–74.

Kim, Nami. "The 'Indigestible' Asian: The Unifying Term 'Asian' in Theological

Discourse." In *Off the Menu: Asian and Asian North American Women's Religion and Theology*, edited by Rita Nakashima Brock, Jung Ha Kim, Pui-lan Kwok, and Seung Ai Yang, 23–43. Louisville: Westminster John Knox Press, 2007.

Kim, Nami, and Wonhee Anne Joh, eds. *Critical Theology against US Militarism in Asia: Decolonization and Deimperialization.* New York: Springer, 2016.

Kim, Richard S. "A Conversation with Chol Soo Lee and K.W. Lee." *Amerasia Journal* 31, no. 3 (January 1, 2005): 75–108. https://doi.org/10.17953/amer.31.3.q6p04504u5t5g8q4.

Kim-Kort, Mihee. *Making Paper Cranes: Toward an Asian American Feminist Theology.* Des Peres, MO: Chalice Press, 2012.

Kimoto, June L. "From Silence to Sounds." In *East Asian and Amerasian Liberation: Proceedings, Second Conference on East Asian and Amerasian Theology, Monday, February 3, 1975, Trinity United Methodist Church, Berkeley, California*, edited by Roy I. Sano, 369–70. Oakland: Asian Center for Theology and Strategies, 1975.

Klein, Naomi. *The Shock Doctrine: The Rise of Disaster Capitalism.* Macmillan, 2007.

Kollontai, Aleksandra. *Make Way for Winged Eros: A Letter to Working Youth Love as a Socio-Psychological Factor. From Symbolism to Socialist Realism.* Boston: Academic Studies Press, 2012.

Kosasa, Karen. "Sites of Erasure: The Representation of Settler Culture in Hawai'i." In *Asian Settler Colonialism: From Local Governance to the Habits of Everyday Life in Hawai'i*, edited by Candace Fujikane and Jonathan Y. Okamura, 195–208. Honolulu: University of Hawaii Press, 2008.

Koyama, Kōsuke. *Water Buffalo Theology.* Maryknoll, NY: Orbis Books, 1987.

Kuan, Jeffrey Kah-Jin, and Mary F. Foskett. *Ways of Being, Ways of Reading: Asian American Biblical Interpretation.* Des Peres, MO: Chalice Press, 2006.

Kung, Lap Yan. *Liberation Theology and Hong Kong's Predicament.* Kowloon: Hong Kong Christian Institute, 1999.

Kwan, Kevin. *Crazy Rich Asians.* Vol. 1. New York: Anchor, 2013.

Kwon, Duke L., and Gregory Thompson. *Reparations: A Christian Call for Repentance and Repair.* Ada, MI: Baker Books, 2021.

Kwok, Pui-lan. *Postcolonial Imagination and Feminist Theology.* Louisville, KY: Westminster John Knox Press, 2005.

Kyung, Chung Hyun, and Hyun K. Chung. *Struggle to Be the Sun Again.* Maryknoll, NY: Orbis Books, 1990.

Lai, Tsz Him. "Understanding the Use of Violence in the Hong Kong Protests." In *The Hong Kong Protests and Political Theology*, edited by Kwok Pui-Lan and Francis Ching-Wah Yip. Lanham: Rowman & Littlefield, 2021.

Lee, Chol Soo. *Freedom without Justice: The Prison Memoirs of Chol Soo Lee.* Edited by Richard S. Kim. Honolulu: University of Hawai'i Press, 2017.

Lee, Christopher. "The Lateness of Asian Canadian Studies." *Amerasia Journal* 33, no. 2 (January 1, 2007): 1–18.https://doi.org/10.17953/amer.33.2.c8053m5q 76215018.

Lee, Erika. *The Making of Asian America: A History.* New York: Simon & Schuster, 2015.

Lee, Eun Ja Kim. "Theological Understanding of Women." In *East Asian and Amerasian Liberation: Proceedings, Second Conference on East Asian and Amerasian Theology, Monday, February 3, 1975, Trinity United Methodist Church, Berkeley, California,* edited by Roy I. Sano, 362. Oakland: Asian Center for Theology and Strategies, 1975.

Lee, Jung Young. *Journeys at the Margin: Toward an Autobiographical Theology in American-Asian Perspective.* Collegeville, MN: Liturgical Press, 1999.

Lee, Robert G. *The Cold War Origins of the Model Minority Myth: Asian American Studies Now.* New Brunswick, NJ: Rutgers University Press, 2010.

Lee, Sang Hyun. *From a Liminal Place: An Asian American Theology.* Minneapolis: Fortress Press, 2010.

Lee, Seulghee. "When Is Asian American Life Grievable?" Tropics of Meta, April 30, 2021. https://tropicsofmeta.com/2021/04/30/when-is-asian-american-life -grievable/.

Leroux, Darryl. *Distorted Descent: White Claims to Indigenous Identity.* Winnipeg: University of Manitoba Press, 2019.

Liu, Catherine. *Virtue Hoarders: The Case against the Professional Managerial Class.* Minneapolis: University of Minnesota Press, 2021.

Lloyd, Vincent W., and Andrew Prevot, eds. *Anti-Blackness and Christian Ethics.* Maryknoll, NY: Orbis, 2017

Lorde, Audre. "The Master's Tools Will Never Dismantle the Master's House." In *Feminist Postcolonial Theory: A Reader,* edited by Reina Lewis and Sara Mills, 25–28. Edinburgh: Edinburgh University Press, 2003.

Loo, Dennis. "Why an Asian American Theology of Liberation?" In *The Theologies of Asian Americans and Pacific Peoples: A Reader,* edited by Roy I. Sano, 209–13. Pasadena, CA: Asian Center for Theology & Strategies, Pacific School of Religion, 1976.

Loo, Leslie. "You Decide! The Dilemma of One Asian Woman." *AmerAsian Theology of Liberation: A Reader* (1973): 374–75.

Lowe, Lisa. *Immigrant Acts: On Asian American Cultural Politics.* Durham, NC: Duke University Press, 1996.

Maghbouleh, Neda. *The Limits of Whiteness: Iranian Americans and the Everyday Politics of Race.* Stanford, CA: Stanford University Press, 2017.

Mandela, Nelson. "'I Am Prepared to Die': Nelson Mandela's Statement from the Dock at the Opening of the Defence Case in the Rivonia Trial." United

Nations, April 20, 1964. https://www.un.org/en/events/mandeladay/court_st
atement_1964.shtml.

Martey, Emmanuel. *African Theology: Inculturation and Liberation.* Eugene, OR:
Wipf and Stock, 2009.

Martinot, Steve, and Jared Sexton. "The Avant-Garde of White Supremacy." *Social
Identities* 9, no. 2 (June 1, 2003): 169–81. https://doi.org/10.1080/13504630320
00101542.

Matsuoka, Fumitaka. *Out of Silence: Emerging Themes in Asian American Churches.*
Eugene, OR: Wipf and Stock, 2009.

McAlister, Melani. "A Kind of Homelessness: Evangelicals of Color in the Trump
Era." Religion and Politics, August 7, 2018. https://religionandpolitics.org/20
18/08/07/a-kind-of-homelessness-evangelicals-of-color-in-the-trump-era/.

McGeeney, Kyley, Brian Kriz, Shawnna Mullenax, Laura Kail, Gina Walejko, Mon-
ica Vines, Nancy Bates, and Y. Garcia Trejo. *2020 Census Barriers, Attitudes,
and Motivators Study Survey Report.* Suitland, MD: US Census Bureau, 2019.
https://www.census.gov/programs-surveys/decennial-census/decade/2020
/planning-management/plan/final-analysis/2020-report-cbams-study-surv
ey.html.

Mignolo, Walter D. *The Idea of Latin America.* Malden, MA: Blackwell, 2005.

Milstein, Cindy. *Rebellious Mourning: The Collective Work of Grief.* Chico, CA: AK
Press, 2017.

Min, Anselm Kyongsuk. *The Solidarity of Others in a Divided World: A Postmodern
Theology after Postmodernism.* London: A&C Black, 2004.

Modood, Tariq. "Political Blackness and British Asians." *Sociology* 28, no. 4 (1994):
859–76.

Molchanova, Violetta S. "Modern Slavery in India: The Essence, Forms, Distribution." *Slavery: Theory and Practice* 4, no. 1 (2019).https://doi.org/10.13187/sl
ave.2019.1.20.

Montgomery, Hanako. "Knife Attacker on Tokyo Train Says He Wanted to 'Kill
Happy Women.'" *Vice*, August 9, 2021. https://www.vice.com/en/article/bvzb
vw/tokyo-train-knife-attack-japan.

Montgomery, Nick, and Carla bergman. *Joyful Militancy: Building Thriving Resistance in Toxic Times.* Chico, CA: AK Press, 2017.

Mrie, Loubna. "Photos: The Secret World of Maids in New York's Richest Neighborhoods." Quartz, August 17, 2021. https://qz.com/634049/photos-the-secr
et-world-of-maids-in-new-yorks-richest-neighborhoods/.

Munoz, Gerardo, and Ángel Octavio Álvarez Solis. "As Free as Blackness Will Make
Them: Interview with Frank B. Wilderson III." Ill Will, September 7, 2020.
https://illwilleditions.com/as-free-as-blackness-will-make-them/.

Murakawa, Naomi. *Ida B. Wells on Racial Criminalization: African American Polit-*

ical Thought. Chicago: University of Chicago Press, 2021.https://www.degruy ter.com/document/doi/10.7208/9780226726076-010/html.

Nelavala, Prasuna Gnana. "Caste Branding, Bleeding Body, Building Dalit Womanhood." In *Dalit Theology in the Twenty-First Century: Discordant Voices, Discerning Pathways*, edited by Sathianathan Clarke, Deenabandhu Manchala, and Philip Vinod Peacock, 266–76. New Delhi: Oxford University Press, 2011.

Nelavala, Surekha. "Visibility of Her Sins: Reading the 'Sinful Woman' in Luke 7:36–50 from a Dalit Perspective." In *Dalit Theology in the Twenty-First Century: Discordant Voices, Discerning Pathways*, edited by Sathianathan Clarke, Deenabandhu Manchala, and Philip Vinod Peacock, 252–65. New Delhi: Oxford University Press, 2010.

Ng, Greer Anne Wenh-ln. "Land of Maple and Lands of Bamboo." In *Realizing the America of Our Hearts: Theological Voices of Asian Americans*, edited by Fumitaka Matsuoka and Eleazar Fernandez, 99–114. Des Peres, MO: Chalice Press, 2003.

Nguyen, Viet Thanh. "Asian-Americans Need More Movies, Even Mediocre Ones." *New York Times*, August 21, 2018. https://www.nytimes.com/2018/08 /21/opinion/crazy-rich-asians-movie.html.

Okihiro, Gary Y. *American History Unbound: Asians and Pacific Islanders*. Berkeley, CA: University of California Press, 2015.

Okihiro, Gary Y. *Third World Studies: Theorizing Liberation*. Durham, NC: Duke University Press, 2016.

Park, Andrew Sung. "Minjung Theology: A Korean Contextual Theology." *Indian Journal of Theology* 33, no. 4 (1984): 1–11.

Park, Kyeyoung. "Black-Korean Tension in America." In *Koreans in the Hood: Conflict with African Americans*, edited by Kwang Chung Kim, 60. Baltimore, MD: Johns Hopkins University Press, 1999.

Park, Soo-jin, and Park Soo-ji. "Gangnam Murderer Says He Killed 'Because Women Have Always Ignored Me.'" https://english.hani.co.kr/arti/english_ed ition/e_national/744756.html.

Pega, Frank, Roman Pabayo, Claire Benny, Eun-Young Lee, Stefan K. Lhachimi, and Sze Yan Liu. "Unconditional Cash Transfers for Reducing Poverty and Vulnerabilities: Effect on Use of Health Services and Health Outcomes in Low- and Middle-Income Countries." *Cochrane Database of Systematic Reviews*, no. 3 (2022). https://doi.org/10.1002/14651858.CD011135.pub3.

Phan, Peter C. *Christianity with an Asian Face: Asian American Theology in the Making*. Maryknoll, NY: Orbis Books, 2015.

Pieris, Aloysius. *Asian Theology of Liberation*. London: A&C Black, 1988.

"Population Estimates, July 1, 2022." US Census Bureau, accessed November 12, 2022. https://www.census.gov/quickfacts/fact/table/US/PST045217.

Postone, Moishe. "Anti-Semitism and National Socialism: Notes on the German Reaction to 'Holocaust.'" *New German Critique*, no. 19 (1980): 97–115. https://doi.org/10.2307/487974.

Prashad, Vijay. *Everybody Was Kung Fu Fighting: Afro-Asian Connections and the Myth of Cultural Purity*. New York: Beacon Press, 2002.

Qin, Amy. "Applying to College, and Trying to Appear 'Less Asian.'" *New York Times*, December 2, 2022. https://www.nytimes.com/2022/12/02/us/asian-american-college-applications.html.

Ragusa, Antonio, Alessandro Svelato, Criselda Santacroce, Piera Catalano, Valentina Notarstefano, Oliana Carnevali, Fabrizio Papa, et al. "Plasticenta: First Evidence of Microplastics in Human Placenta." *Environment International* 146 (January 1, 2021): 106274. https://doi.org/10.1016/j.envint.2020.106274.

Rah, Soong-Chan. *The Next Evangelicalism: Freeing the Church from Western Cultural Captivity*. Downers Grove, IL: InterVarsity Press, 2009.

Ramamurthy, Anandi. *Black Star: Britain's Asian Youth Movements*. London: Pluto Press, 2013

Ramakrishnan, Karthick, and Sono Shah. "One Out of Every 7 Asian Immigrants Is Undocumented." Data Bits, September 8, 2017. https://aapidata.com/blog/Asian-undoc-1in7.

Ramnath, Maia. *Haj to Utopia: How the Ghadar Movement Charted Global Radicalism and Attempted to Overthrow the British Empire*. Berkeley: University of California Press, 2011.

Red Canary Song. "Red Canary Song Response to 8 Lives Lost in Atlanta." Google Docs, accessed August 7, 2022. https://docs.google.com/document/d/1_QomFJnivTZL5fcCS7eUZn9EhOJ1XHtFBGOGqVaUY_8/.

Rickford, Russell. "Malcolm X and Anti-Imperialist Thought." Black Perspectives, February 24, 2017. https://www.aaihs.org/malcolm-x-and-anti-imperialist-thought/.

Rieger, Joerg, and Kwok Pui-Lan. *Occupy Religion: Theology of the Multitude*. Lanham, MD: Rowman & Littlefield, 2013.

Robinson, Cedric J. *Black Marxism, Revised and Updated Third Edition: The Making of the Black Radical Tradition*. Chapel Hill: University of North Carolina Press, 2020.

Rodney, Walter. *The Groundings with My Brothers*. London: Bogle-L'Ouverture, 1969.

Rogers, Katie, Lara Jakes, and Ana Swanson. "Trump Defends Using 'Chinese Virus' Label, Ignoring Growing Criticism." *New York Times*, March 18, 2020. https://www.nytimes.com/2020/03/18/us/politics/china-virus.html.

Roy, Arundhati. "The Doctor and the Saint." In *The Annihilation of Caste: The Annotated Critical Edition*, edited by S. Anand. New York: Verso, 2014.

Sano, Roy I. "A Theology of Struggle from an Asian American Perspective." *Branches* (Fall/Winter 1990): 8–11.

Sano, Roy I. "Ministry for a Liberating Ethnicity." Earl Lectures and Pastoral Conference, First Congregational Church of Berkeley, February 27–March, 1, 1973. Unknown binding.

Ruiz, Lester Edwin J. "Revisiting the Question Concerning (Theological) Contextualization." In *New Overtures: Asian North American Theology in the 21st Century: Essays in Honor of Fumitaka Matsuoka*, edited by Eleazar S. Fernandez, 85. Cambridge, MA: Sopher Press, 2012.

Ruiz, Lester Edwin J. "Towards a Theology of Politics: Meditations on Religion, Politics, and Social Transformation." *Tugón* 6, no. 3 (1986): 32.

Said, Edward W. *Orientalism*. New York: Vintage, 1979.

Sakai, J. *Settlers: The Mythology of the White Proletariat from Mayflower to Modern*. Binghamton, NY: PM Press, 2014.

Sano, Roy I. "Toward a Liberating Ethnicity." Earl Lectures and Pastoral Conference, First Congregational Church of Berkeley, February 27–March, 1, 1973. Unknown binding.

Sattayanurak, Saichol. "The Construction of Mainstream thought on 'Thainess' and the 'Truth' Constructed by 'Thainess.'" Unpublished PhD diss. Chiang Mai University, Thailand.

Seijas, Tatiana. *Asian Slaves in Colonial Mexico: From Chinos to Indians*. Vol. 100. Cambridge: Cambridge University Press, 2014.

Seung, Ai Yang. "Asian Americans." In *Handbook of US Theologies of Liberation*, edited by Miguel De La Torre, 181. St. Louis, MO: Chalice Press, 2004.

Sexton, Jared. "People-of-Color-Blindness: Notes on the Afterlife of Slavery." *Social Text* 28, no. 2 (June 1, 2010): 31–56. https://doi.org/10.1215/01642472-20 09-066.

Shah, Svati P. "South Asian Border Crossings and Sex Work: Revisiting the Question of Migration in Anti-Trafficking Interventions." *Sexuality Research & Social Policy* 5, no. 4 (December 1, 2008): 19. https://doi.org/10.1525/srsp.20 08.5.4.19.

Sharma, Nitasha Tamar. *Hawai'i Is My Haven: Race and Indigeneity in the Black Pacific*. Durham, NC: Duke University Press, 2021.

Shilliam, Robbie. *The Black Pacific: Anti-Colonial Struggles and Oceanic Connections*. New York: Bloomsbury, 2015.

Shubadra, Joopaka. "Arundhati Roy Does Not Know What Caste Pain Is About." Dalit Camera, October 6, 2017. https://www.dalitcamera.com/joopaka-shub adra-arundhati-roy-not-know-caste-pain/.

Slabodsky, Santiago. "It's the Theology, Stupid! Coloniality, Anti-Blackness, and the Bounds of 'Humanity.'" In *Anti-Blackness and Christian Ethics*, edited by Vincent W. Lloyd and Andrew Prevot, 19–40. Maryknoll, NY: Orbis, 2017.

Smith, Andrea. "Heteropatriarchy and the Three Pillars of White Supremacy: Rethinking Women of Color Organizing." In *Feminist Theory Reader: Local and Global Perspectives*, edited by Carole McCann, Seung-kyung Kim, and Emek Ergun, 141–47. New York: Routledge, 2020.

Smith, Ted A. *Weird John Brown: Divine Violence and the Limits of Ethics*. Stanford, CA: Stanford University Press, 2014.

Song, C. S. *Tell Us Our Names: Story Theology from an Asian Perspective*. Eugene, OR: Wipf and Stock, 2005.

Spivak, Gayatri Chakravorty. "Can the Subaltern Speak?" *Colonial Discourse and Post-colonial Theory*. New York: Routledge, 2015.

Sunoo, Harold Hak-won. "Roots of Social Resistance in Asia and Its Impact on Asian Americans." In *East Asian and Amerasian Liberation: Proceedings, Second Conference on East Asian and Amerasian Theology, Monday, February 3, 1975, Trinity United Methodist Church, Berkeley, California*, edited by Roy I. Sano. Oakland: Asian Center for Theology and Strategies, 1975.

Soundararajan, Thenmozi. *The Trauma of Caste: A Dalit Feminist Meditation on Survivorship, Healing, and Abolition*. Berkeley, CA: North Atlantic Books, 2022.

Srinivasan, Amia. "Does Anyone Have the Right to Sex?" *London Review of Books*, March 22, 2018. https://www.lrb.co.uk/the-paper/v40/n06/amia-srinivasan /does-anyone-have-the-right-to-sex.

Swanson, Ian. "Atlanta Killings Underscore Troubling Rise in Anti-Asian Violence." The Hill, March 17, 2021. https://thehill.com/homenews/state-wat ch/543717-atlanta-killings-underscore-troubling-rise-in-anti-asian-violence.

Szasz, Thomas. *The Second Sin*. London: Routledge, 1973

Tachiki, Amy Eddie Wong, and Franklin Ono, eds. *Roots: An Asian American Reader*. Los Angeles: UCLA Asian American Studies Center, 1971.

TallBear, Kim. *Native American DNA: Tribal Belonging and the False Promise of Genetic Science*. Minneapolis: University of Minnesota Press, 2013.

Tan, Jonathan Y. *Introducing Asian American Theologies*. Maryknoll, NY: Orbis Books, 2008.

Tang, Eric. "A Gulf Unites Us: The Vietnamese Americans of Black New Orleans East." *American Quarterly* 63, no. 1 (2011): 117–49.

Tiffany, Kaitlyn. "What Do Female Incels Really Want?" *Atlantic*, May 12, 2022. https://www.theatlantic.com/technology/archive/2022/05/femcel-meaning -female-incel-reddit/629836/.

Tinker, George. "American Indian Theology." In *Liberation Theologies in the United States: An Introduction*, edited by Anthony Pinn and Stacey Floyd-Thomas, 168–80. New York: New York University Press, 2010.

Torre, Miguel A. De La. *Liberation Theology for Armchair Theologians*. Louisville: Westminster John Knox Press, 2013.

Tran, Jonathan. *Asian Americans and the Spirit of Racial Capitalism*. New York: Oxford University Press, 2022.

Tran, Jonathan. "Why Asian American Christianity Has No Future: The Over Against, Leaving Behind, and Separation from of Asian American Christian Identity." *SANACS Journal* 2 (2010): 13–56.

Trask, Haunani-Kay. "Settlers of Color and 'Immigrant' Hegemony: 'Locals' in Hawai'i." *Amerasia Journal* 26, no. 2 (January 1, 2000): 1–26. https://doi.org/10 .17953/amer.26.2.b31642r221215k7k.

Tse, Justin K. H., and Jonathan Y. Tan, eds. *Theological Reflections on the Hong Kong Umbrella Movement*. New York: Palgrave, 2016.

Tseng, Timothy. "Asian American Religions." *Asian American Christianity Reader* (2009): 83.

Tseng, Timothy. "Trans-Pacific Transpositions: Continuities and Discontinuities in Chinese North American Protestantism since 1965." *Revealing the Sacred in Asian and Pacific America* (2003): 241–72.

Tuck, Eve, and K. Wayne Yang. "Decolonization Is Not a Metaphor." *Decolonization: Indigeneity, Education & Society* 1, no. 1 (September 8, 2012). https://jps.li brary.utoronto.ca/index.php/des/article/view/18630.

United Nations. "Statement to the Media by the United Nations' Working Group of Experts on People of African Descent, on the Conclusion of Its Official Visit to USA, 19–29 January 2016." United Nations Human Rights Office of the High Commissioner, January 29, 2016. https://www.ohchr.org/en/statem ents/2016/01/statement-media-united-nations-working-group-experts-peop le-african-descent?LangID=E&NewsID=17000.

Unno, Annusorn. "'Thalu Gas': The Other Version of the 'Thai Youth Movement.'" *ISEAS Perspective*, no. 146 (November 2021): 1–11.

Uprety, Aastha. "Sociologist Tamara Nopper Discusses Anti-Asian Violence and the Limitations of the 'Hate' Framework." *Morningside Post*, April 4, 2021. https://morningsidepost.com/articles/2021/4/2/sociologist-tamara-nopper -discusses-anti-asian-violence-and-the-limitations-of-the-hate-framework.

US Department of Justice. "2020 Hate Crimes Statistics." 2020 FBI Hate Crimes Statistics, accessed April 18, 2023. https://www.justice.gov/crs/highlights/20 20-hate-crimes-statistics.

"USPS Reports Decreased Vacancy Rates in Detroit." Drawing Detroit, April 20, 2021. http://www.drawingdetroit.com/usps-reports-decreased-vacancy-rates -in-detroit/.

Uyematsu, Amy. "The Emergence of Yellow Power in America." *Gidra*, October

1969. Reprinted in Tachiki, Amy, ed. *Roots: An Asian American Reader*. Los Angeles: UCLA Asian American Studies Center, 1971.

Vajiravudh, King. *The Jews of the Orient*. Thailand, Siam Observer Press, 1917.

Veracini, Lorenzo. *Settler Colonialism: A Theoretical Overview*. London: Palgrave, 2010.

Viren, Sarah. "The Native Scholar Who Wasn't." *New York Times*, May 25, 2021. https://www.nytimes.com/2021/05/25/magazine/cherokee-native-american -andrea-smith.html.

Walsh, J. P. M. *The Mighty from Their Thrones: Power in Biblical Tradition*. Eugene, OR: Wipf and Stock, 2004.

Wilderson, Frank. "Gramsci's Black Marx: Whither the Slave in Civil Society?" *Social Identities* 9, no. 2 (June 1, 2003): 225–40. https://doi.org/10.1080/13504 63032000101579.

Wilderson, Frank B. "The Prison Slave as Hegemony's (Silent) Scandal." *Social Justice* 30, no. 2 (2003): 18–27.

Wilkerson, Isabel. "America's 'Untouchables': The Silent Power of the Caste System." *Guardian*, July 28, 2020. https://www.theguardian.com/world/2020/jul /28/untouchables-caste-system-us-race-martin-luther-king-india.

Wilkerson, Isabel. *Caste: The Origins of Our Discontents*. New York: Random House, 2020.

Williams, Rowan. "The Body's Grace." In *Christianity*, edited by Stephen Hunt. New York: Routledge, 2010, 41–58.

Wilmore, Gayraud. "A Revolution Unfulfilled, but Not Invalidated." *A Black Theology of Liberation: Twentieth Anniversary Edition*, edited by James H. Cone. Maryknoll, NY: Orbis Books, 1990, 145–63.

Wolfe, Patrick. "Recuperating Binarism: A Heretical Introduction." *Settler Colonial Studies* 3, nos. 3–4 (November 1, 2013): 257–79. https://doi.org/10.1080/22 01473X.2013.830587.

Wolfe, Patrick. *Settler Colonialism and the Transformation of Anthropology: The Politics and Poetics of an Ethnographic Event*. London: A&C Black, 1999.

Wong, Tanya Chen, Venessa. "Asian Women Don't Feel Safe in Public. Now Some Are Carrying Self-Defense Weapons." BuzzFeed News, April 15, 2021. https:// www.buzzfeednews.com/article/tanyachen/self-defense-weapons-asian-am erican-women.

Wong, Wai-Ching Angela. *"The Poor Woman": A Critical Analysis of Asian Theology and Contemporary Chinese Fiction by Women*. Bern, UK: Peter Lang, 2002.

Woo, Wesley. "Theologizing: An Asian American Perspective." In *The Theologies of Asian Americans and Pacific Peoples: A Reader*, edited by Roy I. Sano, 354–60. Pasadena, CA: Asian Center for Theology & Strategies, Pacific School of Religion, 1976.

Wynter, Sylvia. "Unsettling the Coloniality of Being/Power/Truth/Freedom: Towards the Human, After Man, Its Overrepresentation—An Argument." *CR: The New Centennial Review* 3, no. 3 (2003): 257–337. https://doi.org/10.13 53/ncr.2004.0015.

Yang, Jeff. "The Laguna Woods Shooting Wasn't Driven by Anti-Asian Hate. In Some Ways that Felt Worse." Think, May 22, 2022. https://www.nbcnews.com /think/opinion/laguna-woods-church-shooting-david-chou-taiwan-history -hate-rcna29935.

Young, Alex Trimble, and Lorenzo Veracini. "'If I Am Native to Anything': Settler Colonial Studies and Western American Literature." *Western American Literature* 52, no. 1 (2017): 1–23.

Zesch, Scott. *The Chinatown War: Chinese Los Angeles and the Massacre of 1871.* Oxford: Oxford University Press, 2012.

Zhou, Min. "Are Asian Americans Becoming 'White?'" *Contexts* 3, no. 1 (February 1, 2004): 29–37. https://doi.org/10.1525/ctx.2004.3.1.29.

Zhou, Min, and J. V. Gatewood. *Contemporary Asian America*, 2nd ed.: *A Multidisciplinary Reader.* New York: New York University Press, 2007.

Žižek, Slavoj. *Violence: Six Sideways Reflections.* New York: Picador, 2008.

Zwick-Maitreyi, Maari, Thenmozhi Soundarajan, and Natasha Dar. "Caste in the United States: A Survey of Caste among South Asian Americans." *Equality Labs* (2018): 1–51.